EDUCATIONAL PSYCHOLOGY

Pamela R. Rothstein

An American BookWorks Corporation Project

McGraw-Hill, Inc.

New York St. Louis San Francisco Auckland Bogotá Caracas
Hamburg Lisbon London Madrid Mexico Milan Montreal
New Delhi Paris San Juan São Paulo
Singapore Sydney Tokyo Toronto

Dedication

To John J. Coleman III, M. D., and other surgeons at Emory University (in Atlanta, Georgia) for commitment to their craft and attained excellence in their skill.

Pamela R. Rothstein is pursuing doctoral study at North Carolina State University. She has been an Assessment Specialist for the Houston Independent School District and currently serves as a Human Factors Engineer for the IBM Corporation in North Carolina.

Editor, John Houtz, Ph.D., Fordham University

Educational Psychology

The opinions expressed in this book are those of the author and not necessarily those of the IBM Corporation.

1 2 3 4 5 6 7 8 9 10 11 12 13 14 15 16 17 18 19 20 FGR FGR 9 2 1 0

ISBN 0-07-054027-6

Library of Congress Cataloging-in-Publication Data

Rothstein, Pamela R.
   Educational psychology / Pamela R. Rothstein.
        p.   cm. — (McGraw-Hill college review books series)
   Includes bibliographies
   1. Educational psychology.   I. Title.   II. Series.
LB1051.R685   1990
370.15—dc19   88-13233
                                          CIP

Preface

This book is intended for students in an educational psychology course and for teachers, counselors, psychologists, and others concerned with the design and communication of information, especially for educational purposes. No previous background in education or psychology is assumed.

Because the topics covered correspond to those found in the leading educational psychology textbooks, the book can be used as an overview to the subject and as a text supplement. Teachers and school counselors should find it a clear and convenient source of information for reference and review. It can also serve as a concise text.

Underlying the techniques that have proved successful in the classroom are the theories and studies of many educational psychologists. This book presents the most significant theoretical approaches and research findings and reviews important trends in the field.

Chapters 1 through 3 present an introduction to the field, a practical discussion of effective teaching, and suggestions for appropriate management of classroom behavior. Chapters 4 through 7 introduce development and learning theories and outline physical, emotional, social, and intellectual human growth. Motivational theories and applications for the classroom are presented in Chapter 8. Instructional design, including instructional models and strategies, is discussed in Chapter 9. Chapter 10 provides an overview of research on intelligence and individual differences and general descriptions of commonly administered intelligence tests. The reader is introduced to measurement, evaluation, and different kinds of tests in Chapter 11. An introduction to problem-solving methods and creativity is presented in Chapter 12. Chapter 13 discusses characteristics of special populations, including retarded, learning-disabled, physically handicapped, and gifted children, and the role of the regular classroom teacher in educating these children. Chapter 14 is devoted to the curricular and extracurricular role of computers in the classroom, reflecting the rapidly increasing application of computer science in the field of education. Chapter 15 reviews the trend in educational psychology of researching specific subject areas to determine how each one should be taught.

Each chapter may be read independently and is, for the most part, self-contained. The reader is referred to other chapters for additional material where appropriate.

Acknowledgments

I would like to express gratitude to the following persons for contributions to this book: John Houtz, for conducting the content review of the manuscript and for contributing theoretical and historical perspectives, as well as enthusiasm for this field; Nanako Oguri, for content analysis of educational psychology textbooks during a graduate class project for John Houtz at Fordham University (the content analysis that Nanako and I worked on provided the outline for this book); Jill Conoley Slade, for detailed reviews on classroom management and learning patterns of exceptional children; Carol Tate, for work on second draft revisions; Lawrence Williams and Stella Anderson, for developing figures and additional examples to make the book easier to use and enjoy; Donna Rothstein, for reviewing information and providing examples from a classroom teacher's perspective; Donald H. Mershon, Rick Savage, Michael Rothemich, and Martha Stewart, for additional reviews; Fred Grayson, for continued support and encouragement; Warren Lewis, Dave Griffith, Daniel Carr, and other consultants at the North Carolina State University Computing Center for exceptional consulting services; and, of course, my parents and siblings for their support and enthusiasm.

I would also like to acknowledge the influence of several authors in the field: N. Gage, D. Berliner, T. Good, J. Brophy, J. Glover, and R. Bruner. Their comprehensive tests have contributed to my education and influenced this work.

PRR

Contents

CHAPTER 1

Scope and Purpose of Educational Psychology

This chapter introduces educational psychology, presenting its history, scope, and concerns. It summarizes the contributions of some important individuals in the field and discusses the significance of educational psychology for the classroom teacher.

Definition of Educational Psychology

Educational psychology, a branch of psychology concerned with human learning and development in educational settings, involves scientific study of techniques that can be used to enhance learning. Studies conducted by educational psychologists generally focus on one of the following three areas:

The teaching process (teaching methods, styles, management techniques, etc.)

The learner and the learning process (appllication of principles of

1

cognitive and developmental psychology, taking into account individual differences and learning styles)

The environment (the social context of the classroom or home environment)

The educational psychologist is, in a sense, somewhere between the teacher and the learner in the education hierarchy. Two important functions of educational psychologists are (1) conducting research to learn the most effective ways to teach, and (2) applying research findings from other branches of psychology to educational settings. Research from each of the following fields helps teachers become effective communicators and instructors.

Cognitive psychology emphasizes the role of mental processes in understanding behavior; involves the study of thinking, learning, remembering, problem solving, and to some extent, perceiving.

Developmental psychology is the study of human growth, typically along cognitive, emotional, and physical dimensions.

Social psychology involves study of how social interaction influences behavior.

Educational measurement involves the application of measurement theory to the evaluation of relevant variables such as achievement in educational settings.

Personality theories identify patterns and causes of characteristic behaviors, attitudes, and emotional responses.

Studies of *individual differences* explain characteristics that distinguish one person from another.

Brief History of Educational Psychology

Establishing the Discipline of Psychology

Because educational psychology evolved from the broad discipline of psychology, this history discussion begins with the founding of psychology, in which Wilhelm Wundt and William James played major roles.

Wilhelm Wundt

Wilhelm Wundt is credited with founding the field of modern psychology in 1879 with establishment of the first recognized laboratory for the study of experimental psychology at the University of Leipzig in Germany. During this same time, *Hermann Ebbinghaus* founded a department of psychology at Berlin and *Georg Elias Muller* headed a department of psychology at Gottingen. Each of these individuals made substantial contributions to the field of psychology. Some of Wundt's students, such as *G. Stanley Hall* (who was also one of William James's students), *James McKeen Cattell,* and *Edward Bradford Titchener* helped establish the discipline of psychology in the United States.

William James

However, the establishment of the formal discipline of psychology in this country is usually credited to William James. James (1842–1910) developed and taught the first formal academic psychology course in the United States while he was an instructor at Harvard. In his textbook for this course, *Principles of Psychology,* he described what he believed were the general principles of the field. He also established a small psychological laboratory in America (in 1875, about the same time Wundt established his laboratory) and anticipated many important theories. As an instructor at Harvard, James became increasingly interested in the educational process. In his writing he described psychology as a science and teaching as an art, and he stated that the quality of education depended on the creativity of teachers and on their ability to apply psychological principles.

Founding of Educational Psychology

James also significantly influenced the method of investigation of the learning process. He believed in the importance of natural observation, that is, studying psychology directly in the classroom. This approach is generally referred to as *naturalistic observation* or *field studies.* As an instructor, James recognized the importance of starting where the learner is, a concept that is still valid. During his 30 or more years of study and teaching in the field of psychology, James presented many insightful concepts in a series of famous lectures entitled "Talks to Teachers" (1899).

Edward Thorndike

One frequent problem with observation in the classroom is that the large number of factors operating at any given time make it difficult for the observer to determine precisely what is influencing the learning process. For instance, any number of factors might influence a student's disruptive behavior. The classroom is a large composite structure with many components, and it is often difficult or impossible to completely understand the interrelationship between these components by merely observing the entire system. Edward L. Thorndike (1874-1949) recognized this difficulty and influenced educational psychologists to bring their studies into laboratories where the many variables could be controlled and investigated "scientifically." Whereas William James studied psychology by means of classroom observation, Thorndike conducted experimental studies on animals in a laboratory. While teaching at Teachers College at Columbia University after 1898, he studied the behavior patterns of cats placed in "puzzle" boxes, particularly how long it would take the cats to learn how to escape from the boxes and what rewards were the most effective in eliciting this behavior. Thorndike learned much about this trial-and-error learning. As did James, Thorndike published works of great importance, especially *Educational Psychology*, a textbook first published in 1903. In this text, Thorndike outlined and defined the field of educational psychology.

Throughout the 1930s, under Edward Thorndike's influence, educational psychology became more objective and empirical than it had been under William James and also more narrowly focused. You will read more about the contributions of these two individuals later, but at this point keep in mind the need for both kinds of study in educational psychology. James's studies centered on the classroom itself, whereas Thorndike's studies were conducted in the laboratory, where learning could be measured under more controlled conditions.

John Dewey

Another important contributor to the field of psychology was John Dewey (1859–1952). In the early 1900s, Dewey stressed the importance of studying learning in the actual environment in which the learning was to occur. This is sometimes referred to as an *ecological concept*. Dewey believed that the child was not a passive organism, waiting to receive information, but rather an active learner; therefore, learning should be engineered carefully to guide the child's growth with respect to the child's interests and abilities. Unfortunately, Dewey's ideas were often misinterpreted. Many people misconstrued his approach to mean that the learning experience should center on the child and that children should be allowed to choose their own activities, even to play all day, if that was chosen. Today, however, many of Dewey's ideas, especially his "learning by doing" concept, are implemented as they were originally intended (e.g., the use of learning centers and workshops). Dewey also advocated that the student and the teacher participate equally in the learning process. This view is generally accepted today. Dewey perceived the classroom as a place where learning and living occur simultaneously, thus creating the concept of the classroom as an interactive environment. This is one of the fundamental concepts of contemporary educational psychology.

Educational Psychology in the Early and Mid–1900s

About the same time as Thorndike's text was published in 1910, the first educational psychology journal, the *Journal of Educational Psychology,* was published. Since that time, the field has grown with a proliferation of journals developed to organize a growing body of research in the field. In 1940, *G. Frederick Kuder* founded the *Psychological and Educational Measurement Journal*, and in 1964 the American Educational Research Association began publishing reports of educational research in its own journal and has consistently published studies in educational psychology. By the 1960s the field was firmly established, with several scholarly journals and university programs in educational psychology.

Important Influences on Educational Psychology		
Contributor	Place of Study	Contribution(s)
William James (1842–1910)	Harvard University	Taught first psychology course in the U.S. and wrote *Principles of Psychology*; used natural observation as method
Edward Thorndike (1874–1949)	Columbia University; Teachers College	Wrote *Educational Psychology*; used controlled laboratory studies; discussed trial-and-error learning; documented the law of effect
John Dewey (1859–1952)	Johns Hopkins University	Believed in the ecological concept and that the classroom should be interactive; advocated learning by doing

The Field Today

Today there are professional associations for educational psychologists, such as the American Psychological Association Division of Educational Psychology (Division 15) and the American Educational Research Association. Scholarly journals such as *Contemporary Educational Psychology*, *Educational Psychologist*, *Educational Psychology Review*, and *American Educational Research Journal* continue to be developed and published to meet the needs of contemporary educational psychologists.

In the 1970s and especially the 1980s, leaders in the study of educational psychology have tried to define the field more clearly and differentiate it from other branches of psychology. The field continues to be influenced by work in related areas, particularly cognitive psychology. As educational psychologists incorporate a cognitive perspective today, they attempt to understand how the components in the learning environment affect mental processes. An increasing number of educational psychology textbooks utilize a cognitive psychology approach, and graduate students in educational psychology generally take at least one course in cognitive psychology. The influence of cognitive psychology on education is indicated in the title *Cognition and Instruction*, a journal founded in 1984 by Lauren Resnick.

The present state of educational psychology is quite encouraging. More precisely defined than previously, it is recognized as a field in its own right, capable of utilizing the significant advances in related fields, such as computer science.

Issues Confronting Educational Psychologists

To understand the issues important to educational psychologists, read the list of questions below and try to answer them. Some of the questions are very specific, and others are general; educational psychologists try to answer both types.

1. Does television make children violent?

2. In what academic areas do gender differences exist?

3. What is the best way to improve vocabulary?

4. Does punishment help to eliminate disruptive behavior?

5. How should computers be used in the classroom?

6. What kind of training would be helpful for substitute teachers?

7. How do children learn?

8. How do adults learn?

9. Which teacher behaviors tend to increase student achievement?

10. How do emotions and attitudes affect learning?

11. How should learning be measured?

12. Should instruction methods vary for different age
groups?

This list represents a small subset of the questions and problems
that educational researchers consider throughout their careers. One
aspect of research of this nature, as mentioned before, is that it involves
so many variables (components). What the educational psychologist
must do is first determine which variables are relevant and then decide
how to study them. From their studies, educational psychologists
attempt to derive laws or principles that predict how learning occurs
and how it can be enhanced.

Why Teachers Study Educational Psychology

Understanding the subject matter that you are going to teach to
other people is not sufficient; simply knowing the material does not
ensure that you will be able to communicate it, or that your students will
be able to comprehend it. Studying educational psychology should
enhance your ability to communicate what you know and determine
whether, in fact, your students are learning what you intend them to
learn.

Educational psychology teaches you about managing your classroom to promote learning and minimize disruption. It teaches you how
to present your lessons to both large and small groups—and when to do
which. It also teaches you how to predict certain learning patterns in
students of different ages and from different backgrounds, to comprehend the importance and limitations of the theories employed in
teaching strategies, and to utilize the many tools and techniques that are
available to you, the teacher. Best of all, studying educational psychology will remind you how challenging teaching can be, and how gratify-
ing it is when you make it work for you.

*Educational psychologists incorporate knowledge of the teaching
process, the learning process, and the learning environment in
strategies that are designed to enhance learning. They study topics
such as cognitive and developmental psychology, principles of measurement, and classroom management techniques to determine how to*

create an appropriate learning environment. Educational psychologists also conduct experiments, some in the classroom and some in laboratories, to find their own answers to unresolved questions.

Educational psychology began with William James and Edward Thorndike in the United States in the late 1800s. James showed us that classroom observation provided an important source of information about the learning process. Thorndike went further and insisted that we learn from scientific measurement performed in a laboratory environment. John Dewey was another early contributor to the field. Although he was misunderstood by many people, Dewey introduced important concepts, namely that the child is an active learner and that teachers should reach out to where the student's interests and potentials lie. The field of educational psychology continues to be influenced by work in related fields such as developmental psychology, educational measurement, cognitive psychology, social psychology, personality theory, counseling, individual differences, and most recently, computer science.

Professional Periodicals and Research Materials

Following is a list of professional periodicals in several relevant branches of psychology. Articles that appear in these periodicals present the most current research findings in the field and also represent the basis for new teaching methods and practices.

Adult Education
American Educational Research Journal
Behavioral Science
Change
Child Development
Childhood Education
Clearing House
Contemporary Educational Psychology
Developmental Psychology
Education
Education Digest
Educational Research Quarterly
Educational and Psychological Measurement
Educational Forum

Educational Leadership
Educational Record
Educational Researcher
Educational Technology
Elementary School Journal
Encyclopedia of Educational Research
Exceptional Child
Exceptional Children
Genetic Psychology Monographs
Gifted Child Quarterly
Handbook of Research on Teaching
Harvard Educational Review
High School Journal
Journal of Abnormal and Social Psychology
Journal of Applied Behavioral Analysis
Journal of Education
Journal of Educational Psychology
Journal of Educational Research
Journal of Educational Sociology
Journal of Experimental Child Psychology
Journal of Experimental Education
Journal of Experimental Psychology
Journal of General Education
Journal of Higher Education
Journal of Research and Development in Education
Journal of Teacher Education
Junior College Journal
Merril-Palmer Quarterly of Behavior and Development
Mental Hygiene
Phi Delta Kappan
Psychological Monographs
Psychological Review
Psychology in the Schools
Readings in Educational Research
Review of Educational Research
Review of Research in Education
School Review
Society for Research in Child Development Monographs
Teachers College Journal
Teachers College Record
Theory into Practice
Yearbooks of the National Society for Study of Education

The following important resources provide abstracts (brief summaries) of existing research, review published works, and describe important trends (directions in the field).

American Psychologist–provides information about trends in the field
Annual Review of Psychology-reviews significant work in the past year
Child Development Abstracts and Bibliography–provides abstracts of child development studies from many relevant journals
Contemporary Psychology–reviews new books on psychology
Educational Resources Information Center (ERIC)–publishes three valuable resources: Current Index to Journals in Education (CIJE, an index of articles published in most education-related journals); Research in Education (lists curriculum guides and other information not published in journals); and ERIC Educational Documents Index (index of works found in Research in Education and Office of Education Research Reports)
Psych INFO–provides computer database of psychological studies published in almost all relevant journals; also includes relevant dissertations
Psychological Abstracts–provides summaries of psychology studies published in almost all relevant journals (approximately 900 journals are indexed)
Psychological Bulletin–publishes evaluative and integrative reviews of content and methodological issues in psychology
Psychological Record–publishes theoretical and experimental articles in psychology; also comments on certain articles and book reviews
Psychological Reports–publishes articles with important experimental, theoretical, and speculative contributions to psychology; one-page notes and monograph supplements; and comments on and lists of new books
Review of Educational Research–provides composite articles that combine several articles on a given educational topic
Social Science Citation Index—indicates references where a particular author has been cited
Social Science Index–indexes the most important periodicals in psychology and related fields

The following periodicals frequently present suggestions for different techniques and tools that other professionals have found useful.

Grade Teacher
Instructor
Learning
Psychology Today
Today's Education

In addition, a periodical concerned with a particular field of education might interest you. For example, there are special journals published in arithmetic, coaching, music, geography, and theater. Check with a college or university reference librarian to locate the specific journals that interest you.

Recommended Reading

Cook, T. D., and D. T. Campbell (1979). *Quasi-experimentation: Design and Analysis Issues for Field Settings.* Chicago: Rand McNally. (Provides descriptions of appropriate methods for conducting field research.)

Douglas, N., and N. Baum (1984). *Library Research Guide to Psychology.* Ann Arbor, Mich.: Pierian Press. (Provides sources and relevant information on library research.)

Gage, N. L. (1978). *The Scientific Basis of the Art of Teaching.* New York: Teachers College Press. (Provides a discussion of the art of teaching and its scientific basis.)

James, W. (1899). *Talks to Teachers on Psychology and to Students on Some of Life's Ideals.* New York: Holt. (Provides background on the field of educational psychology with many ideas that are very useful today.)

Kerlinger, F. N. (1973). *Foundations of Behavioral Research,* 2d ed. New York: Holt, Rinehart and Winston. (Presents basic research methodologies.)

Schulman, L. S. (1982). Educational Psychology Returns to the School, in A. G. Kraut, (Ed.), *The G. Stanley Hall Lecture Series, Vol. II.* Washington, D.C.: American Psychological Association. (Provides an analysis of educational psychology and describes where it should go in the future.)

Slavin, R. E. (1984). *Research Methods in Education: A Practical Guide.* Englewood Cliffs, N.J.: Prentice-Hall. (Provides discussion of basic research methods applicable to educational psychology.)

CHAPTER 2

Effective Teaching

As mentioned in Chapter 1, educational psychologists ask both general and specific questions about learning situations. One basic issue they investigate is whether teachers are effective. For the purpose of this discussion, effective teachers are those who design lessons, utilize appropriate teaching strategies, and implement management techniques to optimize learning for all students. After identifying effective teachers, researchers try to determine what makes those teachers effective. A number of factors, such as gender, teaching method, and personality, have been associated with student achievement. For many reasons, these issues are quite difficult to investigate. There are many studies with conflicting results, which further research is trying to clarify. Having reviewed many studies, a few researchers have extracted guidelines for effective teaching. Some of these guidelines are presented in this chapter. You will read about the importance of flexibility, the differences in teaching basic and higher-order skills, and several other guidelines that may improve your ability to teach effectively.

Are There Keys to Success?

The best answer to this question is probably no. Knowledge of the subject matter does not guarantee the ability to teach it. Good communication skills do not invariably indicate the ability to teach students what they need to learn. A teacher's popularity with the students does not necessarily mean that the teacher knows the material or is an effective communicator. In other words, there are no simple answers or guarantees. However, research has indicated that several measures tend to improve one's ability to teach effectively. These guidelines are presented below, but first is a discussion of some controversial research known as the Coleman report. It is important that you are familiar with this work because people still misunderstand and misuse its findings that are related to teacher effectiveness.

The Coleman Report

James S. Coleman (1926–) headed a team of researchers in 1964 who spent 2 years investigating the availability of educational opportunities in the public school systems. The researchers were looking for inequalities based on students' race, color, religion, or national origin. The survey included approximately 4,000 schools, 60,000 teachers, and 600,000 students. The results of the investigation were published in 1966 as *Equality of Educational Opportunity*, which is usually called the Coleman report. Instead of demonstrating inequalities in educational opportunity for different students, the report claimed that almost no particular school-related characteristic had a significant effect on student achievement. In other words, factors such as teacher salary, teacher education, and length of the school day had no relationship to student achievement. On the other hand, social class—a characteristic that teachers cannot affect—did seem to matter. According to this report, students from upper- and middle-class homes appeared to learn better. Because the Coleman report suggested that only one school characteristic, social class, is related to academic achievement, it was disturbing to many educators and researchers. It seemed to imply that nothing teachers do makes a difference.

How should these results be interpreted? Is it true that nothing teachers do makes a difference? When evaluating the validity of the Coleman report, three general points should be considered.

1. The results were extrapolated from *correlational data*; that is, the variables studied were related, but not experimentally manipulated. You will find more about correlation in the chapter on measurement, but for purposes here, correlational means that knowing something about the performance on one variable provides information about performance on the other variable. The variables may vary together, but you do not know whether one variable *caused* the other. As the report indicated, students from upper- and middle-class homes did better, so there is a correlation between social class and achievement. This relation does not mean that one thing caused the other. You *cannot* infer that belonging to an upper-class family caused higher achievement scores.

2. Because the data were averaged together, the beneficial effects to some of the students became less apparent. The research presented in the Coleman report did not investigate how individual students were affected by each variable; rather, student performance as a whole was investigated. What could be overlooked is how individual students benefited in the classroom from a particular variable, such as type of instruction. It is possible that some students benefited from one type of instruction and others did not.

3. Student achievement was measured by standardized achievement tests, which measure only certain kinds of learning. They provide educators with important information, but when considered alone, they do not give a complete picture of a student's academic achievement.

In spite of statistical deficiencies, the Coleman report generated controversy and doubt on the effectiveness of the public schools. However, it had some positive consequences. Research conducted in the last 20 years has indicated that several variables can affect student learning. Some of these variables include teacher behaviors, teaching strategies designed for different groups of students, and teaching strategies applied to different academic subjects. One example of research that was directly influenced by the Coleman report is Goodlad's report (in *A Place Called School*, 1983) that the quality of instruction is poorer in classes for low-ability students than in classes

Important Influences on Educational Psychology		
Contributor	Place of Study	Contribution(s)
James Coleman (1926–)	University of Chicago	Distinguished effective and ineffective teaching methods
Herbert Walberg (1937–)	Purdue and Columbia Universities	Published report on educational opportunity in public schools

for higher-ability students. In these cases, the quality of instruction may affect student achievement.

Factors in Effective Teaching

Flexibility

Unfortunately, no teaching strategy or technique has proved to be effective all the time for all students. One general principle that emerges from the research, though, is a need for the teacher to be flexible—to be trained and competent in different strategies and to be able to apply those strategies at different times for different students.

Enthusiasm

Another significant factor in student learning for which there is some correlational evidence (remember: do not assume causality) is teacher attitude (i.e., enthusiasm). Greater student achievement gains have been associated with more enthusiastic, friendly teachers (Rosenshine & Furst, 1973).

Classroom Management

Classroom management refers to a broad range of techniques used to facilitate instruction, maximize learning time, maintain a pleasant atmosphere, prevent disruptive behaviors, and deal with discipline problems. Refer to Chapter 3 for more information on classroom management.

Knowledge of the Subject, Organization, and Clear Presentation

Knowledge of the subject, organization of the subject matter, and clear presentation are necessary for effective teaching. Information should be presented in a sequence that makes sense to the students and should prepare them sufficiently for practice or exercises. Time should be provided for review and discussion of the material. Examples relevant to the students' own experiences should be provided in the material. Filler words such as "not very," "somehow," and "you know" should be avoided.

The Walberg Report

More evidence for relationships between teaching and student achievement is provided in a report by Herbert Walberg (1984). Walberg (1937–) compiled the results of more than 3000 studies and found that many factors contribute to student learning. The factors over which teachers can have some control are discussed below.

1. Reinforcement facilitates learning. The factor most likely to affect achievement is positive reinforcement. Positive reinforcement is the presentation of a pleasant stimulus after a behavior occurs which increases the chances that the behavior will occur in the future. Praise such as "Chester, finishing all your math problems before recess took a lot of hard work" is a good example of positive reinforcement. For the reinforcement to be effective, it must be specific, contingent on the desired behavior, and not overdone. You should also be aware that reinforcement is more effective with some students, particularly those from lower- and/or working-class backgrounds, than with others. You will read more about this in the chapters on classroom management and learning theories.

2. Efficient use of academic learning time enhances achievement. The amount of time that teachers devote to academic tasks varies. Spending a lot of time on a task does not guarantee that it will be learned, but there is some indication that the efficient use of time affects student achievement.

3. Providing cues and time to answer can improve student perfor-

mance. Effective teachers provide useful cues when students need help. For example, when a student is unsure of the correct response to "4 + 1 = ?", a helpful cue might be, "Is 4 + 1 = the same thing as 5 + 0, and 5 + 0 = ?" Another part of cuing, besides asking helpful questions, is allowing enough wait time. Be sure that the student has enough time to generate a response, without feeling anxious that you will hurry on to someone else. In the movie "The Paper Chase" (and subsequent television series), Professor Kingsfield was notorious for the abrupt manner in which he questioned his law students. Kingsfield provides an excellent example of what *not* to do.

4. Teacher feedback can enhance student achievement. Feedback has also been shown to affect student performance. Walberg found that when teachers graded homework assignments and provided comments, student performance was affected to a greater degree than when homework assignments were not graded.

5. Cooperative learning increases student performance. To establish cooperative learning, use small-group activities to encourage students to participate toward a common goal. For instance, each group consisting of several students could be assigned a special project such as creating a volcano that actually erupts, determining the dimensions of the classroom, and reenacting the signing of the Declaration of Independence. Grading the students based on group performance rather than individual performance may encourage cooperation, reduce competition within the group, and result in increased performance and social awareness.

6. Classroom climate affects student performance. The classroom climate can make a difference in student performance. Walberg found feelings of cohesiveness, satisfaction, goal direction, and friendliness to be conducive to learning. Other research (e.g., Torrence, 1962) suggests that warm, spontaneous, caring teachers foster creative student behavior.

7. Higher-order questions encourage analytical thinking. A higher-order question is one for which a predetermined, correct answer does not exist. The student is compelled to think, analyze, or reason in some manner to create an answer. Asking students to name the first president of the United States is an example of a lower-order question; asking them to explain the importance of presidents is a higher-order question. The latter question enables students to consider the possibilities and explain the complex concept in their own way. Higher-order questions are more likely to increase achievement than are simple, lower-order questions that require rote memorization or mimicking the teacher's words. Again, however, this strategy must be tempered by who the student is. For example, as you will read later, students in primary grades and students learning basic skills will more likely benefit from simple, direct instruction. Higher-order questions are most appropriate for problem-oriented and reasoning tasks.

8. *Advance organizers increase the amount of retained information.* An advance organizer is information presented to the student before a lesson. An effective advance organizer will relate existing student knowledge to the material that will be presented and will indicate what the main points of that material will be. Walberg reports some relationship between the use of advance organizers and student performance. Although other researchers have failed to demonstrate the utility of these organizers in affecting performance, it is common practice to incorporate them in lessons and texts.

Characteristics of Effective Teachers

As discussed earlier, the recent research has tried to pinpoint exactly what behaviors effective teachers exhibit. The following general characteristics and qualities appear to be shared by effective teachers:

1. They are effective classroom managers; that is, they can control the class, handle behavior problems with minimal disturbance to the rest of the class, and utilize class time efficiently.

2. They have appropriate delivery techniques, presenting the lessons in a way that maintains the students' interest.

3. They help the students build self-concept.

4. They go beyond teaching the basic skills and teach critical

thinking and problem-solving skills that will be useful outside the classroom.

5. They evaluate the progress of their students and provide constructive feedback.

6. They are aware of the special needs of some of their students and work to meet those needs wherever possible.

7. They keep abreast of current research so that they can use it to benefit their students.

The Design of Instruction

Appropriate instructional design is crucial for effective teaching. There are both micro (small, specific) and macro (large, general) considerations. Micro considerations relate to how you design the lesson structures. The structure you design depends in part on teaching objectives and student abilities. Macro considerations concern teaching methods you choose. The method you choose depends in part on the age, ability level, and motivation of your students. The subject area you teach is also an important consideration when choosing a teaching method.

Designing Lesson Structures

Before you choose an appropriate teaching method, you must identify the scope of the instruction and the instructional objectives. In teaching a unit on the five senses, for example, will you teach physiology of the eye and the ear? *Instructional objectives* identify the information, skill, or attitude to be learned and the desired level of performance. For example, the student will name the five senses and give examples of each. You also need to consider the *timeframe* of the instruction. Should this unit last 1 week, 1 month, or 30 minutes? If you will teach this information over 1 month, should you present information once a week or once a day? Another consideration is how to relate this information to other events in the students' lives. If you are teaching a unit on the senses, how can you include reference to the bakery that recently opened across from the school, a recent concert by Stevie Wonder, or an annual eye exam?

Before designing a new car, automobile designers are aware of current consumer demand and preferences and, as they develop the design, have specific performance objectives and development timeframes in mind. This process ensures that there is a market for the product they are producing. For example, before a race car is designed, designers try to determine who is likely to purchase the car (men or women, students or professionals, etc.), its passing speed (0–60 mph in 7 seconds), and when it should be available. When the car is built, advertisements are directed to a particular type of consumer and the car sells.

Similarly, understanding the needs of your students, identifying the scope of the instruction, and specifying the performance criteria will help you to design effective lessons.

Choosing a Teaching Method

There are many standard teaching methods from which you may choose. Effective teachers remain flexible and choose instructional methods to meet instructional objectives and student needs and abilities. Several methods are described briefly in this section and in more detail in Chapter 9.

Lecture Instruction

Lecture instruction is the oral presentation of material to a group of students. This format is most appropriate when students are relatively homogeneous, that is, have similar backgrounds and ability. The effectiveness of lectures can be enhanced with supplementary audiovisual presentations (movies, slides, models, tape recordings).

Small-Group Instruction

Small-group instruction is the presentation of material to individual groups of students who may be assigned to work together on the basis of a common characteristic, such as reading ability. When the class consists of students with different ability levels or markedly different backgrounds, small groups may be formed for instructional purposes. Small groups are well suited to provide special training needed by all students in the group and are useful when it is necessary to assess the level of understanding or identify problem areas; this is because students are not as inhibited in small groups, especially when other students in the group share the same problem. Similarly, students who excel in a particular area may be grouped together for enrichment activities.

Although small groups may be useful for instructional purposes, students of all abilities need to work and learn together. Small group assignments should be used to facilitate motivation and learning, but not to discourage students from working with one another. Grouping by academic ability is sometimes unfeasible or unnecessary, as in physical activities, creative activities, role-playing, and social skills development.

Individualized Instruction

Individualized instruction is a process for tailoring instruction to meet the needs of an individual student. This can be implemented with self-paced information units and minimal teacher involvement. When one unit is complete, the student is tested on that unit. After passing the test, the student proceeds to the next unit.

This method can be implemented with tutoring. One instructor (a teacher, adult, or advanced student) teaches one student, tailoring the instruction to meet the specific needs of that student. Again, the pace of the instruction is determined largely by the student.

Certain computer programs are designed specifically to provide individualized instruction. Computers can be used to present, drill, and assess student performance. Individualized instruction, especially tutoring, can be expensive. However, it seems to benefit low-ability students and is often used in special-education and remedial classrooms.

Direct Instruction

Direct instruction is a teacher-centered, structured approach where the students are made aware of the goals, instruction is comprehensive, performance is monitored, and feedback is given (Rosenshine, 1979). Direct instruction is well suited for teaching basic skills and low-ability students. Direct instruction may also be appropriate when you are teaching high-ability students facts (the "who" and the "when").

Open Education

Open education permits students to interact with objects and classmates to encourage learning. In this setting, physical space is open, many materials are available, different age groups may work together, students select their own topics, and instruction is often individualized. Researchers have found greater emotional gains for students in open education programs than in traditional settings.

Mastery Learning

Mastery learning requires students to learn objectives in a particular sequence. They do not advance to a new objective until a specified level of acceptable performance is demonstrated. This approach is appropriate for teaching motor skills, basic academic skills, and low-ability students. The class tends to progress as one unit. While this may not be expedient for higher-ability students who must wait for others to acquire mastery of a given objective, low-ability or slower students are not left behind because instruction does not continue until all students in the class have mastered the material. Additionally, because the material is tested at an individual objective level, specific problem areas are identified and follow-up instruction can be provided.

Discovery Learning

Discovery learning occurs as students learn by doing. Teachers begin lessons with specific examples and stimulate students to discover the general principles from the examples and details. The teacher sets up problems and asks key questions. This approach encourages creative thinking and inductive reasoning. It requires advance preparation from the teacher and assumes that the students have the necessary cognitive skills.

Teaching Different Subject Areas

Educational psychologists now conduct research to determine the most effective ways of teaching different subject areas. They are developing teaching methods for each subject area.

Designing Instruction for Different Students

In this section, many factors previously discussed will be reviewed as they apply to effective teaching for students of different ages and different aptitudes.

Structure and Feedback

Students in the primary grades are most likely to benefit from structured presentations with lots of opportunity for practice (Brophy, 1976). As mentioned in Walberg's research, feedback is also very important. A warm attitude is especially helpful for younger students (Brophy, 1976). Teaching strategies for students in higher grades are more likely to include group discussions and higher-order questions where there is less definite structure. Of course, feedback and reinforcement are still important, but not as critical as they were for the younger students.

Aptitude

Aptitudes vary among students in the same class. Aptitude is a person's ability to perform in a particular area or at a particular task. *Aptitude-Treatment Interaction (ATI)* studies are designed to show how differing aptitudes are affected by various teaching strategies or other treatments. The results of ATI studies demonstrate the need to use different teaching strategies for students with different aptitudes. For example, a study by Peterson et al. (1980) demonstrated that ninth-grade social studies students with high verbal ability performed best when they had been taught by lecture, while students with lower verbal ability performed best when they had been taught using a public-issues approach. (A public-issues approach involves active student participation. Students obtain and organize information from source material and use that information to support their position on a specific issue.) Other studies have revealed similar findings.

Prior Knowledge

Selection of an appropriate teaching strategy is also somewhat dependent on the students' prior knowledge of the material (Rosenshine & Stevens, 1986). If students already know much of the material, the way you present it will be of little consequence, whereas if the students know very little or nothing of the material, the way you present it can make a considerable difference in how much they learn.

Lesson Format

The lesson format is also important. For students with low ability levels, the following format is recommended: make a short presentation, have the students work for a few minutes, then continue by presenting them with more content information in a short presentation, and then have them practice again (Evertson, 1982). This format differs from a more traditional format that would involve one long presentation followed by a long period of solitary seatwork. The recommended format provides small amounts of information each time and does not leave the students to work on their own for long periods.

For higher-ability students, it is important to stimulate them with high-level questions and problems. The presentation format is not as important as it is for lower-level students. Longer lectures can be given and less practice time is needed.

Grading

Lower-ability students should receive grades often to enable them to monitor their progress. When possible, include the students in the grading activity. Students can become more familiar with your expectations when they participate in the grading process. Also, having students correct their own errors helps to ensure that they are learning accurate information.

The Coleman report presented findings suggesting that the primary characteristic that affects student achievement is social class. Although this research was somewhat fraught with methodological problems, the claim spawned much research about the effectiveness of teaching. The research that followed demonstrated many measures that teachers can take to affect student achievement, although there is no one key to success. Some of the behaviors that are important are positive reinforcement, feedback, cues, ample practice, and clear presentations. Creating a pleasant classroom climate is also important. Prerequisites for effective teaching are knowledge of the subject material and skill in classroom management techniques. Research has also demonstrated that a direct instruction method is useful for teaching basic skills and low-ability students. The teaching method used for knowledgeable students is not as important to achievement as is the teaching method used for less informed students. The one finding that is implied repeatedly is the importance of flexibility. Teachers must be able to implement different teaching strategies for different students.

Recommended Reading

Brophy, J. (1982). Successful Teaching Strategies for the Inner-city Child, *Phi Delta Kappan,* 63, 527-530. (Suggestions for teaching inner-city children based on research.)

Epstein, J. (Ed.). (1981). *Masters: Portraits of Great Teachers.* New York: Basic Books. (Essays written by students about their teachers.)

Gage, N. L. (1985), Hard Gains in the Soft Sciences., Bloomington, Indiana: Phi *Delta Kappan.* (Describes many programs and teacher behaviors that affect student learning.)

Good, T., D. Grouws, and H. Ebmeier, (1983). *Active Mathematics Teaching.* New York: Longman. (Describes the development of the Missouri Mathematics Program.)

Hunter, M. (1982). *Mastery Teaching.* El Segundo, Calif.: TIP Publications. (Explains how to conduct lessons, motivate students, and present the material.)

Jencks, C. S. (1972). *Inequality. A Reassessment of the Effect of Family and Schooling in America,* New York: Basic Books. (Presents a comprehensive evaluation and discussion of the data presented in the Coleman report.)

Redl, F., and W. W. Wattenberg. (1959). *Mental Hygiene in Teaching*, 2d ed. New York: Harcourt, Brace, & World. (Provides many suggestions for coping with frustration and also for influencing students.)

Research on Teaching (1983). *The Elementary School Journal.* 83 (4). (A special issue with articles by the leading researchers in the field on effectiveness.)

Rosenthal, R., and L. Jacobson. (1968). *Pygmalion in the Classroom.* New York: Holt, Rinehart and Winston. (Discusses effects of teacher's expectations on student behaviors.)

Walberg, H. (1984). Improving the Productivity of American Schools, Educational Leadership. 41, 19-27. (Presents composite results of many studies on effect of teaching methods on student achievement.)

Wittrock, M. (Ed.). (1986). *Handbook of Research on Teaching*, 3d ed. New York: Macmillian. (An outstanding collection of articles on teaching.)

References

Brophy, J. E. (1976). Reflections on research in elementary schools, *Journal of Teacher Education,* 27, 31-34.

Coleman, J. S., E. Q. Campbell, C. L. Hobson, J. M. McPartland, A. M. Mood, F. D. Weinfeld, and R. L. York. (1966). *Equality of Educational Opportunity.* Washington, D.C.: U.S. Department of Health, Education and Welfare.

Evertson, C. M. (1982). Differences in instructional activities in high and low achieving junior high classes. *Elementary School Journal.* 82, 329-350.

Good, T. (1982). Classroom Research: What We Know and What We Need to Know *R and D Report* No. 9018. Austin: Research and Development Center for Teacher Education, University of Texas.

Goodlad, J. I. (1983). *A Placed Called School.* New York: McGraw-Hill.

Peterson, P., T. C. Janicki, and S. R. Swing. (1980). Aptitude-treatment Interaction Effects of Three Social Studies Teaching Approaches. *American Educational Research Journal.* 17, 339-360.

Rosenshine, B. (1979). The Third Cycle of Research on Teacher Effects: Content Covered, Academic Engaged Time, and Direct Instruction, in P. L. Peterson and H. J. Walberg, (Eds.). (1979), *Research on Teaching: Concepts, Findings, and Implications.* Berkeley: McCutchan.

Rosenshine, B. , and N. Furst. (1973). The Use of Direct Observation to Study Teaching, in R. Travers, Ed., *Second Handbook of Research on Teaching.* Chicago: Rand McNally.

Rosenshine, R., and R. Stevens. (1986). Teaching Functions, in M. Wittrock, (Ed.). *Handbook of Research on Teaching* 3d ed. New York: Macmillan, pp. 376–391.

Torrance, E. P. (1962). *Guiding Creative Talent.* Englewood Cliffs, NJ: Prentice-Hall.

Walberg, H. (1984). Improving the Productivity of American Schools, *Educational Leadership,* 41, 19–27.

CHAPTER 3

Classroom Management

Classroom management refers to a broad range of techniques used to facilitate instruction, maximize learning time, maintain a pleasant atmosphere, prevent disruptive behavior, and handle discipline problems. Classroom management techniques include communication and management skills and instructional tactics. Effective classroom management entails planning classroom activities, setting ground rules, and knowing how to enforce the rules, all the while treating the students with respect.

Classroom management is essential to effective teaching. The more time you spend teaching, the more your students are likely to learn. If you spend most of your time handling (or mishandling) discipline problems, you are cutting short your teaching time. The study of classroom management teaches you the techniques of classroom dynamics and shows you how to use them to your advantage. You learn to maintain a supportive environment, provide opportunities for success, and reinforce appropriate behaviors. These techniques help students behave in ways that facilitate your task of teaching.

Most behavior problems are minor disruptions such as one student's getting up, walking around, or talking in a way that disturbs other students. Common problems are inattention and failure to obey class rules. More serious problems may occur, such as vandalism, fighting, stealing, and showing disrespect. Substance abuse (e.g., marijuana, alcohol) that results in behavior changes is also a potential problem in today's schools. In effective classroom management the emphasis is on prevention rather than on palliative measures such as punishment; potential behavior problems should be detected and kept from developing.

Researchers in Classroom Management

William Glasser

William Glasser (1925–) is known for formulating "reality therapy," a type of psychotherapy designed to help clients handle real-world events, meet their needs, and thus control their own lives. He developed an approach for preventing behavior problems, which he described in his book *Schools without Failure* (1969). He identified several principles, described below, that can be implemented in the classroom environment.

1. *Concentrate on present behaviors; do not dwell on previous ones.* School should be a place where students can be successful.

2. *Establish and enforce reasonable rules.* Monitor student progress and provide reinforcement as much as possible. Demonstrate that you are committed to plans that are made. Do not accept excuses from the students. A student who expresses commitment to something is expected to follow through.

3. *Accept all students as being potentially capable.* Express concern for your students. Respect the students' judgments; ask them for opinions about what they are doing.

4. *Point out to your students how learning in school relates to their experiences outside school.* Involve classroom students in the decision-making process, especially in those decisions that affect them personally.

5. *Do not punish students.* Punishment can generate unwanted

negative consequences. For instance, Glasser maintains that punishing students discourages the sense of responsibility students should have for their own behavior. According to Glasser, students should be responsible for attending class, studying, and learning. (Punishment is discussed further in this chapter and in Chapter 6.)

6. *Hold class meetings to discuss classroom and real-world events that are important to the students.* Glasser suggests discussing social behavior in school, current topics that are on their minds, and school curriculum. Meetings help students learn to solve problems, express opinions orally, and get involved in their own progress. The meetings can also encourage students to participate in classroom management strategies.

Jacob Kounin

Jacob Kounin (1912–) investigated student reactions to teacher control techniques and indicated that the following techniques are most effective for maintaining control.

1. *Demonstrate "withitness" to help maintain control.* Withitness is demonstration of knowledge of things the students care about, such as forthcoming concerts, latest fashions, and classroom activities. Teachers who are aware of what is going on in the classroom and who indicate this awareness to their students have fewer problems than do teachers who are unaware of ongoing problems. Effective managers can prevent further problems by commenting on the problem before it becomes unmanageable.

2. *Handle overlapping situations with ease to facilitate management.* Teachers who can monitor several events simultaneously without chaos tend to be better managers than those who abruptly interrupt one activity to handle a problem with another group.

3. *Maintain momentum to minimize behavior problems.* Students tend to have fewer behavior problems and become more involved in their work when their teachers provide smooth transitions, do not interrupt one task with unrelated activities and discussion, and do not spend too much time giving individual instructions.

4. *Keep the whole class involved to prevent boredom.* Call on all students in your class. Do not repeatedly call on the same few students or follow the same pattern around the room for each class. Teachers who are extremely predictable may find some students bored or inattentive. You should ask a question and then call on students at random. If you ask one student to go to the board to write an answer, involve the rest of the class by having all students write the answer at their desks. Use any technique that seems effective to keep all students participating. For example, during a lecture on the Boston Tea Party, ask individual students how they would feel if the cafeteria cashiers charged them 5¢ extra for milk each day.

5. *Provide variety in the classroom to facilitate good behavior.* Kounin also recommended that teachers provide variety in the classroom, move quickly from one activity to another, and demonstrate enthusiasm.

6. *Be aware of the "ripple effect."* Kounin coined this term. When a teacher reprimands one student, the rest of the class feels the effect and responds to it—analogous to the ripples of water created when a stone is thrown into a pond. A ripple effect may also occur if one student breaks a rule and is not reprimanded and other students subsequently break the rule. To avoid this effect, Kounin suggested the teacher focus on behavior rather than personality, and when reprimanding, avoid angry outbursts.

General Principles of Classroom Management

Recognizing Environmental Factors

An ecological perspective is important for understanding and dealing with behavior problems. Behavior does not occur in a vacuum; it is a response to many environmental factors. Teachers themselves influence student behavior. Realize that as a teacher, you may need to change in important ways before you can expect to see students change. For example, you might habitually shout "Shut up" when you want people to be quiet. This behavior may work well with your friends, but it might escalate the exuberance of noisy students rather than calm them.

Important Influences on Educational Psychology		
Contributor	Place of Study	Contribution(s)
William Glasser (1925–)	Case Western Reserve University	Formulated reality therapy; wrote *Schools without Failure*; advocated helping people control their own lives
Jacob Kounin (1912–)	Case Western Reserve University and State University of Iowa	Identified effective teacher control techniques; coined terms "ripple effect" and "withitness"

You may need to learn a new approach to help your students quiet down. Such approaches are presented in this chapter.

Understanding Student Goals

Another important concept is that behavior is purposive or goal-directed (Dreikurs et al., 1982). According to Dreikurs et al., children do not behave randomly. They act in ways that will meet some need. Generally, children's goals are to seek attention, gain power, seek revenge, or display inadequacy. As you develop strategies for dealing with behavior problems, try to understand the goals underlying them. Do not assume that students misbehave simply to get attention.

Preventing Behavior Problems

Described below are general principles you can use to prevent, or at least minimize, behavior problems, and thereby ensure more time for learning.

1. *Begin implementing classroom management strategies from day 1.* On the first day of school or the first time you work with a new group of students, have specific activities planned. Indicate clearly to your students that you have thought about classroom procedures,

and either spend time with them developing class rules, or post rules in advance.

2. *Provide a physically safe and supportive classroom environment.* As the classroom teacher, you can assure the physical safety and comfort of your students. Make sure that they have adequate restroom breaks and that the classroom is properly ventilated and there are no safety hazards. You can also help ensure that each student feels part of the group. You may want to use group activities to help students feel comfortable during the first few classes.

3. *Design learning activities that will be meaningful to your students and compatible with their interests and abilities.* Understanding developmental principles, age-level characteristics, appropriate academic content, and special interests of your students is important.

4. *Provide opportunities for all students to experience success.* You should provide each student with the opportunity for success. Some students show rapid progress in academic tasks, while others make obvious strides in social tasks. If certain students' academic progress is slow, then point out the success they make in other areas until academic progress can be demonstrated. Another strategy is to break the academic assignment into smaller parts for students not demonstrating success as quickly as others.

5. *Give specific directions and feedback.* Providing feedback to students about their progress helps motivate them to persevere in learning tasks and to enhance their learning.

6. *Encourage students to make decisions and accept responsibility for their work.* You should let students help make decisions. Giving your students feedback on how they are performing and allowing them to help make decisions about what will happen next will provide them with a sense of control. You might provide a list of appropriate curriculum topics and allow the students to determine the order in which they should be discussed or to select two special topics from the list. This sense of control can help students feel more involved and motivated in their schoolwork. Chances of misbehavior may also be reduced.

7. *Openly acknowledge when students are behaving well.* If any or all of your students are behaving well (remaining seated, completing seatwork, being courteous, etc.), you can reinforce this behavior by letting them know that you are aware of it and want them to maintain it. Point out to them that good behavior is essential to a pleasant and productive classroom and that disruptive behavior by even one student might offset or counterbalance the good behavior of other students in the class.

8. *Avoid punishment if at all possible.* There are several possible negative consequences associated with punishment.

a. Strategies you use to punish students may backfire and cause an increase in the inappropriate behavior.

b. Students may become fearful of the person providing the punishment. For example, if a classroom teacher punishes a student, the student may become fearful of that teacher.

c. Students may carry over fear to other situations. For example, if a student is punished during school, the student may become fearful about going to school.

Behavior Modification

Research in operant learning indicates that behaviors that are reinforced increase in frequency or strength; behaviors that are punished and behaviors that are not reinforced will decrease in frequency or strength. Examples of reinforcers are attention, praise, candy, good grades, money, free time, and stickers. More specific terminology and additional information is presented in Chapter 6.

Behavior modification (also known as "b-mod" and "behavior mod") is the application of operant learning principles for the purpose of modifying behavior. The behavior modification approach involves strengthening desired behaviors by reinforcing them and decreasing the occurrence of undesired behaviors by ignoring those behaviors or administering punishment. Many classroom management techniques are based on this approach.

Behavior modification provides many effective strategies for handling, minimizing, and preventing behavior problems.

Extinction

Suppose a student tries to sharpen a pen in the pencil sharpener, then laughs boisterously. By ignoring this inappropriate behavior, the teacher is not reinforcing it and extinction should occur. Extinction means that the behavior will decrease until it no longer exists because it is not reinforced. In this situation, it is important that other students also ignore the inappropriate behavior.

The Premack Principle

Consider a similar example. A student goes to the back of the classroom and sits down at a record player instead of working on a math assignment. The teacher may ignore the student. By ignoring the student, the teacher is not reinforcing the behavior and extinction should occur. However, this student loves music. For this student, simply sitting down and listening to music is reinforcing in its own right because it is enjoyable. In this example, the student may not care (and may prefer) that the teacher ignore the behavior. What should the teacher do? The teacher could talk with the student and come to an agreement that as soon as the math assignment is complete (and 80 percent accurate), the student may spend 10 minutes at the record player. The teacher might even offer to bring in a special record that the student will enjoy. By working with the student, the teacher could help make math work meaningful and enjoyable.

The principle of requiring work first, then providing a reward that the student chooses, is called the *Premack principle.* You may remember a parent or grandparent implementing the same idea by saying "When you finish all your vegetables, you can have dessert" or "When you finish all your homework, you can go outside to play." This technique works well when the student is allowed to choose the reward. Have students make a list of the activities they enjoy most at school, and when you need to implement the Premack principle, the student could select an activity from the list. The Premack principle is helpful for encouraging students to initially engage in a behavior. Once the student engages in the desired behavior, the teacher should help the student appreciate the value of that behavior.

Reinforcers

Behavior modification strategies can also be used to increase appropriate classroom behaviors. For example, when students demonstrate that they have spent an appropriate amount of time on a math assignment, they may be given stickers or praise. The stickers or praise will reinforce (strengthen) the likelihood that students will spend more time on math work. The teacher should select reinforcers according to a student's tastes and interests. For example, candy may not be reinforcing to students who do not like sweets.

Formal and Informal Techniques

Behavior modification techniques can be formal or informal. Several formal techniques are discussed in the section "Dealing with Inappropriate Behavior" (p. 41). Examples of these techniques are individual contracts, group contracts, overlearning, time-out, and token economics. Some informal techniques are discussed throughout this chapter. These techniques tend to be special signals and reminders that help to prevent major problems and increase appropriate behaviors.

Cautions in Using Behavior Modification

Behavior modification techniques can be effective classroom management tools. However, they have generated some criticisms and have some shortcomings. In certain situations ignoring a student's behavior may be dangerous to one or more other students. If one student threatens or attempts to harm another student, the teacher should not ignore the behavior and hope it will disappear, but should intervene to prevent it. Consider a previously cited example with different consequences. A student inserts a pen in the pencil sharpener, sharpens it, and laughs. Subsequently, other students line up at the pencil sharpener, holding pens and smiling. The teacher may try to solve the problem by ignoring all the students—but how much meaningful learning occurs while students stand at the pencil sharpener? The teacher may need to tell the class, specifically, that the behavior is not appropriate.

Important Instructional Tactics

In addition to the research findings and principles described thus far, there are several instructional tactics for maintaining control in the classroom. When you maintain control, you determine how much time is allocated to learning.

1. *Spend time preplanning appropriate lessons and backup activities.* Before you walk into the classroom, know which activities the students can work on and know which lessons you will deliver. Preplanning includes backup planning. If you planned for the students to spend 30 minutes outside at noon and it rains, then you should have other activities planned as alternates. These activities need to be appropriate for the age, ability, and interests of the students. Preplanning also includes having materials ready and accessible when you need them. In the 10 minutes it could take you to walk down the hall to a supply room for colored paper, the students could become animated and mischievous. You might need another 10 minutes to regain control of the class.

2. *In addition to preplanning, set ground rules so that expectations and boundaries are known.* This technique is mentioned repeatedly in research on classroom management. Set ground rules on day 1 and enforce them fairly and consistently. Most research suggests that students be involved in the development of class rules.

3. *Keep the whole class involved so that students do not become distracted or have time to misbehave.* This technique is one of the more difficult ones to implement without practice, but it can become second-nature with a little effort. Keeping the whole class thinking and participating is important. Direct questions to everyone in the class, not merely the best performers. Give everyone a chance to do blackboard work. When you spend time instructing individual students, glance around the room every few minutes to spot any potential trouble or misconduct. When you speak, move around the room instead of lecturing from the same spot every day.

4. *Provide for students with different ability levels so everyone has meaningful work to complete.* In almost every class, there are students with different ability levels. Performance among students will vary and you need to be able to accommodate as many students as possible. There are several implications for the way you deliver

the information and for the follow-up activities you plan. You may need to modify your teaching strategy for the different ability levels. More information or a slower presentation of the material may be needed for the lower-ability students. For higher-ability students, more discussion may be appropriate on complex topics, or less instruction on the basic ideas. The seatwork you give may also need to be tailored to the students' ability levels. For an assignment that you think will take 30 minutes, some students will finish in 15 minutes, some will finish in 30 minutes, some will not finish, and some will never attempt the assignment. You need to have additional activities planned for the students who will finish early, and you need to let the students who do not finish the assignment know when you expect them to finish it. You may decide to assign fewer or less complicated problems to the lower-ability students. Alternatively, you could ask a high-ability student who finishes early to work with a lower-ability student; this is referred to as *peer tutoring*.

5. *Monitor the progress of all your students and adjust lessons as needed.* Be aware of the students' progress and whether they complete their assignments. If students are not doing well, modify the assignment or provide additional instruction. You can expect to have behavior problems if many students are not performing well. Similarly, if most students finish work early and are left with nothing to keep them occupied, they will find things to do on their own.

6. *Model appropriate behavior to help students learn what is expected and appropriate.* Some students develop appropriate behavior and work habits (sitting still, paying attention, not speaking out of turn, etc.) more easily than others; therefore, it is necessary for us to model, or demonstrate, appropriate behaviors and to acknowledge those behaviors in our students. Albert Bandura (1977) has conducted classic work in social learning theory describing how people learn by observing other people. This area of research is discussed further in Chapter 6.

Showing respect for working students by not raising your voice and entering another teacher's classroom politely and cautiously are two ways that you can model appropriate behavior. You should emphasize that good behavior has favorable consequences. Additionally, you can draw attention to students who act appropriately in your own class and in other classes. For example, you could say "Did you notice how quietly Mr. Johnson's class walked to the cafeteria today? I hardly knew they were behind us." Another example is to create a fictional little girl named Allison and say "I think we could all learn something from Allison. She worked hard on her seatwork, finished early, and had 15 minutes left to listen to music. Wouldn't it be nice if everyone worked like that?" Using a fictional student allows you to model the appropriate behavior without generating a "teacher's pet." Although it is appropriate to call attention to students when they are modeling appropriate behavior, do not draw attention excessively to one or two students. This technique could have negative consequences.

Handling Minor Problems

Despite implementation of effective management techniques, minor (and sometimes major) behavior problems are found in many classes. Minor behavior problems may result when students are bored, frustrated, or tired. Boredom-based misconduct can be minimized by varying your teaching materials and approaches. Humor and enthusiasm are also useful. Frustration-based misbehavior can be minimized by dividing difficult material into manageable units and helping students learn to work independently. Fatigue-based problems can be minimized by alternating difficult and easy tasks and allowing frequent breaks.

Have a variety of techniques to prevent these potential problems before they become disruptive. The techniques listed below can be used without disrupting ongoing classwork. These are especially effective for handling minor problems and preventing them from becoming major disruptions to your learning environment.

1. *Use signaling techniques to head off disruptive behaviors.* Examples of signaling techniques are clearing your throat, making a statement to the entire class about the effect a behavior is having, and staring at a misbehaving student. You can develop a special set of signals that the class can help you select. For example, "lights out"

means the class needs to quiet down in 2 minutes, while "hand clap" means to quiet down immediately. Avoid threats and do not offer alternatives that you cannot personally deliver. Do not act or say that you do not like a student, but rather convey that you do not like the particular behavior the student is displaying. Be consistent.

2. *Use " I-messages" to communicate your thoughts or feelings that result from misbehavior.* I-messages are statements the teacher makes about the feelings or thoughts that result from student behaviors. For example, a teacher might say "Watching you get up and down ten times in 10 minutes makes me feel anxious." The use of I-messages gives students feedback about the result of their behavior without passing judgment on them. Especially in classrooms where rapport is already established, I-messages can be very useful management techniques.

3. *Use physical proximity to help decrease inappropriate behavior.* Often an inappropriate behavior will diminish if you walk toward the student while delivering the lesson or monitoring class progress. Sometimes, especially with elementary students, you may touch the children on the arm or shoulder while you stand or sit near them. For certain activities, such as reading in a circle when everyone, including yourself, is sitting down, you should plan ahead of time for certain students to sit near you.

4. *Use humor (but avoid sarcasm) to draw attention to potential behavior problems.* For example, you might say "It seems as though we're preparing for the Boston Marathon the way everyone is moving around today. Perhaps we should prepare a little more for the test next Tuesday and leave running around for after school."

5. *Use reality appraisal to create awareness among the students and help them realize possible consequences of inappropriate behavior.* Reality appraisal is a statement of the actual situation. Use it to ensure that the class is aware of the inappropriate behavior and the consequence that will result. For example, you could say "Five people are out of their seats, not working. There are 10 minutes left to complete page 12. Those not finished in 10 minutes will not have the opportunity to go to learning centers today."

6. *Implement peer monitoring to minimize problems with a particular student.* Especially with students who exhibit chronic behavior problems, peer monitoring can be an effective management strategy. With peer monitoring, a "buddy" is assigned to signal or remind the student when disruptive behavior begins. Both the behavior to be monitored and the type of signal used are agreed on in advance by the students and the teacher. Consider this example: Sarah has a tendency to sharpen her pencil 12 times in an hour. Sarah likes Bob, and Bob is a well-behaved student who generally finishes his work ahead of time. If Bob notices Sarah on her third trip to the pencil sharpener, he will walk to Sarah's desk and ask her how her work is progressing. Sarah understands that this is a cue not to go to the pencil sharpener again. As a further agreement, if Sarah sharpens her pencil only once in an hour, then she and Bob both get 5 minutes of free time at the end of the hour.

Dealing with Inappropriate Behavior

In spite of good planning, setting ground rules, reinforcing appropriate behaviors, and preventing potential problems, there will be some major behavior problems. You should be familiar with (and practiced in) several intervention techniques. As you read about these intervention techniques, think about which ones you will be most comfortable implementing. These techniques require advanced planning. Try to imagine which techniques will be most effective with problem behaviors.

1. *Individual contracts can be used to elicit a specific behavior from one student.* An individual contract is an agreement between a particular student and the teacher that pledges a specified reinforcer for a particular behavior. This type of contract is sometimes called a *contingency contract.* To be effective, contracts should specify a desired, positive behavior. They should include the names and signatures of the people involved, descriptions of mutually agreed-on student behavior, performance level, and reinforcement strategy or reward (called reinforcer).

2. *Group contracts can be used to elicit a specific behavior from a*

collective group of students. A group contract is an agreement between a group of students and the teacher that pledges a specific reinforcer for a particular behavior(s). Students should participate on the negotiating team and agree to the behavior and the reinforcer. The teacher must come through with the agreed-on reinforcer when the class demonstrates the appropriate behavior. The students participate in a group contract on a voluntary basis.

3. *Time-out may be used to remove a student from a situation that is reinforcing an inappropriate behavior*. The student is moved for a brief period of time (3 to 5 minutes) into an area that does not reinforce the inappropriate behavior. One example of this procedure involves physically moving the student from the classroom into the hall. A second example involves keeping the student in the classroom with the teacher turned away from the student. The purpose of time-out is to interrupt the inappropriate behavior. Time-out works best with elementary students. When implementing time-out, tell the student what you are doing, why you are doing it and for how long, and which appropriate behavior needs to be demonstrated. Do not move the student to an isolated, physically uncomfortable, or scary location. And, where necessary, obtain legal consent.

4. *Overcorrection can be used to reduce the likelihood of an inappropriate behavior and increase the likelihood of a related, more appropriate one*. Overcorrection requires the student to retrace steps of the inappropriate behavior, acting appropriately. This process is continued several times until the behavior is thoroughly learned. For example, if a student drops books on the floor, the teacher might implement overcorrection by having the student carry books appropriately several times. This technique is not used in its strict sense in most schools, but there are times when you may find it appropriate. Most typically, it is used with mentally retarded students and primary-grade students.

5. *A token economy can be used for individuals or groups to reinforce appropriate behaviors and establish "costs" for inappropriate ones*. The token economy, originated by Ayllon and Azrin (1968), is widely used in classrooms today. Within a token economy,

certain behaviors merit a specific number of tokens. Tokens are concrete, physical reinforcers, such as poker chips, smiling-face stick-ons or stamps, and points. When a student demonstrates a particular behavior, such as sitting still for 10 minutes or completing a worksheet, the appropriate number of tokens are awarded to that student. At the end of a specified period (one class, one day, or one week), the number of tokens each student has accumulated is totaled. The students then trade in their token for other reinforcers such as free time or a learning center activity. Some token economies include ceilings (i.e., limits) on the number of tokens that can be accumulated; others specify response costs, which are the number of tokens that will be subtracted from the total if specified inappropriate behaviors are manifest. Generally, token economies include instructions for the students, guidelines for giving and taking away tokens, and information about which reinforcers can be purchased with the tokens.

6. *The Good Behavior Game requires students to form teams and compete to demonstrate good behavior.* The Good Behavior Game was developed by Barrish et al. (1969). Basically, it is a game in which two teams compete to demonstrate the most appropriate behaviors. The team that wins receives a reward such as free time or a treat. Performance by each team member is important. The Good Behavior Game requires instructions to the students, guidelines for winning and losing points, and information about the prizes (reinforcers) and how the game will be administered.

7. *Home-based reinforcements are important ways of getting parents involved in resolving behavior problems.* Home-based reinforcements are ways of getting the parents involved by having them administer reinforcers. Getting parents involved helps to ensure that you have their support and that they are aware of the problem behavior(s). An advantage of parental involvement is the addition of reinforcers such as special weekend activities and monetary rewards, which cannot be administered at school. Home-based reinforcers work well with token economies and individual contracts. To administer them, you must have an effective way of communicating with the parents and the parents must agree to administer the reinforcer consistently. Similar to the token economies, a contract agree-

ment with the student must be made. The contract should specify which behavior will be demonstrated and what performance level will be attained.

8. *Retrospective or review discussions provide a time to reestablish rapport.* After a problem occurs and you take action, a follow-up discussion can often be beneficial. In a one-on-one situation, a discussion will enable you to express concern about the student's performance as you try to reestablish rapport. For times when the whole class is involved, summarize the problem and the consequence. Ask the students how the situation can be avoided in the future and make sure that everyone understands.

Communication Skills

Communication skills are essential for effective classroom management. You can facilitate communication in the classroom in several ways.

1. *Give the class your attention.* When the students speak, give them your attention. Listen to what they say. Show respect for them just as you expect them to show respect for you.

2. *Get and keep your students' attention.* Be prepared at the beginning of the class period every day. With this technique, the students adapt the habit of giving you their attention when they enter the room. However, there are also situations for which you need special signals. For example, if you lecture for 10 minutes, assign seatwork for 10 minutes, and then lecture again, you should signal the class in a way that is agreed on by the class, such as saying "At this time, please close your books." The class may appreciate a 2-minute warning before changing activities, and this may ease the transition. Techniques that can help you keep your students' attention include the following:

a. Keep them involved by interjecting questions and getting them to think, rather than merely talking to them, without their participation.

   b. Watch for boredom and fidgeting. Vary activities or provide breaks at those times.

   c. Keep the class aware of the progress that is made with statements such as, "I will talk for 10 more minutes about World War II, then you will have a chance to quiz me."

3. *Ask questions and be receptive to responses.* Teachers frequently ask questions without pausing long enough for the students to think of their responses. The same problem occurs when teachers ask students if there is anything that needs clarification. Rowe (1974) demonstrated that teachers wait for an average of 1 second for students to answer questions. When teachers increased the wait-time to 5 seconds or more, students are more likely to participate, ask related questions, give appropriate, longer answers, and generally appear more confident and involved (Rowe, 1974; Sadker and Sadker, 1986). Teachers tend to provide shorter wait-times for slower students. Especially with slower students, it is important to allow enough time for them to formulate thoughts and generate responses. Try to wait at least twice as long as you think is necessary to see if the class has any thoughts or questions. Asking questions using an open-ended style can also enhance student response. Instead of asking "Are there any questions?" ask "I've seen several inquisitive looks, what questions do you have?" Communicate to the students that you expect them to generate questions and provide thoughtful responses. Communicating positive expectations will help students respond. When students do ask questions, acknowledge well-formulated questions and be receptive to those that are not as insightful. Say some things such as, "That's a very good question . . ." and "I understand the confusion, but the important point is . . . ." You should find that responding to questions in this manner will invite students to listen to what you are saying and encourage them to ask more questions.

Classroom management skills are crucial to establishing a good learning environment. In well-managed classes students know what is expected, feel successful, and continue working, while teachers maintain a no-nonsense, but pleasant atmosphere. A room that is well managed provides more time for learning. Teachers can learn many techniques for handling minor problems to avoid disruptions in learning. Some of these techniques include setting ground rules, getting the students involved, modeling and reinforcing appropriate behavior, and signaling students who are mildly misbehaving. Preventing the major problems is essential to a well-managed class. Even in well-managed classes, some students will need special attention to learn and to maintain appropriate behaviors. Setting up special programs such as token economies and contracts requires extra planning by the teacher and cooperation from the students, but these programs have been successful in reversing inappropriate behavior.

Recommended Reading

Axelrod, S. (1983). *Behavior Modification for the Classroom Teacher*. New York: McGraw Hill. (A book on behavior management written for the classroom teacher.)

Dreikurs, R. B. Grunwald, and F. Pepper. (1982). *Maintaining Sanity in the Classroom: Classroom Management Techniques* 2d ed. New York: Harper & Row. (Presents useful suggestions and discussion that behavior is purposive or goal-directed.)

Emmer, E. T., C. M. Evertson, J. P. Sanford, and M. E. Worsham. (1984). *Classroom Management for Secondary Teachers*. Englewood Cliffs, N.J.: Prentice-Hall. (An excellent source of research-based strategies for dealing specifically with secondary students.)

Evertson, C. M., E. T. Emmer, B. S. Clements, J. P. Sanford, and M. E. Worsham. (1984). *Classroom Management for Elementary Teachers*. Englewood Cliffs, N.J.: Prentice-Hall. (An excellent source of research-based strategies for dealing specifically with elementary students.)

Garrett, S. S., M. Sadker, and D. Sadker. (1986). Interpersonal Communication Skills, in J. Cooper (Ed.). *Classroom Teaching Skills* 3d ed. Lexington, Mass.: Heath. (Provides step-by-step information on communication skills.)

Gordon, T. (1974). *T. E. T.: Teacher Effectiveness Training*. New York: Peter H. Wyden. (A well-known book that deals with many classroom problems and describes techniques such as I-messages and active listening.)

Krumboltz, J. D. and H. B. Krumboltz. (1972). *Changing Children's Behavior*. Englewood Cliffs, N.J.: Prentice-Hall. (A book of practical suggestions based on behavioral principles. This book is appropriate for many people, including both teachers and parents.)

Redl, F. and W. W. Wattenberg. (1959). *Mental Hygiene in Teaching,* 2d ed. New York: Harcourt, Brace & World. (Includes a concise, well-organized discussion of management techniques.)

Swift, M. S. and G. Spivack. (1975). *Alternative Teaching Strategies: Helping Behaviorally Troubled Children Achieve.* Champaign, Ill.: Research Press. (A pragmatic book for dealing with problems such as inattentiveness, impatience, irrelevant talk, and restlessness.)

References

Allyon, T., and N. H. Azrin. (1968). *The Token Economy: A Motivation System for Therapy and Rehabilitation.* New York: Appleton-Century-Crofts.

Bandura, A. (1977). *Social Learning Theory.* Englewood Cliffs, N.J.: Prentice-Hall.

Barrish, H. H., M. Saunders, and M. M. Wolf. (1969). Good Behavior Game: Effects of Individual Contingencies for Group Consequences on Disruptive Behavior in a Classroom, *Journal of Applied Behavior Analysis,* 2, 119–124.

Dreikurs, R., B. Grunwald, and F. Pepper. (1982). *Maintaining sanity in the classroom: Classroom Management Techniques* 2d ed. New York: Harper & Row.

Glasser, W. (1969). *Schools without Failure.* New York: Harper & Row.

Rowe, M. B. (1974). Wait-time and Rewards as Instructional Variables: Their Influence on Language, Logic, and Fate Control. Part I: Wait-time. *Journal of Research in Science Teaching,* 11, 81-94.

Sadker, M., and D. Sadker. (1986). Questioning skills, in J. Cooper (Ed.). *Classroom Teaching Skills,* 3d ed. Lexington, Mass.: Heath.

CHAPTER 4

Development Theories

From infancy to adulthood, humans develop along many dimensions. This chapter concentrates on major theories that describe and predict patterns of intellectual, social, and moral growth. A leading theorist is associated with each category: Jean Piaget with cognitive development, Erik Erikson with psychosocial development, and Lawrence Kohlberg with moral development.

Educators utilize theories of development to gauge what students of different ages are capable of doing and learning. In this way, teachers can prepare lessons that are appropriate to their students' developmental level, taking advantage of what the students are ready to learn rather than assigning material that is either too elementary or too advanced.

Basic Concepts

Over the last several decades, some developmental concepts have been widely discussed and debated. As a student of educational psychology, you should be familiar with these concepts.

Nature/Nurture

One of the most controversial issues has been nature versus nurture. This is the question of which factors determine an individual's intellectual development. Advocates of "nature" believe that hereditary factors are primarily responsible. Hereditary factors are physical and mental characteristics passed from parent to child through the genes. The implications of the nature position are that attributes such as intelligence are inherent, that is, predetermined genetically. Advocates of "nurture" (environmentalists) believe that extrinsic factors (environmental factors) are primarily responsible. Environmental factors are experiences and conditions surrounding an individual. Environmental factors can be material or social, such as vacations spent in Florida, phone calls with a grandparent, homes, cars, televisions, friends, and teachers. Implications of the nurture position are that intelligence and personality are determined or influenced by the type and amount of intellectual and emotional stimulation one receives from the environment.

The nature position was popular for many years, but today it is generally believed that neither factor is solely responsible for a child's development. Instead of focusing on which factor is more important, try to understand the contributions of each factor and use that knowledge to help children develop their potential.

Tabula Rasa: John Locke

An important concept presented by the English philosopher *John Locke* (1632–1704) holds that a child is born with the mind as a blank tablet, or a *tabula rasa*. As the child has life experiences, that tablet, the mind, is filled. Consistent with this concept is the philosophy that any child could succeed in any profession (physician, lawyer, teacher, etc.) if provided with the appropriate experiences. This view that the child's development is shaped by experiences with the environment is shared by behaviorists such as *John B. Watson* (1878–1958) and *B. F. Skinner* (1904–). Watson believed so strongly in the malleability of children that he said he could train a healthy infant to become any type of adult (Watson, 1925). This philosophy implies that great emphasis should be placed on education.

Stages of Development

A third important developmental concept is that growth occurs in stages. Growth stages are periods of major developmental change.

Arnold Gesell

Arnold Gesell (1880–1961) was one of the first researchers to describe developmental stages. Gesell established the Institute of Child Development at Yale University in the 1930s. He observed behaviors in children of different ages and outlined human development. His work, especially the popular books *The Child from Five to Ten* (1946) and *Youth: The Years From Ten to Sixteen* (1956), significantly influenced child-rearing practices among laypersons and professionals several decades ago.

Benjamin Spock

Another well-known figure is Benjamin Spock (1903–). A physician who wrote extensively about child-rearing practices, Spock advocated parental understanding and flexibility in *Common Sense Book of Baby and Child Care* (1985, first published in 1946), which influenced many post-World War II parents.

Developmental Patterns and Variations

Recently, developmental psychologists have learned more about stages of development. The concept of stages is important because it suggests that there are milestones or checkpoints by which we can measure average development. The concept of stages is also fundamental to our knowledge of which behaviors can be expected of children at different ages.

Keep in mind, though, that the theories of cognitive, social, and moral development describe developmental trends, the rates and types of changes seen in average children. In other words, these broad theories describe changes that occur most typically. In reality, the rate of development varies widely among children. For example, a child might be quite advanced intellectually but be immature emotionally; alternatively, a child might excel in mathematics but require remedial work in reading. Some children will lag behind the average in all aspects of development and some will excel in all areas. These developmental differences should be accommodated in the classroom; that is, the needs and abilities of the students should be evaluated as individually as possible and the classwork structured accordingly. One of the fundamental challenges for educators today is to provide for students at different developmental levels in one classroom. One of the great challenges for educational researchers is to determine what can be done to facilitate developmental gains, and then communicate those techniques to educators.

Classroom Applications of Development Psychology

Developmental differences can be attributed to hereditary factors, to environmental deprivation (e.g., malnutrition), or to environmental stimulation (e.g., reading time parents spend with their children). Some students, whose cognitive development is below the class average, may need special help in academic subjects that are especially difficult for them. More advanced students may need enrichment activities. Students whose cognitive development is either far below or far above the class average may benefit from special-education classes either part- or full-time. Special-education classes are designed to accommodate specific developmental differences such as mental retardation, learning disabilities, physical handicaps, visual and auditory impairments, emotional problems, and above-average intelligence. More information on special education is presented in Chapter 13.

To reiterate, the theories described below will help you identify general patterns of expected growth. You should anticipate developmental differences, namely, that students in any one class will function at different levels. When a student deviates so far from the average in a particular area that the student may not benefit from the regular classroom instruction, the student may be placed (part-time or full-time) in a special education class.

Cognitive Development: Jean Piaget

Cognitive development generally refers to abilities to think, learn, remember, perceive, and solve problems. Studying cognitive development provides you with fundamental information for choosing appropriate academic activities for your students. Theories of cognitive development outline the kinds of learning activities that are appropriate for specific age groups. If you are perceptive and familiar with the various stages of cognitive development, you will notice that some of your students are ready for and capable of certain academic activities while other activities are more appropriate for other students. Without this kind of knowledge, you could waste time trying to teach students concepts or skills they are not capable of mastering and could also introduce unwarranted frustration in the learning environment. Two very basic examples are provided to illustrate the point.

Example 1: You are a first-grade teacher standing in front of your class and facing the students. You tell the class "If you need to go to the bathroom, raise your right hand." You demonstrate by raising your right hand. Three children in the class need to go to the bathroom and raised their left hands. These children are unable to reason that since you are facing them, your right hand is on their left.

Knowing that children this age may not realize that your right hand would be on their left, you should turn with your back facing them to demonstrate which hand to raise. After the demonstration, turn around to see which hands are raised. Alternatively, if all students are facing the same direction, you could lift a right hand of a student. In this case you need to consider the cognitive development of the students.

Example 2: Some 5-year-old children are playing cards. Each child learned a certain set of rules for the card game. Each child believes that set of rules is the only "correct" way to play the game. None of the children will agree to change rules because each believes that there is only one "right" way. The point here is that at this stage in moral development, children are rule-bound and unable to change the rules for convenience. Understanding developmental stages helps you understand and predict behavior.

Piaget's Influence

Jean Piaget (1896–1980), a Swiss child psychologist, received a Ph.D. in natural science at the age of 21 and subsequently became interested in child psychology.

While working on a French version of an existing English reasoning test, Piaget became interested in the wrong responses that children

Important Influences on Educational Psychology		
Contributor	Place of Study	Contribution(s)
John Locke (1632–1704)	Christ Church, Oxford	English philosopher; developed concept of *tabula rasa*, child is born with mind as blank tablet
Arnold Gesell (1880–1961)	University of Wisconsin, Clark University, Yale University	Established the Institute of Child Development at Yale University; advocated idea that development occurs in specific sequence of stages; greatly influenced child-rearing practices
Jean Piaget (1896–1980)	University of Neuchatel	Developed the most popular theory of cognitive development
Eric Erikson (1902–)	Psychoanalytic Institute, Vienna	Proposed 8-stage theory of psychosocial development; coined term "identity crisis"
Lawrence Kohlberg (1927–1987)	University of Chicago	Researched moral development in children; identified six stages of moral reasoning

provided. He thought that the wrong responses were a source of very valuable information. As he continued researching, Piaget became convinced that the thought processes of children are basically different from the thought processes of adults. In other words, children are not just little adults, they think and see the world differently from adults. Beginning in 1921 and continuing until his death in 1980, Piaget devoted his studies to understanding cognitive development. Although many researchers have criticized and elaborated on his ideas, Piaget's research has provided the best-known and most comprehensive theory of cognitive development.

Piaget (1952) believed that cognitive development progresses through four stages of growth with different types of thought processes characterizing each stage (and no possibility for skipping stages). Piaget considered interaction with the environment to be an important part of development, serving as the means of obtaining knowledge. In addition to the four stages, Piaget described several important development concepts.

Important Concepts in Piaget's Theory of Stages

Schema

A schema is an organized pattern of thoughts or behaviors that is developed as a result of interacting with objects or people in the environment. A schema can be behavioral (throwing a ball, driving a car) or cognitive (problem solving, categorizing, understanding that there are automatic or manual-shift transmissions). A schema can be relatively simple, such as a baby reaching for a ball; or complex, such as a high-school student solving an algebra problem. When a new experience does not fit with an existing schema, adaptation is necessary. Adaptation is accomplished by the processes of assimilation and accommodation.

Assimilation

Assimilation occurs when the perception of a new experience is adapted to fit with (assimilate into) the existing schema. The perception is information that is filtered or modified to fit with the existing schema. For example, when babies handle new objects the same way they handled previous objects, by grasping, biting, and banging them, they are using existing schemata with unknown objects. In another, more specific example of assimilation, a child who has a cat schema sees a skunk and calls it a cat. The child distorts the perception of the skunk to fit into the cat schema.

Accommodation

Accommodation occurs when the existing schema is altered to handle (accommodate) a new experience. For example, a bicycle rider who only has experience with pedal brakes begins riding a 10-speed bike that has only hand brakes. Accommodation occurs as the original brake schema (information only about pedal brakes) is modified to include knowledge of hand brakes.

Equilibration

Equilibration is the process of restoring balance between what was expected and what was actually experienced. Equilibration occurs as a child assimilates new experiences and accommodates existing schemas. Equilibration, an important part of cognitive growth, involves thought restructuring. When disequilibrium occurs, children have the opportunity to learn and grow. Use this process to your advantage in the classroom. You can spark students' interest by presenting a problem that they cannot quickly solve with existing skills. For example, in a math class, introduce multiplication by asking how much money could be earned in a 40-hour week with an hourly wage of $3.00.

Piaget's Stages of Cognitive Development

Piaget described cognitive development in four stages: sensorimotor, preoperational, concrete operational, and formal operational.

Sensorimotor Stage

The sensorimotor stage begins at birth and ends approximately at age 2. In this stage, children explore the world through their senses and motor skills. Infants' first behaviors are *reflex behaviors,* which do not have to be learned. Examples of reflex behaviors are sucking objects placed in the mouth and grasping objects that touch the palm of the hand. By touching, looking, and tasting, children learn about themselves and the world in which they live. Children begin by exploring their own bodies and continue by exploring objects that are within their range of sight but external to their bodies, such as rattles, balls, and a parent's hand.

Intentionality. One of the most significant developments toward the end of this stage is intentionality, the child's attempt to make certain events occur repeatedly. For example, a child drops a spoon on the floor and an adult picks it up and says "uh oh," and hands the spoon back to the child. Two seconds later, the child drops the spoon on the floor again, the adult picks it up and says "uh oh," and you can imagine how the next 5 minutes go. The child has been intentionally dropping the spoon and eliciting the adult's "uh oh" response.

Object Permanence. At approximately this time, children understand that objects still exist even though they are not directly in sight, such as a ball that is hidden behind a parent's back. This concept is called object permanence. Once children understand that things that are out of sight still exist, they can begin to symbolize these items—and move closer to higher-level thinking.

Trial and Error Learning. You may notice that when infants and young toddlers want to reach something, they will try one time and then give up if they do not succeed. Slightly older children, however, will try one way and then another to reach something they want. For example, a child who wants a toy that is on the bed will try to reach it from one angle, and then move to the other side of the bed to try to reach it. This kind of behavior, called trial-and-error learning, is the beginning of problem-solving behavior. A more advanced form of problem-solving behavior occurs toward the end of the preoperational stage. At this time a child can try alternatives that are not obvious, such as taking the pillow from the bed and using it to knock the toy onto the floor where it can be handled.

Preoperational Stage

The preoperational stage generally occurs from age 2 and lasts until the child is about 6 or 7 years old. At this stage children have the ability to use symbols and share their experiences with others. They also begin to reason, and often their thought processes seem illogical, which can be quite amusing to adults. The child's ability to use language and understand concepts increases at an incredible rate during this stage.

Egocentricity. During the early part of this stage children's views are especially *egocentric,* meaning that their views center on their perceptions. Most likely, such children do not understand that other people have views that are different from their own views. They think everyone sees the world the same as they do. Children at this stage of cognitive development can have a magical way of thinking. Their shadows seem to chase them, characters in storybooks seem real, and objects are assigned lifelike qualities. These children expect adults to view the world the same way. Note that egocentric in this context does not mean conceited.

Irreversibility. Another important concept is that children in this preoperational stage of cognitive development cannot back up and rethink an operation. An *operation* is a reversible mental process such as thinking about pouring milk into a glass after the milk was poured, or cutting a whole pie into eight slices after it was cut. Children at the preoperational stage cannot mentally change directions. Piaget used the term irreversibility to describe this inability to back up and view the operation retrospectively.

Inability to Conserve. A related limitation of the child's thought processes is the inability to conserve. Conservation is the ability to realize that certain properties of an object remain the same even though the appearance of the object has changed. To determine whether a child is capable of conservation, you could try the following. Begin with a colored liquid in a tall glass. Pour all of the liquid into a shorter, wider glass (with the child observing). Ask the child whether either glass contains more liquid and if so, which one. A child unable to conserve will tell you that the taller glass has more liquid. The problem, as Piaget would describe it, is that the child at this cognitive stage focuses on only one aspect, the height of the glass.

Centration. This limitation caused by focusing on one aspect is referred to as centration. You could test the same concept by using two stacks of an equal number of blocks, one set lengthwise and side-by-side, the other set compressed so that it does not stretch as far. The child unable to conserve will tell you that the line of blocks that appears longer contains more (even though the number of blocks is actually the same).

Concrete Operational Stage

The concrete operational stage begins about age 6 or 7 and lasts until 11 or 12.

Reversibility and Conservation. Reversible thinking and the ability to perform operations such as addition and subtraction become possible at the beginning of this stage. Similarly, the child is capable of working through tasks that require the ability to conserve.

Classifying According to One Characteristic. An important ability gained during this stage is to arrange or classify items according to one particular characteristic such as size or color. For example, children become able to stack blocks in pyramid- shaped piles and to place similar-colored items in one group.

Logical Inferences. Following the acquisition of this ability, children become able to make logical inferences. For example, they can reason that if Little John is older than Mary and Big John is older than Little John, then Big John is also older than Mary. The elementary school curriculum, which includes mathematics and basic science skills, reflects the acquisition of these cognitive abilities at this stage.

Class Inclusion. One of the last abilities gained during this cognitive stage is *class inclusion.* When children are capable of class inclusion, they can reason that if there are three boys and two girls in the family, there are more family members than either boys or girls alone.

As you have read and have probably observed, there is tremendous cognitive growth in these elementary-school years. Be careful to realize that the children at this stage are still not thinking like adults. They are still very practical- and concrete-oriented thinkers, and although they can symbolize concrete objects, they have a very limited ability to deal with abstract concepts. Children who are unable to solve word problems when presented only with the word problem may be able to solve the same problem if you provide objects they can manipulate as they work through the problem.

Formal Operational Stage

The formal operational stage begins approximately at age 11 and continues into adulthood. At this stage preadolescents begin to think abstractly and deal with hypothetical situations. They can generate (i.e., form) plausible alternatives and test them "in their heads." Note that not all adults reach this stage of cognitive development.

Limitations of Piaget's Theory

Piaget's descriptions of four stages of cognitive development should be helpful to you in the classroom. However, one criticism of his theory is that at the preoperational stage, he emphasizes children's limitations rather than abilities. It would be helpful, especially for persons dealing with preschoolers, to understand more about what these children are capable of doing and thinking. Moreover, in describing the formal operational stage, Piaget includes children 11 years old and older. It is unlikely that you will notice young adolescents engaging in the formal operations that Piaget describes. Although descriptions of the cognitive processes people are capable of at various ages are useful, it would also be useful for researchers to understand how people progress through one stage and into another. Piaget does not address cognitive development from this perspective.

Classroom Applications of Piaget's Theory

Piaget's findings can be applied in the classroom to help you understand how students perceive and understand situations.

Preschool Through First Grade

Children in preschool and first grade are functioning within the preoperational stage. For these students you should use concrete examples, many visual aids, and objects that the children can manipulate. When presenting lessons and giving instructions, use short sentences with action verbs, and provide the students with a wide variety of classroom experiences and field trips.

Children in preschool through first grade perceive the world very differently from the way adults do. Realize that they are in the preoperational stage, meaning that they are capable of using symbols, but their thoughts are egocentric and their language is limited relative to yours. When you are confused by what they say, ask them to try to explain more fully what they mean. Ask them what they mean by specific words that you find puzzling.

Grades 2 to 4

Children in grades 2 to 4 are most likely functioning in the concrete operations stage. In this stage they base actions on actual experiences and have difficulty dealing with abstractions. Provide concrete examples for them and reference those examples as needed. If you are teaching students about the four basic food groups, mention specific examples in each group. Additionally, you could point out during lunch which foods belong to each food group. Do not expect these children to be able to consider alternatives or hypothetical situations. Provide brief, well-organized lessons and give examples to help explain unfamiliar ideas. Provide opportunity for these students to exercise their increasing ability for logical and analytical thinking. These students will enjoy riddles and academic puzzles.

Grades 5 to 9

Children in grades 5 to 9 are likely to function within the concrete operational stage at some times and the formal operational stage at other times. Be careful to allow these students to fully explain their ideas. During these grades, children develop the ability to explain complicated processes in a logical manner. Provide opportunities for students to practice this skill. High-school students become capable of thinking about abstract and philosophical problems. You may notice a tendency toward preoccupation with these problems rather than more concrete, practical matters. For example, students may be interested in the causes of World War II. Self-analysis also becomes important to these students. Encourage them to examine and discuss their own viewpoints and to carefully consider alternatives.

Social Development: Erik Erikson

Just as children grow cognitively, they also mature socially. Self-concepts, interpersonal skills, and attitudes are continually changing.

These types of social changes certainly affect a student's behavior in the classroom. Social development is influenced by parents, family, teachers, peers, and others. The school is a social as well as an academic institution. Teachers model appropriate behavior and teach students what other adults will expect. Peers influence students' preferences, attitudes, and values. As you read about stages of psychosocial development, notice that different social groups become important at various stages of psychosocial growth. As an educator, you can benefit from understanding which psychosocial crises students may be working through as you are trying to teach them.

Erikson's Stages of Psychosocial Development

Social changes have been plotted in a series of eight stages by Erik Erikson (1902–), one of Sigmund Freud's students who studied at the Vienna Psychoanalytic Institute. Erikson's work is called a *psychosocial theory* because it combines aspects of psychological and social development. Erikson's theory is based on the *epigenetic principle*. In embryology the epigenetic principle refers to the development of certain organs over time and the eventual combination of these organs forming the child. Erikson hypothesized that the personality develops in the same fashion with the ego progressing through a series of stages. The *ego* is the aspect of the mind that controls thinking and reasoning activities. Through the senses, the ego takes in information about the world. The functions of the ego are to distinguish the person from the environment and maintain a balance between the critical and moral aspects of the self. A central idea in Erikson's theory is that each stage involves a particular crisis that must be resolved before the person progresses to the subsequent stage. The stages described below are described more fully by Erikson (1963).

Stage 1: Trust versus Mistrust (Birth to 18 months)

At this stage, where the child is dependent on the immediate environment, there is a need to develop a sense of trust in the world. The mother plays a large part in satisfying this need. If the mother does not consistently satisfy the infant's need for food and affection, a sense of mistrust (fear and suspicion) may develop that may persist throughout the other stages.

Stage 2: Autonomy versus Shame and Doubt (18 months to 3 Years)

At this stage there is a need to achieve some degree of autonomy, that is, to function and perform some activities independently. The term "terrible twos" describes behavior at this stage. Toddlers want to hold on to things and walk where they please. Both parents are important to growth during this stage. Parents who are overly restrictive can lead the child to feel powerless, a feeling that can persist as self-doubt at later stages. Similarly, parents who frequently shame their child risk instilling a sense of incompetence that emerges later on.

Stage 3: Initiative versus Guilt (3 to 6 Years)

During this stage motor and language skills are growing rapidly. Exploration of these powerful skills occurs at this stage as the child's sense of initiative increases. Parents and other family members play a large role in this stage of social development. Permitting a child to run, play, talk, and question things helps the child explore the self and develop initiative. Punishing or restricting displays of initiative may lead a child to feel guilty about functioning independently.

Stage 4: Industry versus Inferiority (6 to 12 Years)

During this stage children enter school, where teachers and peers become important parts of their lives. At this stage children are intellectually curious and want to be creative. When they are encouraged to perform and finish tasks, and are praised for their efforts, they develop a sense of industry. When children are discouraged from trying, fail, or feel that they do not measure up to standards, they develop a sense of inferiority, a negative self-image .

Stage 5: Identity versus Role Confusion (12 to 18 Years)

During this stage young people strive to find out who they are, and look more toward peers than parents to help answer the question. Role confusion is the major crisis at this stage, with particular reference to sexual identity and evaluation of career choices. If adolescents experience continuity in their sense of self, identity develops; otherwise, role confusion results.

Stage 6: Intimacy versus Isolation (Young Adulthood)

During this stage of psychosocial development, there is a need to establish an intimate relationship with someone. Optimally, the relationship will enhance one's sense of identity. Failure to establish an intimate relationship at this point results in feelings, or a lifestyle, of isolation.

Stage 7: Generativity versus Stagnation (Middle Adulthood)

During this stage there is often concern for the next generation, specifically for the welfare and success of offspring; however, it is possible to guide the growth of the next generation through activities other than parenthood, such as teaching and volunteer work. Persons unable to participate in this process may become self-absorbed and stagnate.

Stage 8: Integrity versus Despair (Late Adulthood)

During this stage people reflect about the past and consider their successes and failures. They also face the reality of death. Persons satisfied with what they have accomplished with their lives have feelings of integrity; those who feel unsatisfied with what they have accomplished will feel despair.

Criticisms of Erikson's Theory

Although Erikson's theory is useful because it provides a framework and describes typical behavior in well-delineated, concise categories, it has generated some criticism. Erikson developed these stages on the basis of personal experience and subjective interpretations rather than objective empirical evidence. There have been few empirical studies validating Erikson's work. As did Piaget in his cognitive development theory, Erikson describes events at each stage, but does not explain how one progresses from one stage into another. This information would be useful, especially in clinical environments. Finally, the early stages that describe behavior from ages 3 through 11 tend to focus on the same general concept, namely, that parents should encourage children to function and perform independently.

Classroom Applications of Erikson's Stages

Students will progress through these psychosocial stages as they mature and face new situations or crises. As a teacher, it is important for you to be able to identify any crisis that develops and help the student achieve a positive outcome for that particular stage. Identifying the particular crisis a student experiences will also enhance your understanding of the student's behavior.

Autonomy and Initiative

Allow all children the opportunity for autonomy, and avoid shaming them for undesired behavior. To encourage initiative in children, consider the following suggestions. Allow them to make, and act on, their own choices. You can suggest several activities and allow your students to select one. Encourage children to be active and to make friends. With older preschool children, expect many questions. Be willing to answer their questions, understanding that this is an important part of their development. Design tasks to allow a sense of accomplishment. For elementary-school children design tasks that ensure success, breaking up complex tasks into smaller tasks if necessary. Make sure that the children are aware of the success they experience.

Industriousness

To help students become industrious, consider these suggestions. Give students a chance to be independent. When doing so, anticipate and allow minor mistakes. Provide support when students are frustrated or discouraged. Try not to build competition in the classroom or interrupt your students when they are involved in an activity.

Identity

For secondary students the most prominent crisis is the search for identity. You should provide acceptance of students' appearance, ideas, and opinions. Offer career guidance. Discuss sports, arts, and political role-models. If possible, invite guest speakers for the class or the school. Be aware of who and what are of interest to the students and discuss these topics in class. Help your students work through interpersonal problems. Continuously provide performance feedback, and let students know when they could/should be performing at a higher level.

Moral Development: Lawrence Kohlberg

In addition to studies of cognitive and social growth in children, some very specific research has been conducted on development of moral behavior. Two general findings have been replicated frequently and are especially valuable for educators: (1) Whether a child chooses to act the "right" way depends, to a large extent, on the specific behavior and circumstance. For example, a child who excels in math but not in reading may cheat on a reading test but not on a math test. (2) There is no guarantee that a child who realizes and openly admits that a certain behavior is "wrong" will not indulge in that behavior. For instance, a student who reiterates back to you that stealing is wrong still might steal. Having children memorize rules of good behavior, such as the Ten Commandments and the Boy Scout law, will not necessarily affect the children's decision-making ability. Therefore, it is advisable to reinforce and draw attention to appropriate moral decisions.

Beginning in the 1950s Lawrence Kohlberg (1927–1987) expanded on Piaget's work to investigate stages of moral development. Kohlberg provided 10- to 16-year-olds with narratives of moral dilemmas and asked them how they would respond and why. One of Kohlberg's dilemma narratives is paraphrased below (Kohlberg, 1969, p. 379).

A woman has cancer and is near death. A drug that may save her life is available. The druggist charges $2,000, ten times what it costs to prepare the drug. The woman's husband could collect only half that price. The husband asked the druggist to sell the drug at a lower price and to allow him to pay the balance later. The druggist refused to do this. The husband broke into the store to steal the drug. Should the husband have done that ?

Through use of a complicated scoring system, the responses were evaluated. The results of Kohlberg's work suggest that there are three major levels of moral development: preconventional, conventional, and postconventional. There are two stages at each level, providing a total of six stages of moral development. Kohlberg has revised this hierarchy, and readers may find these stages discussed differently in other sources.

Preconventional Level

The preconventional level is where most children up to age 9 will conform. Kohlberg calls this level "preconventional" because most children at this age do not understand the conventions (mores) of their society. There are two stages at this level.

Stage 1: Punishment-Obedience Orientation

At this stage children's moral decisions are governed by the physical consequences of their behavior. Children submit to the power of those in charge. They are aware that they might get caught or Mommy will be mad, and make choices on the basis of these consequences.

Stage 2: Instrumental Relativist Orientation

At this stage children's moral decisions are based on satisfying their own needs, or at least coming out even. They expect some positive return for obeying rules.

Conventional Level

The conventional level is where most people between ages 9 and 20 will conform. Kohlberg calls this level "conventional" because people at this stage generally follow the conventions (mores) of their society unquestioningly. There are two stages at this level.

Stage 3: Good Boy–Nice Girl Orientation

At this stage the "right" decision is made on the basis of what will please or impress others. There is a need for recognition from parents and teachers. Students will act in ways that make parents proud or teachers and friends impressed. For example, one child may try to make straight A's in school to please parents.

Stage 4: Law-and-Order Orientation

At this stage the "right" decision is based on maintaining social order. Established rules will be obeyed and authority respected. For example, a person may decide not to steal money because the law forbids this.

Postconventional Level

The postconventional level is generally reached by only a small proportion of adults. Kohlberg calls this level "postconventional" because people at this level understand the moral principles that underlie the conventions (mores) of their society. There are two stages at this level.

Stage 5: Social Contract Orientation

At this stage the "right" decision is made on the basis of mutual agreement rather than blind obedience to the rules. Rights of the individual are important in making the right decision.

Stage 6: Universal Ethical Principle Orientation

At this stage the "right" decision is based on self-chosen ethical principles. People at this stage weigh all the factors before making a decision and then strive to apply their principles consistently.

Limitations of Kohlberg's Theory

Although Kohlberg's descriptions of the stages of moral development provide useful information for educators, the validity of his results has been questioned. Kohlberg's theory does not deal with actual behavior and does not seem to clearly define the relationship between moral reasoning and moral behavior. The theory does not explain why persons at different stages may demonstrate the same moral behavior at certain times, or why persons at the same stage of development sometimes demonstrate different moral behaviors.

Classroom Applications of Kohlberg's Theory

The responses of younger children to moral dilemmas will be different from those of older children and yourself. Younger children will probably react on the basis of what they view as right or important. Try to understand their perspective. Develop interesting classroom activitics by presenting moral dilemmas to class members and inviting discussion. Through the discussion you can learn about your students' perspectives and share your thoughts with them.

Kohlberg believes that people progress from one stage to another by interacting with persons who are at the next higher stage (or sometimes the second higher stage). Teachers can assess a student's stage of moral development. After determining the student's current stage, the teacher can present moral dilemmas and work through the solution with the student. The explanations the teacher provides should be arguments appropriate for the next higher stage, helping the student move on to this level.

Theories of cognitive, social, and moral development were presented in this chapter. Each of these theories is a stage theory assuming a natural sequence or progression of growth. Jean Piaget described four stages of cognitive development: sensorimotor, preoperational, concrete operational, and formal operational. Cognitive growth begins with exploration of the world through the senses and progresses to abstract thought and the ability to hypothesize. Erik Erikson described eight stages of psychosocial growth, with a major crisis occurring and needing resolution at each stage. The earliest crisis concerns the child's need to trust the world, and the last crisis concerns the adult's need to achieve integrity, satisfaction with one's life as it has been lived. Lawrence Kohlberg described six stages of moral reasoning that he grouped into three major levels: preconventional, conventional, and postconventional. It is important for educators to understand cognitive, social, and moral development because students' academic abilities are closely tied to growth in these areas.

Recommended Reading

Erickson, E. (1963). *Childhood and Society,* 2d ed. New York: Norton. (Provides a complete description of Erikson's thoughts about personal and social development. This book is not "theoretical.")

Gesell, A., and F. L. Ilg. (1946). *The Child from Five to Ten.* New York: Harper

& Brothers. (A classic, popular book about child development between ages 5 and 10.)

Gesell, A., F. L. Ilg, and L. B. Ames. (1956). *Youth: The Years from Ten to Sixteen*. New York: Harper & Brothers. (This is a classic, popular book about child development between ages 10 and 16.)

Kash, M. M., and G. Borich. (1978). *Teacher Behavior and Pupil Self-concept*. Reading, Mass.: Addison-Wesley. (Presents research describing how teachers can affect self-concept of students and provides many recommendations.)

Kohlberg, L. (1981). *The Philosophy of Moral Development*. New York: Harper & Row. (Description of Kohlberg's ideas on moral development.)

Piaget, J. (1970). *The Science of Education and the Psychology of the Child*. New York: Orion Press. (Piaget's thoughts on education especially with respect to children's varying cognitive abilities.)

Thornburg, H. (1979). *The Bubblegum Years: Sticking with Kids from 9–13*. Tuscon, Ariz.: HELP Books. (Provides an idea of what problems children are dealing with at this age.)

Wadsworth, B. (1978). *Piaget for the Classroom Teacher*. New York: Longman. (Describes the application of cognitive development for educators.)

References

Erickson, E. (1963). *Childhood and Society,* 2nd ed. New York: Norton.

Gesell, A., and F. L. Ilg. (1946). *The Child from Five to Ten*. New York: Harper & Brothers.

Gesell, A., F. L. Ilg, and L. B. Ames. (1956). *Youth: The Years From Ten to Sixteen*. New York: Harper & Brothers.

Kohlberg, L. (1969). "Stage and Sequence: The cognitive-developmental approach to socialization," in D. A. Goslin, (Ed.). *Handbook of Socialization Theory and Research*. Chicago: Rand McNally.

Piaget, J. (1952). *The Language and Thought of the Child*. London: Routledge & Kegan Paul.

Spock, B., and M. Rothenberg. (1985). *Common Sense Book of Baby and Child Care*. New York: Dutton.

Watson, J. B. (1925). *Behaviorism*. New York: W. W. Norton.

CHAPTER 5

Development: Age-Level Characteristics

This chapter presents more information about childhood development with emphasis on the general characteristics of different age groups. Specific behaviors rather than theoretical perspectives are presented. Age-level characteristics will be described for physical, social, emotional, intellectual, and language development.

Understanding developmental progress helps educators build educational programs to fit the needs and abilities of the children. It also helps teachers provide activities that facilitate moving from one developmental stage to the next. By learning the expected developmental level for different age groups, teachers can identify students who are performing significantly behind or ahead of other students and thus help them catch up or more fully develop their special abilities. When you observe a student who seems to be lagging behind the others, you should contact a school counselor, psychologist, or special education teacher for further evaluation of the student. Early identification of developmental problems and implementation of appropriate educational programs can significantly help these children progress. When you observe a student who seems to be developmentally past other students,

*similar steps should be taken so the child can receive enrichment
activities to fully develop special abilities.*

Physical Development

Preschool and Kindergarten

Children ages 3 to 6 years generally have high activity levels and
good control over their bodies. The protruding abdomen that is characteristic of toddlers disappears as the legs and body trunk grow longer.
These physical changes cause the center of gravity to become lower and
result in the increase in control that these children display. They enjoy
physical activities such as running, jumping, and skipping. Partly
because they are so active, these children need rest periods during the
day, even though they might not report feeling tired. You can schedule
two kinds of rest periods: slow, quiet activities to follow the physically
demanding ones and short nap periods where the children lie down to
rest or sleep.

Motor Activities

In preschool and kindergarten children the large muscles in the
arms and legs are more developed than the fine muscles in the hands.
Gross motor activities involve major muscle groups and include activities such as walking and running. *Fine motor activities* require
dexterity and, to a certain extent, precision. Activities that require fine
motor coordination, such as putting together small puzzle pieces and
tying shoelaces, are difficult for children during this period. When you
select materials for these children, choose thick crayons, wide-handled
brushes, and puzzles with a few large pieces rather than many small
pieces. By the end of this period, children can perform gross motor
activities such as going up and down stairs using alternate feet and some
fine motor skills such as cutting and coloring.

Visual Focus

At this age, the lenses of children's eyes do not fully accommodate,
that is, change shape in response to visual stimuli. This makes it
difficult to focus on small objects. Select large objects for activities,

and choose beginning reading materials with large print for these children.

Handedness

Handedness becomes established between ages 3 and 6. Most children are right-handed. Twenty years ago, many teachers tried to train left-handed pupils to use the right hand. This practice is discouraged today. Trying to make a child change can result in the child's feeling guilty and nervous. If you notice a child using the left hand to color, you may surreptitiously place a crayon in the right hand and see what happens. If the child reverts to using the left hand, do not try to force a change.

Primary Grades

Primary grade children share several characteristics with preschoolers—they need rest periods, their large muscles are better developed than their fine muscles, and they may still have difficulty adjusting eye focus between near and far objects (their lenses may not fully accommodate).

Physical Activity

Children age 6 to 9 years are very active, and the same guidelines apply to them as to the 3- to 6-year-olds. However, the 6- to 9-year-olds tend to be more vigorous and accident-prone in physical activities than do younger children. "Wild" is an appropriate adjective to describe their physical play. Also, the increased fidgeting (e.g., fingernail-biting and hand-tapping) and nervous behaviors frequently observed at this age level result from the sedentary activities often required in the primary grades that were not expected in preschool. Sitting still for long periods of time (20 to 60 minutes) is difficult for these children. However, it is also important at this age for the children to learn these social behaviors. You can help the children develop these skills by scheduling interesting activities. For example, provide variety by dividing an assignment into half reading and half coloring. Allow for physical activities such as walking to the board or the teacher's desk. Making the seatwork interesting and providing frequent breaks will help you and the children get through the learning activities with minimal fidgeting and restlessness.

Visual Problems

Two aspects of the visual system are important to development at this time. First, the shape of the lens is still somewhat shallow, making it difficult to adjust focus between near and far objects. This may lead to eyestrain, which causes fatigue. Signs of eye fatigue are blinking and rubbing the eyes. To avoid fatigue, change activities frequently and provide breaks during reading and other close activities. Second, strabismus and amblyopia are eye disorders somewhat common for this age. *Strabismus* is an imbalance in the eye muscles such that both eyes do not work together to provide one picture to the brain. Strabismus can lead to amblyopia, commonly referred to as "lazy eye." *Amblyopia* is any reduction of vision in one eye resulting from squinting or insufficient use of that eye. Children who have either of these conditions may experience double vision and usually compensate by closing one eye, tilting the head, or blinking the eyes. If you notice any of these symptoms, inform the child's parents. Treatment of amblyopia most often involves placing a patch over the stronger eye, which forces the use of the weaker eye. Eye exercises may be suggested, glasses may be prescribed, and sometimes, corrective surgery is advised.

Elementary Grades

In children aged 9 to 12 fine motor skills are usually fully developed. Classroom activities involving arts, crafts, and music are popular and help utilize these newly acquired skills.

Sex Differences in Growth

There is a sex differential for physical growth at this age level. Growth spurts generally occur at age 11 in girls and age 13 in boys. Thus, girls 11 to 14 are frequently taller and heavier than boys of that age. This difference can be embarrassing or awkward for both boys and girls, especially during physical activities. You may need to reassure the boys that they will probably catch up with and surpass the girls in strength and endurance later.

Onset of Puberty

Puberty also begins at this age. The range for girls is 9 to 16, averaging between 12 and 13. The range for boys is 11 to 18, averaging 14. As mentioned earlier, the biological and psychological changes occurring at this time are major concerns of most students, and they are likely to express their curiosity and concerns in your classroom. If your school district permits, you should be prepared to discuss the questions candidly or have someone else provide accurate information.

Junior-High Grades

The physical changes of puberty that began in the elementary grades accelerate in the junior-high years.

Puberty

Puberty brings greater maturation of the sex organs and the appearance of secondary sex characteristics. For females these changes are the development of the breasts, a widening of the pelvis, and a narrowing of the waistline. For males the changes include the development of broader shoulders and some replacement of fat with muscle. Changes that occur in both sexes are the appearance of hair on the face, body, underarms, and pubic areas, in addition to skin and voice changes. As a result of puberty, many students in this age group are self-conscious of their appearance and some experience physical awkwardness.

Maturation Differences

Research has been conducted to determine the effects of early and late maturation on students' well-being. The findings have been mixed. Some students benefit from early maturation. They grow more independent and self-confident. Others find early maturation is a difficult problem to handle. The early and late bloomers in your class may appreciate a little extra attention, especially early-maturing females and late-maturing males. To the extent that it is appropriate in your school district, you may help the students through this awkward time by talking openly with them and scheduling time for grooming activities.

Secondary Grades

One major physical characteristic of adolescents aged 16 to 18 is an increase in sex drive. Many students in this age group engage in sex, often without using birth control.

Sexual Problems

Even though students observe peers suffering negative consequences, they do not believe the same thing will happen to them. With the increase in sexual behaviors comes the risk of illegitimate births and sexually transmitted diseases. If the school system does not object, the teacher may provide information about birth control and sexually transmitted diseases, emphasizing the importance of grooming and hygiene. As in the earlier years, appearance is important and information about physiological changes is necessary. Teachers should demonstrate acceptance of students' physical appearance during these years.

Sex Education

Recognizing the need for education in this area, many schools are responding with sex education courses and making counselors available for discussions with students. Additionally, schools may provide special library books and audiovisual materials to help provide information. Sex education in a class setting or in textbooks and other reading materials sometimes generates controversy. Some parents do not feel that school is the appropriate place for this kind of program, while others are grateful to the school for sharing the responsibility of providing sex education for their children. However, with the spread of acquired immune deficiency syndrome (AIDS), information on the prevention of sexually transmitted diseases can be life-saving.

Social Development

Preschool and Kindergarten

Children aged 3 to 6 engage in several types of play, sometimes with other children and sometimes beside other children without playing with them. The spontaneous play groups are likely to be small, not organized, and subject to change. Children of this age may quarrel frequently, but they are quick to forgive and forget. They enjoy being dramatic and inventive, often drawing ideas from cartoons they have seen. The sex roles that are modeled on television and by parents and teachers affect the way the children play. As a result, you may notice girls acting more dependent and less achievement-oriented. This early age is a good time to encourage girls to be more achievement-oriented and boys to be more emotionally responsive.

The major types of children's play you may notice are

Solitary play–A young child plays with a toy and does not pay attention to other children in the room.

Onlooker behavior–A young child watches other children playing and may comment on their play, but will not join the group.

Parallel play–A child plays beside another child, perhaps with the same toy or engaging in the same game, but will not join the other child. For example, two children building roads for their trucks will build two roads rather than work together to build one road.

Associative play–A child plays with other children, but the play is unorganized, without assignment of roles or a clear purpose for the activities.

Cooperative play–A child plays with other children and the play is organized with some assignment of roles. There may be an end result, such as, an art project or a play. Children often play doctor or house, alternating roles.

Primary Grades

Children between ages 6 and 9 are likely to have best friends and selected enemies. Children this age are likely to play in small groups, with organized rules. Children will learn games in a given situation with one set of rules. Often they encounter another child who has learned a different set of rules. These children seldom resolve differences between sets of rules. Quarrels are frequent, and you may notice some children punching and kicking others. You will probably observe the children quite absorbed with playing by the rules, and, in general, very enthusiastic.

Elementary Grades

Social interaction for children between ages 9 to 12 is especially important because the peer group becomes a powerful influence on social behavior, often more powerful than the adult influence. You will notice many of these children acting with similar mannerisms, frequently dressing and talking the same, mimicking role-models such as the California Valley Girl popular in the mid-1980s. In general, much social behavior at this age is determined by what is "in." Students seek the attention of their peers, and this can be disruptive in the classroom. It is sometimes wise for the teacher to ignore minor attention-seeking behaviors, to achieve the extinction of these behaviors, through non-reinforcement, as mentioned in Chapter 3. If the behavior disrupts other students, however, the teacher could reprimand the misbehaving students and design a particular behavior modification program to reduce or eliminate this inappropriate behavior (see Chapter 3).

A positive characteristic of children this age is an increase in sensitivity to others' feelings. With strong peer influence, others' feelings are not always considered, but children of this age can understand how they might offend others and can empathize with them.

Junior-High Grades

Following the patterns begun in elementary school, peer pressure is the major influence of social behavior for students aged 12 to 15.

Students of this age can be encouraged to think through their actions and predict the consequences. You can encourage these students to consider alternative approaches and the consequences. These students begin to be interested in student government activities that give them the opportunity to establish some of their own policies. In class, discussions of moral and political behaviors can be stimulating, but it is sometimes difficult for students to openly express or defend minority opinions. The tendency for students to conform to the peer group by acting, dressing, and eating alike is still very strong, and students of this age are generally concerned with their self-image, or acceptance by their peers—more so than in previous years. Vandalism and other more serious behavior problems tend to occur at this age, especially in boys.

Secondary Grades

Although peer pressure is still a most important influence on day-to-day behaviors, parents and teachers can have important impact on long-term decisions, such as career or college choices. Students this age begin to act more mature and are usually receptive to the respect adults give them. Deeper friendships are nurtured by students in high school than by younger students, perhaps as more long-term and far-reaching decisions are made. It seems especially important to young women that intimate friendships are established at this time in their lives.

Emotional Development

Preschool and Kindergarten

Children 3 to 6 years old will express their emotions openly, sometimes verbally and at other times physically. Jealousy is an emotion often seen in this age group, particularly with respect to attention that the teacher has given to certain students. You may want to help the children recognize value in expressing emotions verbally rather than physically. Emotional outbursts are usually short-lived and soon forgotten, so do not feel obligated to intervene whenever there is a conflict. You can help minimize these problems by changing activities frequently and providing ample rest time and snacks.

Primary Grades

Children aged 6 to 9 are most likely to want to please you, the teacher. They are eager helpers, and you can use this to your advantage. They need your praise. Partly because they want to please you, they are quick to be offended by criticism or lack of attention. They also, like most people, have a difficult time dealing with failure. It is important to provide situations in which all of your students can be successful. Children this age still have difficulty putting themselves in someone else's place, and are often insensitive to other's feelings. Watch for this sort of insensitivity and try to intervene.

Elementary Grades

Emotionally, these years may be difficult for children, especially as puberty approaches. Conflicts develop between behaviors expected by peer groups and those expected by adults. This is an important time to maintain communications and make sure that the ground rules are understood. It is also important to be aware of what is "in" and acknowledge it as important to the students. Behavior problems are more frequently manifested at this age and delinquency increases.

Junior-High Grades

With the many changes occurring in the junior-high student's life—puberty, identity confusion, and cognitive development—this transition period is one fraught with particular stress. It is common to see students between ages 12 and 15 moody and depressed. You may also find some students preoccupied with their concerns and not attending to lessons you have prepared. Whenever you can, work their concerns, physical appearance, sex roles, and other life- related issues into your lessons.

Drug Abuse

Drug abuse among teenagers is one of the most serious problems facing schools. Students entering junior high (approximately 12 and 13 years old) are experimenting with alcohol, marijuana, and other drugs. Students are increasing their use of drugs, using more potent drugs, and starting at an earlier age than students did a few years ago. Teenagers who are most likely to experiment with drugs have low self-esteem, lack strong values, and are particularly influenced by their peers. Children of substance abusers are also likely to experiment with drugs.

Drug education programs in the schools are becoming an important part of the curriculum. In a program called DARE (Drug Abuse Resistance Education) started in Los Angeles, police officers go into classrooms to talk to fifth and sixth graders. The officers explain why students should not try drugs, why drugs are dangerous, how to resist peer pressure, how to increase self-esteem, and how to build assertiveness. Elementary, junior-high, and senior-high classroom teachers are encouraged to participate in drug education and prevention programs.

Teachers can obtain additional information from The American Council for Drug Education in Rockville, Maryland; The National Clearinghouse for Alcohol and Drug Information in Rockville, Maryland; and The National Parents' Resource Institute for Drug Education (PRIDE).

Secondary Grades

The most common emotional problem for students aged 16 to 18 is depression, especially in females. Common symptoms are crying, sulking, and suicidal thoughts.

Suicide Prevention

Teenagers *do* attempt suicide. You should be aware of the symptoms: unsuccessful attempts to deal with a problem, deterioration of meaningful relationships, giving away possessions, telling another person that suicide is being contemplated, and severe depression. If a student openly admits to be considering suicide, inform a counselor. Do not ignore the symptoms. If the student has a well-thought-out plan, immediate intervention is needed. Never hesitate to refer a student to a counselor, suicide-prevention center, or mental health clinic. In many school districts there are school programs and support services available to handle emotional problems such as depression and contemplated suicide. A school counselor or psychologist can assess the severity of a possible problem. Subsequently, the school may get parents involved and begin a treatment program. When the problem is judged to be sufficiently severe, the student may be referred to other professionals for additional help.

Juvenile Delinquency

Another serious problem that may intensify during this time period is habitual delinquency. Delinquents are frequently low- achievers with poor family relationships. Often these students are from impoverished homes and believe they will not do well in school, frequently because they receive little or no encouragement from their family or peers. There may be economic and social pressures for the student to drop out of school. It can be very difficult for these students to see that the long-term reward of a good job after graduation is more beneficial than dropping out. Teachers need to use every method at their disposal to encourage these students to stay in school and to reinforce behaviors incompatible with delinquency.

Intellectual Development

Preschool and Kindergarten

Children between ages 3 and 6 like to talk. (Language development is presented in a subsequent section of this chapter.) Common and most appropriate activities for these children are variations of the show-and-tell theme. Over the last few years, teachers have begun to substitute other names for this kind of communication game such as show-and-share and share-and-tell. Sometimes a child brings a toy to class and discusses it, or passes the toy around for each child to hold. Variations of the game include sharing toys and stories related to a specified theme and sharing stories without presenting toys. Children this age also have very active imaginations. Their attention spans are relatively short.

Primary Grades

Like 3- to 6-year-olds, primary-grade children like to talk, especially when a significant adult in their life is listening. It will probably be easier for you to have a child talk than read or write. Almost certainly you will need to help them develop listening skills. In general, young children are eager to learn. Their eagerness to learn and their willingness to please make teaching young children a pleasure for many adults. In addition to being eager to learn, they are also eager to report (tattle) on other children. Do not always assume a child tattles because that child is angry or needs attention. Many times, children tattle because the way a rule was interpreted differed from their literal interpretation and they want the record set straight. If you work with primary-grade children, you will most likely need a strategy for dealing with tattle-tales.

Elementary Grades

In this age group gender-related differences in intellectual abilities are apparent. Girls tend to do better in verbal tasks such as reading and spelling and also in mathematical computation. Boys tend to do better in mathematical reasoning and spatial problems. At this age, girls tend to earn higher grades in school. Some of these differences will even out over the next few years, but you may want to encourage students to work a little harder on their weaker areas. Memory and attention span have increased relative to preschool days. Children this age are intellectually curious. They are likely to begin collecting things. They set high standards for achievement, desiring to be the best in their class, and often set themselves up for failure because they set unrealistic goals. These children want to be independent and need emotional support from adults.

Junior-High Grades

The students undergo several transitions in cognitive development between ages 12 and 15. They become capable of formal thought and are able to consider extenuating circumstances in moral judgment. The rate of transition varies from student to student; you will find students at several levels in your classroom—and group discussions will reveal this. Also, a student who demonstrates the ability for formal thought one day will not necessarily do so on another day about a different topic. When you present abstract information to students in this age group, it is important to check with the students to determine how well they understood this information. When discussing moral issues, you may also notice that some students can more easily consider extenuating circumstances than other students can. You may find that small-group discussions work well with students at this age; in small groups it is easier for the minority opinion to be heard and considered.

As students become more capable of formal thought, encourage them to become more involved in current events. Political issues are important and stimulating topics that these students are able to work with.

Students in junior high school have increased attention spans relative to elementary students, but preoccupation with other concerns, such as puberty and self-identity, sometimes makes concentration difficult.

As students become more capable of abstract thought, problem solving, and critical thinking, the school curriculum should be geared to provide appropriate experiences. Emphasis should move away from rote memorization and unquestioning acceptance of factual information. Teachers should concentrate on stimulating interest in the "why" and "how" behind curriculum material. Schools have been criticized for adhering to the "basics" and requiring students to learn things without understanding why these things are important. This approach can produce apathy in students and dull their skills rather than enhance their intellectual growth. Explaining to students why it is important to learn history can be helpful in generating student interest. Helping students investigate the causes or precipitating events of a war and discussing how war can be prevented can facilitate the development of cognitive abilities in this age group.

Secondary Grades

The ability to work with formal thought is one characteristic of students aged 16 to 18. Even though the ability exists, you may not see it exercised well. Instead of straight lectures, you may structure your lessons to encourage abstract and problem-solving behaviors by the students. Present information with key pieces missing or hidden and have the students fill in the gaps. Group discussions are important but should be conducted without students feeling a pressure to perform in front of their classmates. Also realize that having the ability to engage in formal thought does not mean that students can theorize scientifically or rationally. You can help develop their abilities by suggesting methods for thinking through problems and encouraging their creativity—when it is well-directed. These students demonstrate increased ability to take perspective and solve problems.

Language Development

Closely related to intellectual development is language development, the vehicle through which intellectual development is most often expressed. An important aspect of language development is the relationship between thinking, speaking, reading, and writing.

Researchers are investigating how language develops and is related to thinking. Generally, children seem to develop language while developing cognitive abilities. They look for patterns and invent rules to put the pieces together.

Birth to 1 Year

The earliest speech sounds produced are crying and cooing. These sounds are common to all children. Cooing (expressing vowel sounds) begins as early as 3 to 5 weeks after birth. Near the fourth month, infants begin babbling, producing vowel and consonant sounds without specific meaning. Social interaction becomes very important. Infants will babble in response to adults who speak to them. Between the ninth and tenth months infants are capable of *echolalic babbling,* imitating sounds others make. At this point, babies who are deaf may become silent. Somewhere between 9 and 18 months most children utter their first word. They can say "mama" when they need something. The first words are typically labels for objects and actions. During the *holophrasic stage,* children this age speak only one word "sentences" to communicate, but can use *intonation* to convey meaning. Intonation is variation in inflection. During the first year, the child's vocabulary grows tremendously.

2 to 3 Years

Sometime near the second year the child begins putting two words together, in what is called the *two-word stage.* This then progresses to *telegraphic speech,* meaning that it is understandable, but words arc missing. Essential content words such as nouns and verbs are used. Less functional words such as articles and pronouns are omitted. Examples are "all gone" and "mommy more." For example, a child says "Mommy more" to mean "Mommy, I want more milk right now." Additionally, speech is *propositional,* meaning that the child implies more than can be produced with existing vocabulary and ability. Syntax is rather primitive, especially at the beginning of this stage; important words are omitted. Rules of grammar are overregularized, so children misuse plurals and the past tense. *Overregularization* is the application of rules where they do not apply. For example, after learning to add "ed" for past tense, a child might overregularize and say "Daddy goed." Another example of overregularizing is adding "s" to render words plural; a child might say "mouses" instead of "mice." *Overgeneralization* may also be seen at this stage when children call all men "daddy" or all four-legged animals "doggy."

Between the second and third years, the child may ask many questions, sometimes using unintelligible jargon interspersed with meaningful words. Children this age like to hear themselves and often demonstrate *echolalia,* repeating what is heard.

By the third year the *mean length of utterance (MLU)* for most children is between 3.5 and 4 words. MLU is the average number of words or *morphemes* (morphemes are the smallest meaningful unit of speech) in an utterance. Many sentences have a subject, a verb, and an object, though many grammar rules are not applied. By this time, most children have a vocabulary of approximately 900 words, and they can tell stories and express how they feel.

The speech sounds mastered by most children this age are the consonants p, b, m, w, and h and all vowels.

4 to 5 Years

As a very general figure, 4-year-old children have a typical MLU of four words. They can tell lengthy stories. The typical vocabulary is 1500 words. Children this age still make grammatical errors, which generally disappear with increased practice. Stopping the child to correct errors only slows the child down, and may introduce unnecessary frustration. If a child uses a word incorrectly, you may try repeating with the correct word, but do not make the correction obvious. For example, a child says "I helded the doll." You may repeat "You held the doll? You like to hold the doll, don't you ?" This procedure seems to be very effective for helping children learn appropriate grammatical rules.

Some reading and language arts programs take into account the kinds of errors children this age will make. The emphasis of these programs is not on correcting the errors, but rather on the meaning and experience of the material. Generally, these programs are called *language experience programs.* The teacher will stimulate discussion and have a child tell a story and will then record on large paper what the child said. The child later reads and sometimes writes (copies) the story. This experience allows the child to focus on communication and not get bogged down by errors that will most likely pass with a little more experience. This kind of program does not suggest that you specifically reinforce incorrect grammar. Although these programs do not focus on proper spelling and grammatically correct sentences, some teachers prefer to correct minor spelling and grammatical errors as they record what the child said. However, the incorrect grammar or spellings should not be the focal point of the experience. The point of this approach is to teach the children that what can be said can also be written, and what can be written can also be read, and that all the information can be communicated to other people.

Again, as a general figure, by age 5 most children have a vocabulary of about 2200 words and are likely to string 5 words together to make sentences. These children can count to 10, name objects, and state their name and age.

Speech sounds mastered by most children aged 4½ are t, d, n, g, k, y, and ng.

6 to 7 Years

Between ages 5½ and 6½ most children use all the basic rules of grammar, including proper use of plurals, possessives, verb tense, and syntax (sentence construction). Most 6-year-olds have a vocabulary of 8000 to 14,000 words.

Speech sounds mastered by children aged 6½ are sh, zh, l, th, and j. Speech sounds mastered by children aged 7½ are s, a, r, and wh.

Most girls have mastered all speech sounds by age 7; most boys have mastered all speech sounds by age 8.

Human development follows fairly predictable patterns. Age-level characteristics for physical, social, emotional, intellectual, and language development were presented. Knowing what characteristics and behaviors to expect of children at different ages helps you develop teaching strategies that will most benefit your students. It also helps you determine the kinds of information and skills worth spending time on. Another important reason for learning these characteristics is to be able to screen children who are lagging behind developmentally or are experiencing emotional problems. You can often help these students by consulting their parents or classmates or referring them to counselors, and sometimes by being a good listener yourself.

Recommended Reading

Adelson, J. (1972). The Political Imagination of the Young Adolescent. In J. Kagan and R. Coles, (Eds.), *Twelve to Sixteen: Early Adolescence.* New York: Norton. (Presents useful information regarding changes in the young adolescent.)

Bradley, D. F. (1988). Alcohol and Drug Education in the Elementary School. *Elementary School Guidance & Counseling, 23,* 99-105.

Burnett, C., G. Mendoza, and S. Secunda. (1975). *What I Want to Be When I Grow Up.* New York: Simon & Schuster. (A delightful book written by actress Carol Burnett.)

Chomsky, N. (1968). *Language and Mind.* New York: Harcourt Brace Jovanovich. (A classic presentation of the theory of transformational grammar.)

Elkind, D. (1981). *The Hurried Child. Growing Up Too Fast Too Soon.* Reading, Mass.: Addison-Wesley. (An excellent, popular book on current factors affecting child development.)

Hall, E., M. Perlmutter, and M. Lamb. (1982). *Child Psychology Today.* New York: Random House. (Presents an overview of many development topics.)

Lerner, R. M., and D. F. Hultsch. (1983). *Human Development: A Life-Span Perspective.* New York: McGraw-Hill. (Presents general coverage of social, personality, and physical development.)

Miller, George A. (1981). *Language and Speech.* San Francisco: Freeman. (A very readable presentation of language development.)

Thomas, M. (1974). *Free to Be You and Me.* New York: McGraw- Hill. (A popular book written by actress Marlo Thomas.)

CHAPTER 6

Noncognitive Learning Theories

Two kinds of noncognitive learning theories—behavioral and humanistic theories of psychology—are discussed in this chapter. They are noncognitive theories because they do not try to explain learning as a function of processes in the "black box"—the mind. Functions of the mind, such as thinking, remembering, and problem solving, are not directly observable. You cannot see the thinking process. While cognitive theories describe, explain, and predict what occurs in the mind during these nonobservable processes, behavioral theories describe, explain, and predict learning as a result of observable behaviors only.

Behavioral theories emphasize how persons and objects in the environment influence behavior. When the behavioral theories are applied to the learning environment, they produce teacher-centered approaches to education. The behavioral theories discussed in this chapter were developed by John B. Watson, Ivan Pavlov, and B. F. Skinner.

Humanistic theories of psychology emphasize the importance of the affect (emotional reactions to real-world events) on behavior. They stress the importance of the relationship between student and teacher and maintain that students should be offered many choices in the learning process. When humanistic theories are applied to the learning environment, they produce student-centered approaches. The humanistic theories discussed here were developed by Abraham Maslow, Carl Rogers, and Arthur Combs. These noncognitive learning theories can be applied in designing instructional materials and classroom environments that are conducive to learning.

Behavioral Theories

The behavioral theories to be discussed here are classical conditioning, operant conditioning, and social learning. First, however, is a brief history of behavioral psychology.

History of Behavioral Psychology

Behavioral psychology has been evolving since the middle of the nineteenth century as a reaction to an earlier theory called *functionalism.* Some of the theorists who paved the way for behaviorism are Alexander Bain, Edward Thorndike, and John Dewey.

John B. Watson and the Introduction of Behaviorism

John B. Watson (1878–1958) is generally credited with introducing behavioral psychology in its modern form. While teaching at Johns Hopkins University in 1913, Watson published the article "Psychology as the Behaviorist Views It" in the *Psychological Review* and introduced behaviorism to Americans.

According to Watson, behaviorists try to predict responses based on knowledge of preceding events called *stimuli.* They also try to predict which stimuli were present during a given response. Behaviorists learn how to predict behavior, which is any observable action, by observing people interacting with their environment and noting changes. Behaviorists also want to control behavior. Once they observe how interacting in an environment changes behavior, they can recreate situations that will increase or decrease behaviors. The ability to control behavior can be applied in classroom management for purposes of discipline and also for structuring lessons and other classwork designed to optimize academic performance. Teachers need control over many student behaviors, for example the number of times students run to the pencil sharpener, ask for help, and talk out of turn. Teachers also need to understand how they can influence academic behaviors such as the amount of time students spend reading and working on math problems. Behavioral theories provide this kind of information.

Most behaviorists concentrate only on observable behaviors, not the cognitive processes that may occur with the observable actions. However, Watson did some investigation of subvocal speech as a means of learning about thoughts and feelings. *Subvocal speech* is inaudible movement of the lips, tongue, larynx, and other speech mechanisms similar to movements made during regular speech. People sometimes use subvocal speech during cognitive processes, such as when trying to remember a phone number. More recent researchers, the *neobehaviorists,* have continued this type of study.

Behaviorism From 1920 to 1960

In the 1920s Ivan Pavlov published *Conditioned Reflexes,* which describes the behavioral theory of classical conditioning. In the 1930s the prominent behaviorists were John Watson, Edward Tolman, Edwin Guthrie, and B. F. Skinner. Tolman introduced the first cognitive-behavioral theory. Guthrie had a strong associationist influence that helped shape modern behaviorism. Skinner began work at this time that in the 1940s and 1950s became known as operant conditioning, the most popular behavioral theory. Other important developments at that time were Clark Hull's logicodeductive theory and William Estes's work on the effects of punishment. Additionally, Skinner continued publishing, and with books such as *Walden Two* and *Science and Human Behavior,* he popularized operant conditioning and became the dominant figure in behavioral psychology.

Behaviorism Since 1960

In the 1960s the influence of behaviorism began to be replaced by humanistic theories and a few years later, by cognitive theories of learning. One major behavioral concept introduced in the 1960s by Martin Seligman (1942–) was the concept of *learned helplessness,* the feeling that one cannot be successful or independent.

In the 1970s and 1980s, M. J. Mahoney, D. H. Meichenbaum, David Watson, and Roland Tharp published much work that supports the potential of cognitive behaviorism. The cognitive-behavioral approach uses behavioral methodologies to investigate the effect of cognitive processes on behaviors. What people say to themselves (for example, "I know I can do it, just concentrate, okay, here goes") may have important effects on subsequent behavior. Studies in cognitive behaviorism will probably increase during the 1980s and 1990s.

Today, even without recent theoretical advances in behaviorism, the principles that underlie the theory are still valuable to the classroom teacher. Many classroom management techniques are based on behavioral concepts. A major influence of behavioral psychology has been to document observable effects of interactions between the students and the environment in which they function.

Classical Conditioning: Ivan Pavlov

Classical conditioning occurs when an event that is not typically related to a reflex response acquires the ability to elicit that reflex response. Ivan Pavlov (1849–1936), a Russian physiologist, is credited with observing and reporting about classical conditioning. In the late 1800s and early 1900s he studied the digestive system of dogs, which eventually led him to describe a type of behavioral learning termed *classical conditioning*. Pavlov attempted to determine the length of time between when a dog was fed and when it would begin to secrete digestive juices (i.e., salivate). He observed that the time interval changed as the experiment was repeated. Initially, the dogs salivated after they began eating. On later trials, the dogs salivated when they saw the food coming, before beginning to eat. Eventually, the dogs salivated as soon as they saw or heard the experimenter approaching.

Pavlov designed a set of experiments to test this phenomenon systematically. He sounded a bell immediately before a dog was fed and noted that the dog salivated. Pavlov continued pairing the two stimuli, the sound of the bell and the presentation of food, several times. After several paired presentations, Pavlov presented only one stimulus, the ringing of the bell. When he did this, Pavlov observed the dog salivate, even though no food was presented. Because of the experimental method used to systematically investigate this phenomenon, the kind of learning described by Pavlov has been called classical conditioning. Some researchers call it respondent conditioning.

Important Influences on Educational Psychology		
Contributor	Place of Study	Contribution(s)
John B. Watson (1878–1958)	University of Chicago	Founder of American behaviorism; declared he could train any child for any specialty
Ivan Pavlov (1849–1936)	University of St. Petersburg; Russian Military Medical Academy	Established principles of classical conditioning; provided foundation for learning theories; received 1904 Nobel prize for work on primary digestive glands
Burrhus F. Skinner (1904–)	Harvard University	Established principles of operant conditioning; developed behavior modification techniques; maintained that learning cannot occur without reinforcement
Albert Bandura (1925–)	University of Iowa	Promoted social learning theory
Abraham Maslow (1908–1970)	University of Wisconsin	One founder of third-force (humanistic) psychology; proposed theory of motivation on basis of hierarchy of needs
Carl Rogers (1902–1987)	Columbia University	Developed nondirective approach to counseling

Important Influences on Educational Psychology *(cont.)*		
Contributor	Place of Study	Contribution(s)
Arthur Combs (1912–)	Ohio State University	Humanist; believed that teachers should try to understand what is happening from student's point of view.
Martin Seligman (1942–)	Princeton University; University of Pennsylvania	Conducted research on learned helplessness

The learning that occurs in classical conditioning begins with an unconditioned stimulus that elicits an unconditioned response (reflex). *Unconditioned stimuli* (UCS) are events that elicit involuntary reflex actions such as the startle reflex. *Unconditioned responses* (UCR) are the actions that occur naturally and do not have to be learned. In Pavlov's example food is the UCS and salivation is the UCR. No one had to teach the dog to salivate when food was presented; it was an automatic response.

The second step in classical conditioning is to pair a conditioned stimulus with the UCS that already elicits the UCR. A *conditioned stimulus* (CS) is a novel event that does not already elicit the desired response. In Pavlov's example the sounding of the bell (the CS) was paired with the presentation of food (the UCS) and the salivation (the UCR) continued to occur. At this point, the salivation is still considered an unconditional response. The final step is to sound the bell (CS) without the presentation of food. If classical conditioning has occurred, that sound will elicit salivation and the dog's response will have been conditioned, that is, learned and associated with the CS. Therefore, the dog's salivation has become a *conditioned response* (CR) to the sounding of the bell.

Food presented

Dog salivates

Food paired with bell
several times

Dog salivates

After several pairings with
the food, the dog will salivate
when hearing only the bell.

Dog salivates

Fig. 6.1 Pavlov's Classical Conditioning

Operant Conditioning: B. F. Skinner

One limitation of classical conditioning is that it describes learning associated only with reflex behaviors, such as salivating, and does not explain how new behaviors are acquired. Edward Thorndike's work (1913) with cats placed in puzzle boxes (described in Chapter 1) established the basis for operant conditioning, which explains how people acquire new behaviors. These boxes were described as "puzzles" because the cat had to pull out a bolt to escape from the boxes. Thorndike placed food outside the boxes. On initial trials, the cats fumbled around until they accidentally discovered how to pull the bolt to get out of the cage. On later trials, the cats could pull the bolt out more quickly and received food, which was satisfying. Thorndike called this phenomenon the *law of effect*, which states that actions that produce satisfaction or rewards will be repeated in similar situations.

Burrhus Frederick Skinner (1904–) noticed the limitations of classical conditioning and built upon Thorndike's law of effect. Skinner investigated other associations between stimuli and responses. The type of learning that Skinner describes is called operant conditioning. Some researchers also call it *instrumental conditioning*. Operant conditioning involves learning voluntary responses and strengthening or weakening those responses by the consequences, the reinforcers.

Most of the research that Skinner conducted involved an apparatus that Skinner designed which has come to be known as the *Skinner box*, a small cage with a built-in lever (or bar) and a tray. Outside the box is a container of food pellets. When the lever is pressed, a food pellet can be rolled automatically into the box and onto the tray.

For a typical experiment Skinner would place a hungry rat inside the box. The rat would discover the lever and notice that pressing the lever delivered food pellets on the tray. Once this was learned, Skinner provided food pellets only under certain conditions, and the rat would learn what these conditions were and press the lever more frequently when they occurred. For example, Skinner would provide pellets when the bar was pressed only after a tone was sounded. The rat learned that pressing the lever when a tone was sounded resulted in delivery of food pellets, but pressing the lever when there was no sound did not produce food pellets. We "know" that the rat learned this response to the tone because the rat pressed the lever frequently when the tone was sounded and infrequently when the tone was not sounded. The term *operant* conditioning was chosen because the rats "operated" the bar to receive food.

Social Learning Theory: Bandura

Albert Bandura (1925–) is responsible for the classic work in the area of social learning theory, a third type of behavioral learning theory (Bandura, 1977). Social learning theory describes the process of observational learning. People learn new behaviors through two kinds of observational learning, vicarious conditioning and modeling.

Vicarious Conditioning

In vicarious conditioning a student's behavior will increase or decrease in relation to the rewards or punishment that someone else received for similar behavior. Consider this example: Bob usually picks on little John and little John does not retaliate. One day Bob sees Stuart call little John a "twit." Little John hauls off and hits Stuart. In the future Bob stops picking on little John. Or consider another example in which younger siblings observe praise that parents give older siblings for being responsible or getting good grades. Through vicarious conditioning, the younger siblings learn the behaviors that elicited the parental praise.

Modeling

The second type of observational learning is imitation or modeling, where a behavior is increased after an observer sees another person demonstrating the behavior. The observer does not have to see the person reinforced or punished for the behavior. Sometimes the observer learns the behavior simply to imitate the model, or at other times, learns the behavior in anticipation that it will increase a certain skill level. Examples of observational learning are: an unpopular high-school student watches a popular high-school student and begins using similar hand gestures, a junior-high athlete observes a professional athlete chewing tobacco and later tries it, a home economics student observes the instructor gently folding egg whites and later mimics the gentle folding behavior. The major point of social learning theory is that people can learn new behaviors by watching others and practicing. The modeling process is facilitated by similarity between the model and modeler (person learning through observation).

Elements in Observational Learning

According to Bandura (1986), there are four important elements in observational learning: attention, retention, production, and motivation or reinforcement.

1. *Attention*. For observational learning to occur, students have to

attend to the to-be-learned behavior. If they do not see, hear, or otherwise experience the new behavior, it will not be learned. As the teacher, you can facilitate observational learning by emphasizing relevant events (or behaviors).

2. *Retention.* To imitate a behavior, students must retain (remember) what they observed. You can facilitate retention by encouraging students to rehearse information or behaviors and by providing cues.

3. *Production.* After the behavior has been attended to and retained, it must be practiced until it can be produced well. During the production stage, students will practice a new behavior until they can reproduce it like the model. During this stage, you can provide feedback and encouragement until new behaviors are mastered.

4. *Motivation and Reinforcement.* Once the new behavior is acquired, it will be demonstrated when there is appropriate motivation, or incentive. Subsequently, appropriate reinforcement of the new behavior when it is demonstrated will strengthen it and help to ensure it will occur again. Referring to the preceding example, the home economics teacher could further reinforce the gentle folding behavior by complimenting the student or assigning a good grade. The unpopular student's new gestures would be reinforced if other students paid attention when those gestures were used.

Behavioral Principles

To implement behavioral theories, you need to understand the relationships between stimuli, reinforcements, and responses because these relationships determine whether learning will occur. The following are important terms and principles of behaviorism.

Reinforcement

Reinforcement is any event or consequence of a behavior that results in an increase in the frequency of that behavior.

Classes of Reinforcement. There are two classes of reinforcement, positive and negative.

Positive reinforcement is the presentation of a stimulus after a behavior occurs that increases the strength or likelihood that the behavior will be repeated. The stimulus is usually pleasant, such as a hug, monetary rewards, time for social talking, or candy. If a student gets all A's on a report card, and the parent gives the student $5, and the presentation of the money increases the likelihood that the student will try for all A's next time, then the money was a positive reinforcer.

Negative reinforcement is the removal of an aversive or unpleasant stimulus that increases the strength or likelihood that a behavior will be repeated. Examples of aversive stimuli that may be removed are events or objects that cause loud noises and work that students do not want to do. For instance, if a young child is frightened when a large door closes with a loud bang, the child may not want to close the door. A parent who removes the loud noise that occurs by cushioning the frame of the door has removed an aversive stimulus. If the child is then more likely to walk through that door and close it, then the behavior was negatively reinforced. If an annoying buzzer rings when you sit in your car without a seatbelt, you might fasten the seatbelt to turn off the buzzer. In this example, you fasten the seatbelt (increase the desired behavior) to turn off the buzzer (remove the aversive stimulus). Do not confuse negative reinforcement with punishment. Remember that reinforcement means increasing behavior. Negative reinforcement means removing an aversive stimulus to increase the behavior .

Schedules of Reinforcement. Reinforcement schedules determine the timing of the presentation of the reinforcers.

Initially, *continuous reinforcement*, meaning that the reinforcer is presented every time the behavior occurs, is used to strengthen behaviors when they are first learned. An example would be giving a child a gold star for every homework paper completed.

After a behavior is mastered, *intermittent reinforcement* is used to maintain the behavior. On intermittent schedules a behavior is not reinforced every time it occurs. An example would be giving a child a gold star on certain homework papers. An intermittent schedule is very powerful because students do not know when to expect the reinforcer, so the behavior is maintained. It also takes less time to implement.

There are four types of intermittent reinforcement schedules. Two of these schedules are based on the behavior ratio, meaning the number of responses that should occur between reinforcements. The other two schedules are based on time intervals, meaning the amount of time that elapses between reinforcers.

Fixed ratio–A reinforcer is presented after the desired behavior occurs a specified number of times. For example, a teacher gives students 20 math problems on a worksheet. The teacher offers to check every 10 problems. Students are likely to work quickly through the first 10 problems, and then take a break before tackling the next 10.

Variable ratio–A reinforcer is presented after the behavior occurs at varying times. For example, the teacher might give students 20 math problems on a worksheet, have them begin working, and tell them that anyone who has finished 8 problems can come to get the work checked. Subsequently, the teacher might tell students that anyone who has finished 15 problems can come to get the work checked. With this variable-ratio schedule, the students are more likely to work steadily because they cannot predict when the reinforcement will come. This schedule is effective in maintaining behavior over long periods of time. Behaviors maintained on this schedule tend to be quite resistant to extinction (disappearance of a learned behavior).

Fixed interval–A reinforcer is presented after the first occurrence of a behavior when a given amount of time has elapsed, for example, 5 minutes. A teacher trying to reinforce quiet behavior using a fixed-interval schedule will check every 5 minutes to see if the class is quiet. If the class is quiet, the reinforcement is given. When this kind of schedule is used, the desired behavior tends to increase just before the reinforcer, which comes at a predictable time. There is also a good chance for a decrease in the appropriate behavior and/or an increase in the undesired behavior right after the reinforcer is given. For example, a teacher walks around the lunch tables every 5 minutes to make sure the students are quiet. The students are most likely to be quiet immediately before the 5-minute check and are most likely to become boisterous right after the check, when there is a safe period.

Variable interval–A reinforcer is presented after the first occurrence of a behavior when different time periods have elapsed. For example, after the first occurrence of a behavior, a reinforcer is presented after 5 minutes, then after 3 minutes, then after 10 minutes. A teacher trying to reinforce quiet behavior using a variable-interval schedule will check at different intervals to see if the class is quiet. If the class is quiet, the reinforcement is given. When this kind of schedule is used, the desired behavior tends to be more constant than when a fixed interval is used because the reinforcer is not presented at predictable times. There is also less likelihood of a break in the behavior right after the reinforcer is given. For example, a teacher walks around the lunch tables 5 minutes after the class sat down to make sure the students are quiet and if so, to praise them for this. Three minutes later, the teacher walks around again. Ten minutes after the second check, the teacher walks around again. The next day the teacher uses a different variable schedule, perhaps a 5-minute check, then a 7-minute check, then a 2-minute check. Each time the class is quiet during the check, they are praised.

Extinction

Extinction is the decrease and eventual disappearance of a learned behavior. When behavior is not reinforced, it gradually disappears and becomes extinct. In the experiment with Pavlov's dog, when food was not presented when the tone was sounded, then the salivation response to the sound of the bell eventually became extinct. In other words, the food reinforced the salivation when the tone was sounded and when that reinforcement did not continue, then the salivation response to the tone disappeared. Sometimes teachers try to extinguish inappropriate classroom behavior by ignoring it, assuming that the student will give up after failing to attract attention or elicit a response from the teacher or other students. The expectation is that giving attention to the problem is reinforcing it, strengthening it, and that if the reinforcement is not provided, the behavior will eventually become extinct.

Punishment

To psychologists punishment is any stimulus that decreases the strength or frequency of a behavior. There are several possible negative consequences associated with punishment, however, and its use in the classroom is generally not recommended, as mentioned earlier (Chapter 3).

1. Punishment may cause an increase rather than a decrease in the inappropriate behavior.

2. Punishment may generate fear toward the person providing the punishment. For example, if a classroom teacher punishes a student, the student may become fearful of that teacher.

3. Punishment may generate fear toward another situation. For example, if a student is punished during school, the student may become fearful about going to school.

There are two kinds of punishment, presentation punishment and removal punishment.

Presentation punishment is the presentation of a stimulus after a behavior that causes a decrease in the behavior. Common presentation punishments include spanking, demerits, and extra writing assignments. A teacher observes a student talking out of turn and gives the student one demerit. The student is less likely to talk out of turn later. The demerit was a presentation punishment.

Removal punishment is the removal of a stimulus after an undesirable behavior that causes a decrease in that behavior. Common removal punishments are curtailment or confiscation of privileges, such as watching television and using a family car. For instance, a parent notices a child speaking disrespectfully to another adult. The parent takes away the child's television privileges for a week. If the child becomes less likely to speak disrespectfully, then removal punishment was implemented successfully.

Stimulus Generalization and Discrimination

Stimulus generalization takes place when a learned response to one stimulus also occurs when a similar stimulus is presented. For example, Pavlov's dogs learned to salivate to one particular tone, but they could have generalized and subsequently salivated when other tones were presented. In another example, a student who has difficulty in one math class may generalize and learn to expect difficulty in subsequent math classes.

Stimulus discrimination takes place when a learned response to one stimulus is not made when similar stimuli are presented. For example, Pavlov's dogs could learn to discriminate between tones when food would be presented after one particular tone, but not after other tones.

Shaping

Shaping is reinforcement of gradual change in behavior until a desired behavior is achieved. The gradual change is brought about by appropriate use of reinforcers and punishment. A teacher has one student who does not play with the other students at recess. The teacher may try to shape the child's social behavior by gradually involving the student and reinforcing the *approximations* (small steps) of appropriate behavior. For example, one day the teacher talks to the student (this student enjoys talking with the teacher) while other children play at a distance. A few days later, the teacher talks to the student while other children play nearby. A few days later the teacher has another student enter the conversation between the shy student and the teacher. A few days later that second student talks only with the shy student. The teacher is not involved, but later praises the shy student for spending time with the second student. These approximations eventually lead to the shy child's joining the rest of the class during some recess activities.

Cueing

Cueing provides a stimulus that sets up the appropriate behavior. This is important because it helps the desired behavior occur so that it can be reinforced. If you cannot elicit a desired behavior, or a part of that behavior, then you cannot reinforce it. A teacher who reminds the class that two demerits are given for speaking out of turn, before the students speak out of turn, is implementing cueing.

Classroom Applications of Behavioral Theories

There are a number of ways to apply behavioral theories in the classroom. First, be aware that some of the students' emotional reactions are learned associations. For example, a child who is afraid of swings may have learned to associate falling down and getting hurt with the sight of a swing. If this were the case, you might have success getting the child to swing over time by implementing a shaping procedure. Shaping could be used to gradually change the behavior until a desired behavior is achieved. You could first break the swinging task into smaller steps such as having the child walk to the swingset, talk with friends near the swingset, sit on a swing without swinging, and later, swing with you standing nearby. It is important to make each small step a positive experience for the child. You could also reinforce the appropriate behavior at each step up to and including when the complete swinging behavior is demonstrated. Another application of behavioral theories is to make learning tasks fun, or at least pleasant experiences. Help associate school and learning with pleasant feelings by minimizing competition and providing occasional treats.

Operant Conditioning

Operant conditioning can be applied in many ways in the school setting. Most behavior modification techniques utilize operant conditioning. For example, reinforce the appropriate behaviors. Take time to commend students when they are working hard or being cooperative, especially in difficult circumstances. If it seems that reinforcers are not working, check that the reinforcers you chose are really reinforcing to the students. You might also check the reinforcement schedule you are using. Make sure that you are using the most appropriate one for the kind of problem you have. If you have trouble eliciting behaviors so that they can be reinforced, begin using cues to set up the behaviors you want to see. Then, when the students approximate the behavior you want, reinforce the approximation.

In a recent article, Skinner (1984) specified four guidelines based on behavioral principles that can be used to improve teaching. Skinner suggested that teachers (1) be very clear about what they are going to teach, (2) make sure that prerequisite skills are mastered before introducing more complex concepts to the students, (3) not force all students to progress at the same pace, and (4) use programmed instruction (PI). Programmed instruction will be covered in Chapter 9 under "Individualized Instruction," but the basic ideas are to present lessons that are divided into small steps and to provide immediate performance feedback. Students progress through these lessons at their own pace.

Social Learning Theory

Social learning theory can also be applied in the school setting. The behaviors of other students and the classroom teacher often serve as models for young students. The teacher may display enthusiasm for math, be prompt in coming to class, be polite to other teachers, and so on. All of these behaviors may be learned through observational learning in the classroom. Teachers can also take advantage of vicarious conditioning by praising desired behaviors in front of many students.

Humanistic Theories

The second major category of learning theory presented in this chapter is the humanistic learning theory, which investigates the effect of emotional and interpersonal behavior on learning. Humanistic theories developed in the late 1960s and early 1970s in response to discontent with behavioral approaches. Behavioral approaches were criticized for not considering how students feel about themselves or their teachers. Humanists argued that these feelings are important to learning. Behavioral approaches were also criticized for being too simplistic. Humanists argued that teachers need to be concerned with more factors than those considered by behaviorists. Learning in a classroom environment is more complicated than classical conditioning experiments conducted in a laboratory. Behavioral theories have also been criticized because they fail to explain how learning occurs. For example, consider language acquisition. Behavioral explanations are limited because they do not help us understand how language is acquired (except that speech sounds and appropriate means of communication are reinforced).

The humanists, in general, believed that education should involve the development of both the intellect and the emotions. The goal of this approach is to help develop students' personalities, values, social skills, and self-concepts in concert with academic achievement. Humanists might argue that it is more important for students to become responsible, caring adults than to score a few points higher on an achievement test.

Many social factors also influenced the development of the

humanistic perspective. For example, after World War II there was an upsurge in American technology. There were also strong civil rights movements during this period, and generally there was concern with productivity and efficiency. At that time a number of books were published that described what was wrong with American schools, for example, Silberman's (1970) *Crisis in the Classroom*, Neill's (1960) *Summerhill: A Radical Approach to Child Rearing*, and Holt's (1964) *How Children Fail*. Criticism of the educational system grew and confidence declined. Humanists began to argue that education should incorporate awareness of emotions and feelings, and that behaviorists and cognitivists were "dehumanizing" education.

The three individuals who had the greatest impact on the humanistic movement were Abraham Maslow, Carl Rogers, and Arthur Combs.

Abraham Maslow

Abraham Maslow (1908–1970) is known for proposing humanism (Maslow, 1968), otherwise known as *third-force psychology*. Drawing on his work in motivation, Maslow argued that inasmuch as healthy children seek fulfilling experiences they should be allowed to make choices and control much of their own behavior. Parents and teachers, in addition to providing children's basic needs, should give them room to grow by encouraging them to function independently and to take control of their own lives. Maslow also presented a major theory of motivation that describes children's needs in more detail. His need theory of motivation is discussed in the next chapter.

Carl Rogers

Carl Rogers (1902–1987) developed a new approach to psychotherapy, the *client-centered approach* (also called *nondirective therapy* and a person-centered approach). Rogers emphasized that the client is the central figure. The therapist does not tell the client what is wrong and what to do, but rather helps the client solve the problem. The therapist establishes a warm and accepting attitude toward the client and demonstrates sincere empathy. In this environment the client becomes more self-accepting and self-aware and is better able to solve personal problems without the help of a therapist. In addition to being a psychotherapist, Rogers was a professor of psychology. He believed that these same techniques could be applied in educational settings. According to this approach, known as the *learner-centered* approach, teachers should be sincere, trusting, and empathetic with students. As in to Maslow's view, the learner-centered approach results in the students gaining greater control over their educational experiences.

Arthur Combs

Arthur Combs (1912–) believed that self-perception is very important and that teachers should help students develop positive self-concepts. Combs held that behavior is a direct result of what the person is perceiving at any given point in time. The implications of this position are that teachers should try to understand what is happening from the student's point of view. Combs saw the teacher as one who facilitates learning and encourages students. Combs (1965) believed that effective teachers are knowledgeable of their subject material, use many instructional methods, are sensitive to others' feelings, believe their students can learn, and help students develop their learning potential and positive self-concepts.

Classroom Applications of Humanistic Theories

Soon after the popularity of humanistic education peaked, a "back to the basics" trend appeared. Researchers cannot adequately answer the question, "How effective was humanistic education?" However, several general guidelines derived from humanistic education are useful for today's teachers:

1. Trust students and allow them to make choices in the learning process. With some control over what they learn, your students are likely to be more highly motivated and appreciate the value of their education.

2. Be sincere, warm, responsive, and empathetic toward your students. Learn your students' names and use them in class. Praise their work when appropriate. Communicate the belief your students are capable, responsible people. Help them develop positive self-

concepts. Within reasonable limits, share your own feelings and reactions with them.

In addition to these general guidelines, the following classroom activities and procedures are advocated by humanists:

1. Provide activities that allow students to explore their feelings and emotions. For example, have open discussions about current events and the impact they may have.

2. Following unusual experiences, discuss thoughts and feelings with small groups of students.

3. Encourage students to keep diaries or other journals. Some students will enjoy audio or video tape recording of thoughts and feelings instead of writing.

4. Encourage students to empathize with other students. Design role-playing exercises and other sociodramatic games to help students learn to identify with others. For example, have a student play the part of a teacher who catches a student cheating on an exam, or have a tough student play the part of a wimp in a pretend fight.

5. Help students become more aware of their values by implementing values clarification activities. Students may need help identifying their values, claiming their values, or acting consistently with their values. Simon et al. (1972) provided 79 strategies to help students with values clarification. These strategies give students practice identifying their values and publicly sharing them.

6. Implement pass/fail grading rather than traditional A, B, C, D, F grading. Pass/fail grading may reduce competition between students and help teachers to be viewed as facilitators rather than judges.

Behavioral and humanistic learning theories were discussed in this chapter. Behavioral theories include classical conditioning, operant conditioning, and social learning. In classical conditioning, a conditioned stimulus is paired with an unconditioned stimulus until it can elicit a conditioned response. Classical conditioning involves automatic reflex responses. Operant conditioning involves learning new be-

haviors that are voluntary. The behaviors are learned because of the presentation of reinforcing consequences. Social learning theory describes how new behaviors can be learned or existing behaviors changed by direct observation of other people.

Humanistic proponents such as Maslow, Rogers, and Combs emphasize the human aspect, emotions, and interpersonal relations in the school environment. They believe that students should be given choices in their education. They also believe that teachers should develop warm, trusting environments in which children can explore and grow.

Recommended Reading

Bandura, A. (1986). *Social Foundations of Thought and Action: A Social Cognitive Theory.* Englewood Cliffs, N.J.: Prentice-Hall. (A recent description of Bandura's theory which integrates behavioral and cognitive perspectives.)

Canfield, J. T., and H. C. Wells. (1976). *100 Ways to Enhance Self-Concept in the Classroom: A Handbook for Teachers and Parents.* Englewood Cliffs, N.J.: Prentice-Hall. (Describes many interesting activities designed to improve self-concept.)

Lane, H. (1976). *The Wild Boy of Averon.* New York: Bantam Books. (The story of Jean-Marc Itard's work to civilize a boy found in a French forest.)

Maslow, A. H. (1968). *Toward a Psychology of Being,* 2d ed. Princeton, N.J.: Van Nostrand. (Describes the propositions that define Maslow's view of humanistic psychology.)

Miller, N. E. , and M. J. Dollard. (1941). *Social Learning and Imitation.* New Haven: Yale University Press. (A classic text that describes the basis of social learning theory.)

Neill, A. S. (1960). *Summerhill: A Radical Approach to Child Rearing.* New York: Hart. (Describes Neill's unique school which was designed in London in the early 1900s to fit the child.)

Read, D. A., and S. B. Simon. (Eds.), (1975). *Humanistic Education Sourcebook.* Englewood Cliffs, N.J. : Prentice-Hall. (A collection of ideas teachers can use to implement humanistic ideas in the classroom.)

Rogers, C. (1980). *A Way of Being.* Boston: Houghton Mifflin.

Simon, S. B., L. W. Howe, and H. Kirschenbaum. (1972). *Values Clarification:*

A Handbook of Practical Strategies for Teachers and Students. New York: Hart. (Provides 79 ideas for helping students with values clarification.)

Skinner, B. F. (1968). *The Technology of Teaching.* New York: Appleton-Century-Crofts. (Discusses the application of operant conditioning techniques and how they apply to the teaching profession.)

Skinner, B. F. (1948). *Walden Two.* New York: Macmillan. (Describes Skinner's idea of a utopia.)

References

Bandura, A. (1986). *Social Foundations of Thought and Action: A Social Cognitive Theory.* Englewood Cliffs, N.J.: Prentice Hall.

Bandura, A. (1977). *Social Learning Theory.* Englewood Cliffs, N. J.: Prentice-Hall.

Combs, A. (1965). *The Professional Education of Teachers.* Boston: Allyn & Bacon.

Holt, J. (1964). *How Children Fail.* New York: Pitman.

Maslow, A. H. (1968). *Toward a Psychology of Being.* 2d ed. Princeton, N.J.: Van Nostrand.

Neill, A. S. (1960). *Summerhill: A Radical Approach to Child Rearing.* New York: Hart.

Silberman, C. E. (1970). *Crisis in the Classroom.* New York: Random House.

Simon, S. B., L. W. Howe, and H. Kirschenbaum. (1972). *Values Clarification: A Handbook of Practical Strategies for Teachers and Students.* New York: Hart.

Skinner, B. F. (1953). *Science and Human Behavior.* New York: Macmillan.

Skinner, B. F. (1984). The Shame of American Education. *American Psychologist, 39,* 947-954.

Thorndike, E. L. (1913). Educational Psychology, in *The Psychology of Learning,* Vol. 2. New York: Teachers College, Columbia University.

Watson, J. B. (1913). Psychology as the Behaviorist Views It. *Psychological Review, 20,* 158–177.

CHAPTER 7

Principles and Models of Cognitive Learning

This chapter describes four models of cognitive learning and shows how the principles derived from these models can be used in the classroom. These models differ from noncognitive models by speculating about phenomena that cannot be seen. For example, you cannot observe how a student remembers information. From test scores, teachers can learn about a student's level of performance, but test scores do not indicate why some events are easier to remember than others. The cognitive models explain how people learn, retain, and retrieve information. Educational psychologists study cognitive learning models in order to better understand how learning takes place. The more you understand about how learning occurs, the better able you are to help make it happen.

Brief History of Cognitive Psychology

Early Developments

Many psychologists in the late 1800s, William James and Sigmund Freud, for example, were interested in understanding mental processes. A common method of investigation at that time was introspection (self-observation and disclosure). Then, in the early part of the twentieth century, John B. Watson argued that mental processes could not be measured objectively and that introspection could not be verified. Psychologists shifted their research focus from mental processes to observable behavior. The result of this shift was a relatively inactive period for cognitive psychology research.

Use in World War II

Subsequently, during World War II, psychologists were needed to conduct human factors research on training, selection, and performance of military personnel. *Human factors* is the study of human performance, preference, and safety in human/machine systems. In doing this research, psychologists studied complex tasks, such as piloting airplanes. A rebirth in cognitive psychology occurred as psychologists returned to universities and theorized about the underlying mental processes involved in these complex tasks.

Recent Trends

Several other events since the 1950s have contributed to the resurgence of interest in cognitive psychology. When a famous linguist, Noam Chomsky (1959), argued that Skinner's behavioristic explanation of language development was inadequate, psychologists began to realize the limitations of the behaviorist perspective. Ulric Neisser's *Cognitive Psychology* (1967) helped redefine and draw attention to the field. Another important event was the rapid development of computers, which provided powerful tools for studying underlying mental processes.

Cognitive Science

A subsequent field emerged in 1976, called cognitive science, which overlaps cognitive psychology. Cognitive science integrates research in cognitive psychology, artificial intelligence, and linguistics, utilizing computer simulations and logical analyses. The journal *Cognitive Science* is a good reference for learning more about the scope of the field.

Gestalt Psychology

One of the first cognitive theories was developed in the early 1900s by three German psychologists, Wolfgang Köhler (1887–1967), Kurt Koffka (1886–1941), and Max Wertheimer (1880–1943).

The word *Gestalt* means pattern, form, or configuration. Gestalt psychologists assert that people learn things by arranging them in patterns and viewing the relationships among the items, sometimes oversimplifying them.

Laws of Perceptual Organization

Several principles and laws of Gestalt psychology describe how people organize perceptual stimuli into meaningful information. Included are:

Law of good figure—Patterns are seen in the simplest way possible. This is the central principle of Gestalt psychology. It is also referred to as the *law of Prägnanz* (*Prägnanz* is German for "good figure"), and sometimes as the *law of simplicity*.

Law of proximity—Things physically close together are organized into units.

Law of similarity—Things that look alike are organized together.

Law of contiguity—Points that would create a straight or smooth line if connected will be organized together.

Law of closure—Figures that are not complete (having gaps) will be remembered as if they were complete.

Principle of Summation

One of the most famous Gestalt concepts is that the whole is more than the sum of its parts. For example, as you read the words on this page, which are actually a series of lines and curves, you perceive more than merely lines and curves. You read words and obtain meaning from them. Similarly, when you look at your best friend, you see more than skin, eyes, a nose, and a mouth. You recognize a friendly face.

Figure-Ground Principle

Another important contribution of the Gestalt psychologists is the figure-ground principle. As you look at or hear complex stimuli, you will focus on a basic figure and allow the rest of the stimuli to remain less distinct. This principle also applies for an ambiguous stimulus with two possible figures; only one figure is perceived at a time. The meaningful stimulus is perceived as the figure, and the other stimulus is perceived as the background. Characteristics that determine which stimulus is perceived as the figure are symmetry, convexity, area, and orientation. Stimuli that are symmetrical (balanced), convex (bulging outward), larger, and vertical or horizontal are most likely to be perceived as the figure.

Köhler's Experiment

A classic illustration of Gestalt psychology was conducted in 1916 by Wolfgang Köhler. Köhler used a chimpanzee named Sultan to demonstrate learning as the perception of new relationships, sometimes called *insight*. Placed in a cage with a variety of playthings, including some sticks, Sultan discovered that he could use the sticks to reach things outside the cage beyond his arm's reach.

One day, Köhler placed a banana outside Sultan's cage, beyond the reach of Sultan's sticks. Failing to reach the banana, Sultan threw down a stick and stormed off to another part of the cage. While sulking, he saw a larger stick outside the cage. Sultan jumped up, used a short stick to reach and rake in the larger stick, then used the larger stick to rake in the banana. Sultan solved the problem by perceiving relationships in a new way, that is, by using the first instrument to obtain the second, larger instrument, which would be used to obtain the desired object. Because Sultan perceived relationships between the objects in a new way, he demonstrated insight, an indication of learning. Subsequent researchers observed that animals without raking experience and animals who did not happen to see the banana and the long stick did not solve this problem.

Limitations of Gestalt Principles

Gestalt principles have several limitations. For example, the law of good figure (law of simplicity) does not specify how one determines which of several figures is the simplest. In addition, the role of familiarity in perception is typically not considered in discussions of figure-ground perception. Stimuli that may be meaningful or appear familiar will probably be grouped together; traditional Gestalt psychologists did not take this into account. A more general problem is that Gestalt psychologists do not specify the conditions under which any given law will determine perception. For example, if the laws of simplicity and similarity both apply to a set of stimuli, one cannot predict which law will govern the perception of those stimuli. Another general problem with Gestalt psychology is that the principles are used to describe a situation rather than to explain what is happening. A more useful approach would provide the missing explanations.

Classroom Applications of Gestalt Psychology

Although the Gestalt principles are not widely applied in educational settings, one application is to provide opportunity for insight by letting students make mistakes and solve problems on their own.

Field Theory

Kurt Lewin

Kurt Lewin (1890–1947) used the Gestalt principles in the 1950s to develop a cognitive theory called field theory. The name *field theory* comes from a related concept in physics called "field of forces," which refers to the way metal filings are arranged in certain patterns when they

Important Influences on Educational Psychology		
Contributor	Place of Study	Contribution(s)
Wolfgang Köhler (1887–1967)	Berlin	Cofounder of Gestalt psychology movement; advocated insight as component of problem-solving process
Max Wertheimer (1880–1943)	Berlin and Würzberg	Cofounder of Gestalt psychology; emphasized teaching for understanding, teaching the whole picture
Kurt Koffka (1886–1941)	Berlin and Edinburgh	Cofounder of Gestalt psychology; wrote *Principles of Gestalt Psychology* (1935)
Kurt Lewin (1890–1947)	Berlin	Advocate of Gestalt psychology; developed field theory of motivation

are placed near a magnet. Lewin's theory explains that human behavior is affected by two factors, positive and negative forces called *valences,* and the direction of those valences, called *vectors*. Lewin also used the concept of *life space.* A person's life space includes everything in that person's environment. Within the environment, some people and objects will be ignored, some will receive minimal attention, and some will be significant. People and objects that are important have a high positive valence, and the individual is attracted to them. People or objects with a negative valence will be avoided if possible.

Classroom Applications of Field Theory

Field theory teaches us to look at a student's behavior from the student's own perspective. Students engage in behaviors that involve them with persons and objects they are attracted to. They will shy away from people and things with negative valences. You may be able to help students concentrate on things you think are important by first understanding what attracts them. If you are teaching an aspect or period of history that does not particularly interest some of your students and you know that those students are interested in famous scientists, you might elaborate the history lecture to include relevant scientists of that period.

Network Models

Network models, developed within the last 20 years, were designed to explain how certain types of information are represented in human memory. For example, Collins and Quillian (1969) proposed a network model of semantic memory. *Semantic memories* are facts, concepts, and principles not related to specific events. Examples of semantic information are: states are bigger than cities, Atlanta is the capital of Georgia, birds have wings. School learning usually involves semantic memory. This model maintains that semantic information is connected in a huge network with related information connected hierarchically. General categories, such as plants, are easy to access in memory. Very specific information, such as information about a specific kind of plant, is deep within the hierarchy. To access information about the gardenia, for example, a person searches first for the general category of plants, then for the information about gardenias. Searching through this hierarchy takes time; specific information takes longer to retrieve than information about general categories.

Information Processing Model

The information processing model is a popular explanation of human cognitive processes. The model utilizes concepts and terminology from linguistics, information theory, and computer science to describe human thought processes. The human being is considered an information processing system that senses, stores, encodes, and retrieves information much as a computer does. Mental events are discussed as information that is transferred from input to output, that is, from the original stimulus to the final response.

Methods of Investigating Mental Processes

Within the information processing framework, psychologists have developed several methods for investigating mental processes. Three of these methods are:

Verbal reports–reports taken before, during, and/or after performing a task to help researchers learn about thinking and reasoning processes. During verbal reporting, persons state out loud what they are thinking. Ericsson and Simon (1980) call this "thinking aloud" and stress that persons should not state how they are thinking, only what they are thinking. Trying to say how one is thinking can make the task more difficult by increasing the demands on working memory and reasoning processes.

Latency data–the speed of responses. Researchers measure the amount of time between stimulus presentation and response generation. Computers are useful tools for collecting latency data because they can be programmed to accurately record response times. When latency increases (more time between stimulus and response), researchers infer that more mental processing occurred. Latency data is often collected on a secondary task while a person is performing a primary one. Researchers might vary the difficulty of the primary task. If the response time to the secondary task increases, researchers infer that more processing was needed for the primary task. Latency data is collected as a way of quantifying cognitive processing.

Eye fixations–data that describe where a person is looking at any given time. Researchers have used eye fixations to study problem-solving strategies. For example, a researcher might present a picture of folded paper on a computer screen and ask a participant to determine what the paper would look like unfolded. By recording eye fixations, researchers can determine what aspect of the problem (the folded paper) the participant focuses on and how that person progresses through the task. The eye fixations of successful and unsuccessful problem solvers can vary significantly. An important application of this kind of research is teaching unsuccessful problem solvers to approach the problem the same way the successful problem solvers did.

Models of Memory

One of the most common applications of the information processing model describes human memory. Two widely accepted models of memory have been proposed, one by Craik and Lockhart (1972) and the other by Atkinson and Shiffrin (1968).

Levels of Processing Model

Craik and Lockhart proposed a model which maintains that information is subjected to varying levels of mental processing, and that information received thorough processing will be remembered. For example, your students might try to memorize state capitals by saying them repeatedly. To increase the likelihood of their remembering, you might have them learn special facts about the capitals, show them pictures or filmstrips of the capitals, take them on imaginary trips to the capitals, and so on. According to the levels of processing model, the more deeply students process the names of the capitals (by working with greater levels of detail), the more likely they will be to remember them.

Information Processing Model

An information processing model of memory based on work by

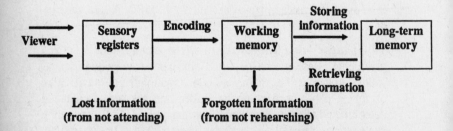

Fig. 7.1 Information Processing Model

Atkinson and Shiffrin (1968) is shown in Fig. 7.1. The boxes represent different processing states, and the lines represent how information is transferred from one state to another. These states and processes are discussed in detail following the diagram.

Sensory Registers

Stimuli enter the body through *sensory receptors*. The primary sensory receptors of cognitive information are the eyes and the ears. Information entering these receptors must be held for a brief period of time in order to be perceived. The sensory register holding visual information is called *iconic memory*. The sensory register holding auditory information is called *echoic memory*. The duration of iconic memory is less than 1 second, while echoic memory can last for up to 4 seconds.

To appreciate the importance of memory at this part of the processing system, imagine someone reading aloud to you the following sentence: "Can you remember the first part of this sentence while I am speaking the second part?" If your echoic memory were not functioning, how could you make sense of the sentence? You need to be able to remember a certain amount of information while hearing additional information so that the whole sentence will have meaning. The same phenomenon is true of iconic memory, your memory for rapidly fading images. It seems to make sense that the duration of iconic memory is so brief. If iconic memory lasted for several seconds, you would still see the words on the top of this page as you try to read this sentence. You can imagine what a confusing display of information that would be!

Working Memory

From the sensory registers, some information is lost. Other information, which is *attended to,* "moves" into working memory and is encoded. *Encoding* means that further processing of the information occurs based on what the information looks like, sounds like, or means. At this point in the system thinking occurs. For example, after you look up a phone number, you begin *rehearsing* the number by reciting it over and over. You rehearse the information to keep it in working memory.

The information is not a permanent part of your memory at this time. If someone interrupts you and you stop rehearsing the number, you will probably have to look it up again. The representation of the phone number will be gone. Working memory is activated when information is first received from the sensory registers and also when information from long-term memory must be utilized.

Limitations of Working Memory

Working memory is limited in the number of items and the amount of information it can maintain. Information that is not rehearsed will remain in working memory for a limited time, about 20 seconds. However, by rehearsing the information you can keep it in working memory indefinitely, though this may prevent you from encoding additional information. Most people can hold between five and nine pieces of information in working memory. Noting that the limitation is seven pieces of information plus or minus two pieces (from five to nine) and that the finding is so robust, George Miller (1956) described the capacity as the "magical number seven, plus or minus two." Some tests of intelligence measure the capacity of the working memory and factor it into the intelligence quotient (IQ).

Obviously, your students know more than seven plus or minus two things. The information they have acquired over a lifetime and permanently stored in the long-term memory is also available.

Chunking Strategy

One way to hold more information in working memory is to use a strategy called chunking. Chunking means to group several individual pieces of information into a single piece. For example, try to remember these numbers in order: 193756224. If you chunk them into groups, such as 193 756 224, you reduce the number of bits (pieces of information) to be remembered from nine to three. A second way to chunk the information is by grouping the information into meaningful units. For example, if your mother was born in 1937 and your street address is 224 South Hampton, then these chunks might be easy to remember: 1937 56 224.

Serial Position Effect

A second, well-documented finding about working memory is that the location of information in a list can determine how likely it is to be remembered. In general, information at the beginning or end of a list is more likely to be remembered than information in the middle. This finding is called the serial position effect. The information processing model attributes serial position effects to a limited-capacity working memory. When all the to-be-remembered information is not rehearsed, some of the information is lost. Remembering items at the beginning of the list is called a *primacy effect*. The primacy effect occurs when the first items in a list are maintained in working memory. Remembering items at the end of the list is called a *recency effect*. The recency effect occurs when the items at the end of the list are maintained the best. If you ask students to memorize a list of difficult spelling words, you may discover that they "learn" the words at the beginning and the end of the list the best. This is most likely to occur if they begin at one end of the list whenever they practice the list and if they do not use any other memory aids. You might suggest that they break the list into small groups before they begin memorizing, or that they start memorizing at different places in the list each time they study. Memory aids are discussed later in this chapter.

Long-Term Memory

Long-term memory (LTM) is the permanent storehouse of information. First dates, special birthday parties, capital cities, and other information accumulated throughout one's lifetime is stored in long-term memory. Researchers now believe that LTM has an unlimited capacity, meaning that most people have the ability to store as much information as they would like. However, the ability to store the information is different from the ability to access the information. Many researchers try to find out what happens to information you cannot remember that you used to "know." They are trying to determine whether all information that was once stored in LTM is maintained or if some of the information eventually disappears. The question is, is the information there and difficult to *retrieve* (i.e., pull back into working memory), or is it gone?

As has been mentioned briefly, there is an interchange of information between working memory and LTM. Acting on the information in

working memory helps transfer it into LTM where it is stored until
needed. Later, the information is retrieved from LTM and utilized from
the working memory.

Semantic and Episodic Memory

Some researchers consider two categories of memory, semantic and
episodic. *Semantic memory* is information concerning facts, concepts,
and principles. Examples of semantic memory are: Atlanta is the capital
of Georgia, Birds have wings, $2 + 3 = 5$, and All people should be free.
Episodic memory is information about specific events. Examples of
episodic memory are memories of your sixteenth birthday party, your
first date, and going to Atlanta. Most school learning utilizes semantic
memory.

Declarative and Procedural Memory

Sometimes researchers categorize knowledge (memories) as declarative and procedural. *Declarative knowledge* includes facts and
beliefs. Examples of declarative knowledge are: there are 50 states in
the United States, my friend likes me, and yesterday you studied for 6
hours. *Procedural knowledge* is memories of processes (things one
knows how to do). Examples of procedural knowledge are driving a
car, tying a shoe, and playing cards.

A Computer Analogy

The growth of the computer science field has helped cognitive
psychologists in important ways. Traditionally, computers have been
used as models of human memory processes. More recently computers
and special software have been used to test cognitive learning theories
by simulating cognitive processes. The following paragraph describes
how computers are used as a model of human thought.

Information is entered into the computer's temporary storage from
an external source, such as a keyboard, a joystick, or another computer.
If the information is in a format that the computer can understand, and
if an application provides appropriate directions, the information can
be transferred and stored in a permanent location such as a floppy disk,
a hard drive, or a compact disk for later use. To use the information,
applications must search the permanent storage location, retrieve the

appropriate information, and transfer the information back to the computer's working memory where it will be processed. Information temporarily stored in the computer's limited working memory—random-access memory (RAM)—and stored permanently will be lost when the computer is turned off.

Memory and Forgetting

Many research studies have been conducted to help psychologists understand how people remember (and forget) information. Researchers try to determine how memories are stored and under what conditions people are most likely to remember things. This next section describes some reasons for forgetting information and some methods you can use to help your students remember things.

Forgetting

Why do we forget certain things and events? Researchers agree that there are two basic reasons for forgetting: decay and interference.

Decay Theory

According to decay theory, over time, without rehearsal, information representation becomes weak and eventually disappears.

Interference Theory

According to interference theory, new information interferes with old information and the old information is eventually lost. There are two kinds of interference: proactive and retroactive (sometimes called proactive and retroactive inhibition).

Proactive interference occurs when old information makes it difficult to remember new information. For example, a student learns to spell "believe" with the "i" before the "e" and then has trouble remembering to spell "receive" with the "i" after the "e."

Retroactive interference occurs when new information makes it difficult to remember old information. For example, a student's native language is English. The student can spell the English word *lottery*, and later learns the French word *loterie*. On a subsequent English assignment, the student provides the French spelling of the word instead of the English spelling.

Repression

Some researchers (e.g., Freud) discuss forgetting due to repression. *Repression* occurs when people resist remembering unpleasant experiences.

Remembering

Some memories are constructive and others are reconstructive.

Constructive Memories

Constructive memories are recalled in the same way they were interpreted when the event occurred. For example, at a swimming pool you see John trip over a chair and fall into the water. At that time you infer that the chair caused John to fall. A subsequent constructive memory is that John tripped over the chair and fell into the water.

Reconstructive Memories

Reconstructive memories are based on inferences made at the time of recall together with some of the original information. A subsequent reconstructive memory would be if you did not remember what John fell over and inferred that it was a table because there must have been several tables around the pool. Your reconstructive memory would be that John fell over a table into the pool.

Recall and Recognition

Some memory tasks are more difficult than others. You may ask students to *recall* information without cues or you may ask them to *recognize* the correct information. An example of recall occurs for fill-in-the-blank tests. Students have to remember the correct answer without hints. Recall tends to be more difficult than recognition. Recognition memory is needed for multiple-choice tests where the correct answer is provided with several incorrect choices. The students must recognize the correct answer, not generate it.

One problem students sometimes have with recall tasks is the *tip-of-the-tongue phenomenon*, the feeling of knowing something without being able to produce it. Students may claim that they "see" the answer to a question—that it is right there on the top half of the first page of the book—but they can't reproduce it. Similarly, they may be able to write down the first letter of the answer, but not complete the word.

Schema

One term frequently mentioned in memory research is schema. Schemata are structures used to make complex events make sense. For example, consider the following events: a hostess seats you, a waiter takes your order, a person next to you asks for the time, you help yourself to the salad bar, your dinner is served, you pay for your meal, you leave the restaurant as other people enter, and so forth. Most people will recognize that all these events may occur when they go out to eat. They are part of a restaurant schema. An actual restaurant schema could include each of these events and many more. The schema helps you organize several events into one meaningful event and anticipate what might occur next. Many researchers believe that without schema, complex information would be difficult to understand and remember.

Teaching for Retention

One of the most important objectives teachers have is to see their students leave the classroom knowing more than when they entered. It is important that students remember what you teach them, not only to pass tests, but also to have information they can apply in subsequent learning environments. Researchers have noted several factors that determine whether people will remember things. You can incorporate these factors as you plan lessons.

Distribution of Practice

Retention is enhanced when information is distributed over time. When students cram for a test, a process called *massed practice,* they may remember the information for a test the next day but are likely to forget it soon after the test. Similarly, if you discuss a topic extensively in one lesson and never mention it again, students are less likely to remember it than if you break it into smaller parts and present it over a

2-week period. Distributed practice helps minimize fatigue and lack of motivation and reduces the risk of primacy and recency effects.

State- and Context-Dependent Retrieval

Some studies have shown that people remember things best when they are in the same situation during both learning and recall. This factor can be considered in two parts. *State-dependent retrieval* means that people remember best when they learn and recall while under the same state—for example, sobriety versus intoxication. *Context-dependent retrieval* means that people remember best when they learn and recall while located in the same environment, such as a particular classroom or a particular time of day. State-dependent retrieval is probaby not something that will affect classroom learning, but context-dependent retrieval may. If your students are accustomed to having math class in your classroom immediately after lunch, you would optimize test performance by administering math quizzes right after lunch in your classroom rather than at the end of the day in the cafeteria.

Depth of Processing

The more information is analyzed and associated with other information, the more likely that it will be remembered. It is important that the material be meaningful to the students. You can accomplish this in several ways:

1. Relate new lessons to old ones.

2. Use many analogies and examples.

3. Explicitly state how the lesson affects the students. Tell them how they will be able to use the information later in life.

4. Use terminology that the students understand.

5. Ask questions to determine whether the material is meaningful to them and to clarify misinterpretations. Making information meaningful is probably the single best way to ensure that it will be remembered.

Mnemonics

Mnemonics are memory aids. They are strategies such as pictures, instructions, new words, and lists of several words that help in the recall of information. Mnemonics are generally used when the items to be remembered are not inherently meaningful and thus require rote memorization. Mnemonics provide associations between known and unknown information. Recall of the unknown information is facilitated by its association with the known information. For example, to remember the names of the Great Lakes, *H*uron, *O*ntario, *M*ichigan, *E*rie, and *S*uperior, students might use the acronym HOMES to remind them of the first letter in each name. Common academic mnemonics are "i before e, except after c" and "Columbus sailed the ocean blue in fourteen hundred and ninety-two."

Imagery

Many of the methods use imagery as a memory aid. Imagery is the use of mental images to represent information and preserve some of the physical attributes of that information. Visualizations you create in your mind are one form of mental imagery. For example, to remember the French word for cheese, *le fromage,* you might visualize a package of cheese labeled *Le Fromage* on a restaurant table in Paris.

Chain Method

The chain method of aiding memory, sometimes called the *link method,* uses visual links created between the items in a list to help recall of those items. To remember to run three errands, for instance to the bookstore, the supermarket, and the post office, create a visual chain that links the three errands together. For example, picture a book-sale sign in the supermarket window, and then inside the supermarket, picture a special postal area.

Keyword Method

The keyword method uses associations between new words and familiar words that sound similar. The keyword method has been especially useful when teaching students new words in a foreign language. Two steps are involved. First, find a part of the foreign word that sounds like an English word; that is the keyword. Next, form a visual image that associates the keyword with the English meaning of the word. For example, the Spanish word for duck is *pato* (pronounced pot-o). The keyword could be *pot*. The visual image that associates pot with the meaning *duck* could be a duck with a pot over its head. After students create this image, they can use it to remember the meaning of pato.

Pegword Method

The pegword method uses modified images of to-be-remembered items associated with known words to aid recall. The already known (familiar) words provide a "peg" to which new items become associated. To use the pegword method, begin with a list of words that you know. For example, by remembering an old nursery rhyme you probably already associate two with shoe, four with door, six with sticks, and eight with gate. Therefore, there is no problem remembering the four images shoe, door, sticks, and gate. Next, use modified images to associate the items to be remembered with the words in the list you already know. To remember to pick up four things at the supermarket, for example, aspirin, toilet paper, apples, and beef, use four modified images. For example, the shoe becomes a shoe with a large bottle of aspirin rather than a foot in it, the door becomes a door wrapped with toilet paper, the sticks become candy apples, the gate becomes a gate cemented in beef instead of dirt. When you get to the supermarket, use the nursery rhyme to remember the four words and use the associated modified images to remember the four items.

Loci Method

The loci method is another memory aid similar to the pegword type. To use the loci method, make associations between to-be-remembered items and places rather than images of known words. For example, use rooms in your house that you can walk through and modify those images to include the items you need to remember. To remember to pick up four things at the supermarket, aspirin, toilet paper, apples, and beef, use four modified images. For example, the toilet paper becomes toilet paper streaming from the trees in your front yard, the aspirin becomes a huge bottle of aspirin blocking the entrance to your house, the apples become an apple pie a la mode waiting for you in the foyer, and the beef becomes a cow standing in your kitchen. When you get to the supermarket, walk through your house, seeing the modified images to help you remember the four items.

Acronyms

An acronym is a word formed from the first letters of other words. Acronyms can be used to help students remember lists. For example, an existing acronym, APA, can help them remember American Psychological Association. The acronym FACE can be used to remember the names of notes (F, A, C, E) in the spaces of a treble clef. Students can create their own acronyms to provide cues that will help them remember words. For example, students needing to remember four capital cities might create an acronym from the first letters of each city.

Acrostics

A similar technique is to form a sentence or phrase with each word corresponding to the first letter in the words that need to be remembered. This kind of sentence mnemonic is called an *acrostic*. Most musicians are familiar with the sentence "*E*very *g*ood *b*oy *d*oes *f*ine." The first letter of each word stands for a line in the treble clef. Those letters are e, g, b, d, and f. Another sentence, "*A*ll *c*ows *e*at *g*rass," is used for remembering spaces in the bass clef.

Metacognition

Metacognition means thinking about thinking. This process occurs during working memory. Metacognition strategies improve problem-solving and study skills. Recent researchers discuss two kinds of metacognition: knowing about cognitive processes and monitoring cognitive processes.

Knowing About Cognitive Processes

Knowing about cognitive processes means that a person knows about cognitive strengths and weaknesses. For example, a teacher who has difficulty remembering students' names may keep a seating chart for each class. High-school students who know they have better math skills than reading skills may choose to pursue college degrees in a math field rather than becoming English teachers.

Monitoring Cognitive Processes

Monitoring cognitive processes means, for example, that a student who is reading and comes across a sentence that is not understood will back up and reread the sentence. Students who do not monitor this process proceed over the sentence without realizing the problem. People are not necessarily aware of this type of monitoring behavior.

Classroom Applications of Metacognition

Talking with students about metacognitive behaviors can help them improve cognitive skills. For example, try to make poor readers aware of the need to reread information they do not understand. Also, suggest that they summarize each unit of information (pages, chapters, etc.) as soon as they finish reading.

Applications of Cognitive Learning Principles

Listed in this section are several memory and learning principles that are derived from laboratory learning research and can be applied in the classroom. These principles can be employed by teachers using the strategies specified here. Some citations to the applicable laboratory research are provided. Additional information is provided in the chapter on instructional models (Chapter 9).

1. *Concentrate on the fundamentals at first.* As a result of limited sensory stores and limited-capacity working memory, we have limited ability to process information (Cook, 1986). When teaching new material, present only one method, even if several methods exist. Leave the details and more complex concepts to a later presentation. Minimize the amount of rote memorization expected of students. After the basics are covered (and this may happen sooner for some students than others), present alternative methods and shortcuts.

2. *Get the students involved.* The deeper we process information, the more likely it is that information will be retained (Craik and

Tulving, 1975). Use many hands-on exercises. Require students to solve problems rather than simply follow rote instructions. Use visual aids in addition to presenting information orally.

3. *Make time for overlearning.* Overlearning improves retention over time by building strong associations between stimuli and responses. Build repeated practice sessions into the daily activities. Review the basic skills before teaching advanced skills. Especially when there is potential for previous learning to interfere with current learning, emphasize overlearning of correct information. However, when implementing these overlearning strategies, be careful not to bore the student. Give interesting new examples and summarize information rather than simply repeat the instructions.

4. *Break complex or lengthy lessons into small chunks.* Presenting information over a spaced time helps people retain information better than presenting information in a massed manner (i.e., a short time frame) because more and sometimes better associations are formed. (Underwood, 1970). Present one chunk, then let the students rest or practice or change activities. Later, present a second chunk, and repeat. Note: In addition to simply spacing these chunks over time, it is important to reiterate the lesson learned in the first chunk and to relate the second chunk to the first.

5. *Relate new information to old (familiar) information to facilitate organization and retrieval.* Information is linked together in a complex network (Ausubel, 1960). Give students a roadmap of the lesson. Use opening statements that provide a framework for subsequent information. These advance organizers show students where you are going and give them a place to put the new information. Analogies and metaphors are good tools to help you link information together.

6. *Present the most important information early in the instructional period; then summarize the most important principles at the end.* When a long chain of information is to be learned, the information most likely to be remembered is that which occurs earliest or last (Craik, 1970). Be careful that the summary occurs while the students are still attentive. For example, 2 minutes before recess or lunch,

students may be hungry or restless, in which case the summary may not be heard well. Additionally, teach students to utilize appropriate rehearsal techniques, such as chunking.

7. *Plan the presentation of a series of lessons so that it follows some logical or temporal progression.* Instruction is more easily learned if it follows a logical sequence (Hilgard and Bower, 1975). For example, to use a computer, one would first turn the computer on, then insert a diskette, then start a software package. Therefore (assuming some knowledge of concepts), the instructional sequence of this information should be: (a) turning the computer on, (b) inserting the diskette, and (c) starting the software package. As another example, when learning to recite all 50 states, the lessons might be presented in either a geographical or alphabetical progression.

8. *Teach students about mnemonic strategies and encourage them to use them, especially for rote memory tasks.* Mnemonic strategies aid memory by creating associations among information.

9. *Help students minimize forgetting that results from disuse by having them apply what they learn.* Forgetting occurs when information is unused, repressed, or interfered with. Encourage students to repeat and review information. Relate lessons to previous material. Ask questions that require students to think about previously learned material. Help students minimize forgetting that results from repression by establishing a pleasant environment. When scary or embarrassing events occur, try to focus on other things, and later emphasize any positive aspects. Help students minimize forgetting that results from interference by changing activities frequently, providing distributed study times in the same environment, encouraging students to learn things thoroughly, and encouraging students to make things meaningful for themselves.

10. *Teach students to monitor their learning strategies, identify problem areas, and develop plans for efficient learning.* Metacognitive strategies can make learning more efficient by helping students become more aware of cognitive strengths and weaknesses. For

example, poor readers need to realize that they should reread information that they do not understand.

11. Students can implement several of the principles described above by using the following study strategy known as PQ4R (and sometimes SQ4R), which stands for Preview, Question, Read, Reflect, Recite, and Review (Thomas and Robinson, 1972). This study strategy implements previous principles 2, 3, and 5. Additionally, PQ4R implements principles based on studies of context-dependency and the use of mnemonic devices. Very briefly, the PQ4R method suggests the following:

a. Have a set study schedule. Study in the same location.

b. Preview (or survey) the material. Use the headings.

c. Question. Ask your own questions.

d. Read. Read carefully to answer the questions you asked.

e. Reflect. Think about material already known and how it relates to new material. Try to think of examples.

f. Recite. Stop periodically and try to recall what you have read.

g. Review. Review immediately after studying and again before an exam.

The cognitive learning principles of Gestalt psychology, field theory, information processing model, and network models provide frameworks that help you design lessons students can learn and remember. Gestalt psychology explains how people recognize information even when it is distorted and how people perceive patterns. Field theory describes the importance of understanding behavior from the viewpoint of the learner, because at any given time the learner is attracted to certain objects and repelled by others. The most prominent cognitive model today is the information processing model. Using analogies to how computers operate, this model helps explain how people store and retrieve information. The most recent models of human memory are network models, which also draw analogies from computer systems. Network models maintain that certain kinds of memory are hierarchi-

cally related to specific pieces of information located in different places in the brain.

Human memory is generally considered a multistore process including a sensory storage; a temporary, limited-capacity working memory; and a permanent, unlimited-capacity long-term memory. Two important techniques for increasing retention include the distribution of practice and making information meaningful. Special techniques, called mnemonics, help students with rote memorization tasks. Metacognition, which is knowing about and monitoring cognitive processes, can play an important role in efficient processing of information.

Recommended Reading

Anderson, J. R. (1985). *Cognitive Psychology and Its Implications* (2d ed.). San Francisco: Freeman. (Explains the basic terminology and principles of cognitive psychology and provides many examples; is easy to follow and useful as reference material.)

Bigge, M. L. (1982). *Learning Theories for Teachers* (4th ed.). New York: Harper & Row. (A good source for behavioral and cognitive learning theories.)

Boring, E. G. (1950). *A History of Experimental Psychology* (2d ed.). New York: Appleton-Century-Crofts. (History of Gestalt psychology is presented in the Chapter 23; in general, this book is an excellent source about the history of psychology.)

Lorayne, H., and J. Lucas. (1974). *The Memory Book*. New York: Ballantine Books. (A popular "how to" book on memory improvement.)

Royer, J. M., and R. G. Allan. (1978). Principles of Cognitive Learning Theory for Classroom Use, in *Psychology of Learning: Educational Applications*. (Chapter 5). New York: Wiley, (Discusses the information processing model and how it applies to the classroom setting.)

Zechmeister, E. B., and S. E. Nyberg. (1982). *Human Memory: An Introduction to Research and Theory*. Monterey, Calif.: Brooks/Cole. (Provides a thorough presentation of the research and findings of human memory.)

References

Atkinson, R. C., and R. M. Shiffrin. (1968). Human Memory: A Proposed

System and Its Component Processes, in K. Spence and J. Spence, (Eds.). *The Psychology of Learning and Motivation*, Vol. 2. New York: Academic Press.

Ausubel, D. P. (1960). The Use of Advance Organizers in the Learning and Retention of Meaningful Verbal Material, *Journal of Educational Psychology*, *51*, 267-272.

Chomsky, N. (1959). Verbal Behavior (a Review), *Language, 35*, 26-58.

Collins, A. M., and M. R. Quillian. (1969). Retrieval Time from Semantic Memory, *Journal of Verbal Learning and Verbal Behavior, 8*, 240-247.

Cook, M. S. (1986, December). Cognitive Psychology and End-User Training. Paper presented at the Data Training Conference and Exposition, Washington, D.C.

Craik, F. M. (1970). The Fate of Primary Memory Items in Free Recall," *Journal of Verbal Learning and Verbal Behavior*, 9, 143–148.

Craik, F. I. M., and R. S. Lockhart. (1972). Levels of Processing: A Framework for Memory Research. *Journal of Verbal Thinking and Verbal Behavior, 11*, 671–684.

Craik, F. M., and E. Tulving. (1975). Depth of Processing and the Retention of Words in Episodic Memory. *Journal of Experimental Psychology: General*, *104*, 268-294.

Ericsson, K. A., and H. A. Simon. (1980). Verbal Reports as Data, *Psychological Review*, 87, 215–251.

Hilgard, E. R., G. H. and Bower. (1975). *Theories of Learning*, (4th ed.). Englewood Cliffs, N.J.: Prentice-Hall, (pp. 607–609).

Miller, G. A. (1956). The Magical Number Seven, Plus or Minus Two: Some Limits on Our Capacity for Processing Information, *Psychological Review*, *63*, 81-97.

Neisser, U. (1967). Cognitive Psychology. New York: Appleton.

Thomas, E. J., and H. A. Robinson. (1972). *Improving Reading in Every Class: A Source Book for Teachers*. Boston: Allyn & Bacon.

Underwood, B. J. (1970). A Breakdown of the Total Time Law in Free-Recall Learning, *Journal of Verbal Learning and Verbal Behavior, 9*, 573-580.

CHAPTER 8

Motivation

This chapter discusses the importance of motivation in learning environments. Students sitting in a classroom are unlikely to learn unless they are motivated to do so. Therefore, a large part of teaching involves motivating students to learn what you have planned. Factors that influence motivation and several prominent theories of motivation are discussed in this chapter. These theories span cognitive, behavioral, and humanistic domains.

Factors in Motivation

Motivation, a prerequisite to learning, is the influence of needs and preferences on behavior. It affects the direction a student takes, activities a student chooses, and the intensity with which a student engages in an activity. A number of factors enter into motivation, including basic needs such as sustenance, and higher-level needs such as the need to know and understand ideas and phenomena. Other factors include the need for success, sexual gratification, and projection and maintenance of a positive self-image. The theories that researchers have developed to account for motivational factors are presented below.

Most of these theories have direct implications for managing the learning environment.

Behavioral Perspective: Extrinsic Motivation

Behavioral learning theorists (e.g., Skinner) and social learning theorists (e.g., Bandura) believe that people are motivated to obtain reinforcers and avoid punishment. Extrinsic motivation is administered from an external source and is not inherent in the behavior itself. For example, a student gets all A's on a report card, and the parent gives the child $5. The money is an extrinsic motivator. Common extrinsic motivators are money, praise, free time, special time with the teacher, and special privileges.

The behavioral perspective on motivation helps explain why students prefer particular subjects, spend time on assignments they prefer not to do, and try to please some teachers. According to the behavioral perspective, something in the environment reinforces these behaviors, or these behaviors help the student avoid some punishment. Once you determine which events are reinforcing and which events are punishing, you can utilize these events for motivating the students.

Use moderation when administering extrinsic reinforcers. Do not overdo it. Some students may feel that you are trying to manipulate them and may resent having to do what you want to earn your approval. Additionally, students may only engage in the desired behavior in order to earn the reinforcement without understanding the long-term benefit. In such cases the students may be too dependent on you. Use extrinsic reinforcement to help students initially, but follow up by helping them understand the value of the desired behavior so that they will want to adapt for its inherent benefit, not merely to please you or to receive the reinforcer.

Cognitive Perspective: Intrinsic Motivation

Cognitive interpretations of motivation emphasize intrinsic motivation. Intrinsic motivators lead the student to engage in the behavior because of the inherent value of doing so. Examples of intrinsic motivators are the feeling of satisfaction that working on math problems produces and the feeling of pride that learning to spell words correctly causes. The more students are motivated by intrinsic factors, the less motivation the teacher has to provide. The cognitive perspective on motivation helps you understand why you do not always have to provide reinforcement, why trying to solve a problem excites some students and frightens others, and why some students will not work unless they are graded or receive a reward. Generally, the cognitive perspective maintains that people are motivated to create a sense of equilibrium or competence rather than receive an external reinforcement. People are naturally motivated to explore, learn, and have fun (e.g., White, 1959). Some students will engage in learning tasks simply for the sake of learning.

Humanistic Perspective: Abraham Maslow's Hierarchy of Needs

The humanistic perspective of motivation is that people behave to satisfy needs. The most prominent humanistic theory of motivation was proposed by Abraham Maslow (1908–1970). Maslow (1954) developed a hierarchy of needs that he believed represented motivational factors throughout the lifetime. The needs are categorized as deficiency needs and growth needs. *Deficiency needs*, the lowest four needs in the hierarchy—food and water, safety, love, and esteem—are no longer motivators once they are satisfied. *Growth needs* are motivators once basic needs are met. Maslow believed that the more growth needs are met, the more motivated a person becomes to learn and to grow.

A significant concept in Maslow's theory is *self-actualization*, one's ultimate goal in life—to attain one's full potential. Self-actualization includes having a good sense of self, being recepive toward others, appreciating a variety of experiences, having an efficient perception of reality, and being creative, spontaneous, and independent. Maslow (1968) estimated that fewer than 1 percent of all adults attain self-actualization. The seven need categories in Maslow's hierarchy are as follows:

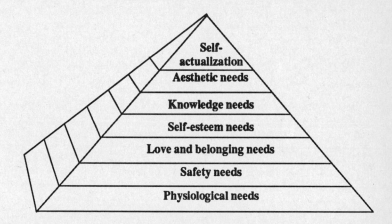

Fig. 8.1 Maslow's Hierarchy

1. *Physiological needs*—Sustenance and physical comfort are crucial to a student's performance in the classroom. Those who are hungry, thirsty, or in need of a restroom break will be motivated to fulfill those needs rather than spend energy learning.

2. *Safety needs*—Students need security, protection, and stability. For most students in American schools these needs are already satisfied. In schools where they are not, such as those in crime and drug-plagued inner cities, learning can suffer.

3. *Love and belonging needs*—Students need to feel accepted, receive affection, and be part of a group. Students who feel excluded or rejected may have difficulty attending to academic lessons. It is important to try to help students meet this need in the school environment.

4. *Positive self-regard and self-esteem needs*—Students need to feel good about themselves. Again, you as a teacher can do much to provide successful experiences for students.

5. *Need to know and understand*—Once the deficiency needs are satisfied, people are motivated to learn about the world around them.

6. *Aesthetic needs*—A second growth need is to appreciate and enjoy the beauty in the world.

7. *Need for self-actualization*—The highest growth need and the one that very few people ever achieve, this is the need to fulfill one's potential in life.

According to Maslow, growth proceeds through an endless series of choices in which people strive to meet deficiency needs and achieve growth needs. Maslow's perspective on motivation helps you understand why some students have difficulty working right before lunch and early in the morning when they are hungry; why some students are more likely to learn in a relaxed, positive atmosphere; and why some students seem to care more about learning and exploring than do other students.

One problem in applying Maslow's hierarchy of needs is the difficulty in determining which needs have not been met. It is unlikely that all your students are trying to meet the same need. Furthermore, helping students meet their needs can be difficult and time-consuming.

Achievement Motivation

Particularly relevant to motivation in a school environment is the study of the motivation to achieve. David McClelland (1917–) postulated that there is a general human tendency to achieve success and avoid failure (McClelland and Atkinson, 1948). McClelland (1961) conceived the term *achievement motivation,* meaning that people have a need for achievement. Some of your students will seem more interested in striving for success, while others will seem more motivated to avoid failure (Atkinson, 1964). This motivational tendency plays an important role in the choice of study partners, the amount of time students persist on a task, and the activities students choose.

Fear of Success

Some interesting research on the differences between males and females in achievement motivation was conducted by Matina Horner (1968). Horner had male and female university students spend 4 minutes writing a story based on the statement "At the end of first-term

Important Influences on Educational Psychology		
Contributor	Place of Study	Contribution(s)
Abraham Maslow (1908–1970)	University of Wisconsin	Cofounder of third-force (humanistic) psychology; proposed theory of motivation on basis of hierarchy of needs
David McClelland (1917–)	Wesleyan University; University of Missouri; Yale University	Developed theory of need achievement and techniques for measuring achievement
Martin Seligman (1942–)	Princeton University; University of Pennsylvania	Conducted research on learned helplessness
Leon Festinger (1919–)	College of City of New York; State University of Iowa	Researched cognitive dissonance
Sigmund Freud (1856–1939)	University of Vienna	Constructed first major theory of personality development; emphasized importance of sexual and aggressive drives in determining behavior

finals Anne finds herself at the top of her medical school class." Horner analyzed the theme of the stories that were produced. She found that 65.5 percent of the women's stories reflected a general theme of fear of success, such as Anne would lose her friends or Anne would feel guilty about the success. In contrast, only 9 percent of the men's stories reflected a fear-of-success theme. Subsequently, Horner had these students engage in both competitive and noncompetitive activities. In these activities the women who wrote stories with the fear-of-success theme performed much better in the noncompetitive activities. Horner then suggested that many women are motivated by a fear of success, especially in competitive situations. Horner's finding generated much research over the next few years. The result has been a well-documented generalization that many women fear success.

As a classroom teacher, you can help young men and women be motivated by achievement rather than failure by providing activities that they can master. When students master tasks, encourage them to take pride in their accomplishments. Encourage women to participate in traditionally male-dominated activities and encourage men to participate in traditionally female- dominated activities.

Failure Avoidance

Another interesting finding on achievement motivation is that students who are motivated to avoid failure are likely to choose tasks that are either too difficult or too easy for their current skill level. Atkinson and Litwin (1960) discovered that in a ring-toss game failure-avoiders will stand too close or too far from the target while success-seekers stand at an intermediate distance from the target. Atkinson and Litwin suggested that failure-avoiders stand far away so that if they fail no one will blame them or stand so close as to ensure success. This finding has important implications for the classroom teacher. You may discover that students who choose extremely easy tasks or extremely difficult ones are not attempting to be disruptive, but are trying to preserve their self-image in an uncertain situation.

Learned Helplessness

Yet another significant aspect of achievement motivation is the occurrence of learned helplessness, which is an extreme avoidance response. Students experiencing learned helplessness think that there is no possibility for success. They expect to fail. Martin Seligman (1942–) has been a major contributor in this area of research (e.g., Hiroto and Seligman, 1975).

Try not to become frustrated with students experiencing learned helplessness. You can help them by breaking tasks into activities that will allow them to be successful, providing immediate feedback about their performance, and demonstrating consistent expectations of them.

Attribution Theory

In addition to being motivated for success or to avoid failure, students are motivated by what they think caused the success or failure. This area of motivation research is called attribution theory. It is closely related to achievement motivation.

Causal attribution theories investigate the relationship of perceived causes of events to subsequent behaviors. Students who attribute success to random chance (luck) will not be highly motivated to attempt the same task another time. Students who perceive success as the result of hard work and natural ability will most likely be willing to attempt the same task or a more difficult one another time. Basically, attribution theory investigates reasons why students think they did or did not perform well. It asks the question "To what do students attribute their success or failure?" Most research indicates four common reasons attributed for success or failure: ability, effort, task difficulty, and luck. Irving B. Weiner has conducted much of the attribution research (e.g., Weiner, 1979). Weiner found that high-achieving students and low-achieving students attribute success to different factors. High-achievers attribute success to ability and effort and attribute failure to not trying hard enough. Low-achievers attribute success to luck and attribute failure to lack of ability. In other words, low achievers perceive success as something that merely happened, perhaps by accident. These attributions are difficult to change.

Locus of Control

The concept of locus of control (Rotter, 1954) is important in attribution theory. *Locus* means location, and locus of control refers to the place where responsibility is attributed. People with an internal locus of control assume responsibility for things themselves, believing that they cause their own success. People with an external locus of control attribute behavior and similar phenomena to external forces beyond their control. They believe that factors such as the weather,

luck, or other people are the cause of their success. Usually students
with an internal locus of control who want to succeed in school will
work hard to do so. Students with an external locus of control, who
believe that success is due to external factors, are not as likely to work
hard to succeed. However, locus of control can vary according to
subject matter and activities. For instance, a student with an internal
locus of control in math may demonstrate an external locus of control
in verbal tasks.

Classroom Applications of Attribution Theory

You can apply the concepts of attribution and locus of control in
the classroom to understand how students approach tasks and how they
interpret the feedback you provide. You should be aware that students
who expect failure and then do fail will not be motivated to work hard.
In turn, they are likely to fail again, and again and again, as they
continue to expect failure. This series of events is commonly known as
a *self-fulfilling prophecy*, meaning that a person expects something to
happen and acts in a way that makes the event happen in the predicted
manner.

The research on need achievement and attributions presents interesting results, but a major limitation to these perspectives is the difficulty of observing the phenomenon. Additionally, need achievement and
attributions can vary from one person or activity to another. Finally,
perhaps most frustrating to the classroom teacher is the fact that these
motivators are resistant to change.

Cognitive Consistency Theory: Leon Festinger

You read earlier that the need to maintain a positive self-image is
considered a fairly strong motivator by the humanistic psychologists
(see Maslow's hierarchy of needs). One aspect of this need is the
necessity to maintain a balance between how one acts and what one
believes. For example, Cindy believes she is a good student, so she is
likely to act in ways that good students act. It is also important to act
consistently from one occasion to another. Barry is known for being a
Dallas Cowboys fan. Even though the Cowboys lost three games in a

row, Barry will continue to support them. People are motivated to maintain these types of consistency. Psychologists who study this particular kind of motivation refer to the phenomenon as the need to maintain cognitive consistency, or equilibrium. The theories that describe our motivation to maintain equilibrium are called cognitive consistency theories, or sometimes *cognitive dissonance theories*. The best-known theorist in this field is Leon Festinger (1919–), who proposed the theory of cognitive dissonance.

Festinger's Research

According to Festinger (1957), people experience tension when one belief or behavior is inconsistent with another. To resolve this tension people may change behaviors or beliefs or make excuses to justify the inconsistency. For example, Mary considers herself to be a good student and usually gets good grades, but she fails a math test. She experiences some tension because failing a math test is inconsistent with the image of being a good student. To resolve the inconsistency, she excuses the bad grade by remarking that the questions were tricky. Another way Mary might resolve the inconsistency is by promising herself to study harder the next time or do an extra-credit paper.

Festinger (1957) conducted a classical study of cognitive dissonance. He paid college students to participate in a boring task. Some of the students were paid $1; others were paid $20. He asked all the students how interesting the task was. (Remember that all the students participated in the same task.) Festinger found that the students who were paid $1 said the task was interesting, but the students who were paid $20 said the task was boring. Festinger explained the difference in perception as follows. The students who were paid $1 would feel foolish for participating in a boring task, so they changed their perception of the task in order to enjoy it and to justify their involvement. The students who were paid $20 participated for the money, so it did not matter to them that the task was boring. They did not have to modify their perceptions because there was no dissonance.

Areas of Cognitive Dissonance Research

There are four areas of cognitive dissonance research:

1. *Postdecisional dissonance*–Once a decision is made, the negative aspects of what was chosen and the positive aspects of what was rejected cause dissonance. Dissonance in this situation is usually reduced by focusing on the attractive aspects of what was chosen and the negative aspects of what was rejected. For example, you decide to buy a new car. You are debating between a Toyota Corolla and a Nissan Sentra. You decide on the Nissan Sentra, but you experience some dissonance because the Toyota Corolla has some very attractive features. To reduce the dissonance you think of the following: the Corolla was too expensive, anyway. Besides, the dealer could not deliver for 3 months. You really like the Nissan Sentra. It has good gas mileage and the dealer had just the right color in stock.

2. *Forced compliance*–When a person has adequate justification for doing something with a negative connotation, such as being paid to lie, then there is little dissonance because the person was obligated to comply. However, if the person lies with insufficient justification, then dissonance occurs. In this situation people generally adjust their attitudes in favor of the lie and therefore reduce the dissonance. Festinger's study described above (participants in an experiment listened to a very boring lecture) is an example of a forced-compliance situation. The fact that some participants were paid $20 reduced the dissonance they might have felt for waiting through the boring lecture. Those subjects had to comply to receive the nice payment. On the other hand, the persons who were paid only $1 experienced dissonance because there was no apparent reason for them to wait through the lecture. These participants were not forced to comply (because they did not receive the attractive $20 payment). In fact, these participants were likely to lie to reduce their dissonance. They were likely to say the lecture was sort of interesting (even though they were bored) to help justify waiting through it.

3. *Exposure to information*–People can reduce dissonance by seeking out new consonant information and avoiding new dissonant information. This method works well unless the dissonance becomes so great that it is easier to obtain more dissonant information and change one's attitude in favor of the dissonant opinion. For example, if your students have a generally favorable attitude toward the presi-

dent of the United States, and you ask them to read a newspaper for a week and then bring to class a list of four things they learned about the president, they are likely to bring in four items that concur with their original attitude.

4. *Social support*-To increase consonance, people seek out other people with similar attitudes or behaviors. To decrease dissonance, people will try to discredit other people with different attitudes or behaviors. For example, Mark is trying to decide which group of students to join during recess. One group is playing basketball and the other group is going exploring in the woods. Mark experiences dissonance. He resolves this dissonance by thinking that the children playing basketball are getting good physical exercise, which is the purpose of the recess period. He then joins the group playing basketball.

Classroom Applications of Cognitive Dissonance Theory

In general, people will try to reduce cognitive dissonance by changing their attitudes, changing their behaviors, seeking support for their cognitions, and rejecting dissonant cognitions. This theory is useful for understanding why students seek certain information and why students concur with others. One problem in utilizing this theory is that it is sometimes difficult to know when two cognitions are dissonant. Additionally, you cannot always predict which method a student will use to reduce the dissonance.

Sigmund Freud— Sexual and Aggressive Drives

Although Freud's work on motivation does not receive much attention today, one cannot conclude a discussion of motivation theories without paying him homage.

Theory of Motivation

Sigmund Freud (1856–1939) believed that human motivation was primarily a function of the unconscious. He maintained that cognition and emotion worked together as a source of motivation. Freud postulated that motivation was a function of two instinctual drives: a sexual drive and an aggressive drive. The presence of one of these drives creates a state of tension, and people are motivated to reduce the tension through either fantasy or overt behavior. Freud's theory is considered a *tension-reduction theory*.

Significance of Freud's Work

Although Freud has many critics who contend (among other criticisms) that he overemphasized biological factors at the expense of social factors, he has influenced the way we think about motivation, development, and personality. Freud was the first theorist to draw attention to the concept of the unconscious. Freud's work significantly influenced our current views of child and personality development. He emphasized that serious psychological conflicts can exist at very young ages, and that those conflicts can persist and affect adult life. Freud outlined the type of questions that must be answered to develop a comprehensive theory of personality.

Classroom Applications of Freud's Theory

Because of his emphasis on sexual drives, Freud's work is especially relevant to junior- and senior-high classes. During and subsequent to puberty, most students display increased interest in biological and physical changes. Making plans for an upcoming dance or for a Friday night football game may be more interesting to these students than the fundamentals of algebra or English grammar. You should incorporate the interests of the students into your lessons and utilize their preoccupations as potential reinforcers. For example, allow students who finish work early to gather in the back of the classroom and listen to records or have group discussions; provide interesting books about romance and human biology for leisure-time reading; sponsor dances and get students on planning committees; hold open, candid discussions with students after basic assignments are completed; and do whatever you can to demonstrate the relevance of classroom work to life after school.

Motivating Students in the Classroom

The wide variety of motivational theories are testimony to the complexity of behavior. Research in each area presented is ongoing. According to the existing research, there are many things you can do in the classroom to help motivate the students to learn what you are trying to teach.

1. *Try to ensure that students' basic needs are met.* This means encouraging students to eat breakfast, to use the restroom when breaks are provided, and to wear appropriate clothing. It also means maintaining a physically safe environment and helping all students feel part of a group.

2. *Be specific about what your students are to learn.* Make your expectations known. Make sure that students know what to do to complete a task and how to get started.

3. *Choose appropriate reinforcers.* Remember that the effectiveness of a reinforcer depends on how rewarding it is to the person you are reinforcing. If you do not know what students consider rewarding, you need to ascertain this. For example, giving candy to a child who does not like or cannot eat sweets may not be rewarding to that child.

4. *Do not rely on extrinsic reinforcement.* Use extrinsic reinforcement initially, but help students appreciate and enjoy learning for the sake of learning. Help them become independent by encouraging them to rely on intrinsic reinforcement.

5. *Promote expectations of success.* Help all students, especially females, to be successful. When students are successful, help them acknowledge the ability and effort that led to their success. Sometimes you will need to break tasks into smaller activities to help ensure that students can be successful.

6. *Allow students some control and choice in their learning activities.* Give them room to explore and grow.

7. *Provide a variety of activities and try to make them interesting.*

Take into account individual differences by providing activities appropriate to students at different ability levels.

8. *Provide frequent and informative feedback.* Let students know how they are performing. Inform them of their strengths or weaknesses and indicate specifically how they can improve their performance.

9. *Encourage students to set goals for themselves and to work toward these goals.*

Thorndike first demonstrated a link between learning and motivation and called it the law of effect. Behaviorists discuss this link in terms of extrinsic reinforcers that increase the strength of behaviors. Cognitive theorists add the concept of intrinsic reinforcement, specifically, that people are sometimes motivated to do things based on inner preferences. Humanistic theorists such as Maslow and Rogers maintain that motivation is based on fulfilling deficiency needs such as food, safety, and social acceptance, and growth needs, including the need to learn and to understand.

A strong motivator is the need to achieve. Sometimes people are motivated toward success and at other times are motivated to avoid failure. Another major theory, cognitive dissonance theory, states that people are motivated to maintain a sense of cognitive equilibrium. They will change attitudes or behaviors to render dissonant cognitions more consistent.

The factors that motivate behavior are numerous and complex. Within the classroom, the teacher must utilize these factors to motivate the students to attend to and learn what is taught. Teachers can achieve this objective by ensuring that basic needs are met, using appropriate reinforcers, making lessons interesting, giving students choices, and ensuring that students have opportunities for success.

Recommended Reading

Arkes, H. R., and J. P. Garske. (1982). *Psychological Theories of Motivation* (2d ed.). Monterey, Calif.: Brooks/Cole. (Presents in-depth discussion and critiques of the major motivational theories.)

Aronson, E. (1984). *The Social Animal* (4th ed.). New York: Freeman. (Provides an informative and delightful description of dissonance theory, attribution theory, and other relevant motivational work.)

Brophy, J. (1981). Teacher Praise: A Functional Analysis, *Review of Educational Research, 19,* 557- 576. (Provides valuable information about using praise in the classroom.)

Glasser, W. (1969). *Schools without Failure.* New York: Harper & Row. (Building on the work of achievement motivation, Glasser argues that if students are to succeed in life, they should first experience success in school.)

Maccoby, E., and C. Jacklin. (1974). *The Psychology of Sex Differences.* Stanford, Calif.: Stanford University Press. (Presents research on differences between males and females in several academic tasks.)

Maslow, A. H. (1968). *Toward a Psychology of Being* (2d ed.). New York: Van Nostrand. (Maslow's description of his theory and the basic propositions of growth psychology.)

Pearce, J. C. (1977). *Magical Child.* New York: Bantam Books. (Provides an interesting discussion on the impact of child-rearing practices on the motivation and goals of today's children.)

Wlodkowski, R. J. (1978). *Motivation and Teaching: A Practical Guide.* Washington, D.C.: National Education Association. (Provides information about motivation and ideas for applying the information in the classroom.)

References

Atkinson, J. W. (1964). *An Introduction to Motivation. Princeton,* N.J.: Van Nostrand.

Atkinson, J. W., and G. H. Litwin. (1960). Achievement Motivation and Test Anxiety as Motives to Approach Success and Avoid Failure. *Journal of Abnormal and Social Psychology, 60,* 52-63.

Festinger, L. A. (1957). *A Theory of Cognitive Dissonance.* Evanston, Ill.: Row, Peterson.

Hiroto, D. S., and M. E. P. Seligman. (1975). Generality of Learned Helplessness in Man. *Journal of Personality and Social Psychology, 31,* 311-327.

Horner, M. S. (1968). Sex Differences in Achievement Motivation and Performance in Competitive and Non-competitive Situations. Unpublished doctoral dissertation, University of Michigan.

Maslow, A. H. (1954). *Motivation and Personality.* New York: Harper & Row.

Maslow, A. H. (1968). *Toward a Psychology of Being* (2d ed.). New York: Van Nostrand.

McClelland, D. C. (1961). *The Achieving Society*. Princeton, N.J.: Van Nostrand.

McClelland, D. C., and J. W. Atkinson. (1948). The Projective Expression of Needs: II. The Effect of Different Intensities of the Hunger Drive on Thematic Apperception *Journal of Experimental Psychology*, *38*, 643-658.

Rotter, J. (1954). *Social Learning and Clinical Psychology*. Englewood Cliffs, N.J.: Prentice-Hall.

Weiner, I. B. (1979). A Theory of Motivation for Some Classroom Experiences. *Journal of Educational Psychology*, *71*, 3-25.

White, R. W. (1959). Motivation Reconsidered. The Concept of Competence. *Psychological Review*, *66*, 297-333.

CHAPTER 9

Instructional Models and Strategies

Instructional models describe learning under various conditions and help researchers develop comprehensive theories. They provide a generalized framework within which to design instructional strategies. Two of the most popular models are Jerome Bruner's discovery approach and David Ausubel's reception learning. Instructional strategies are different methods of approaching the teaching task, for example, learning centers, peer instruction, or programmed instruction, depending on the objectives of the lesson and the students' abilities. This chapter begins with a discussion of the basic tools of instruction: educational goals, instructional objectives, task analysis, lesson plans, and lesson development.

Goals, Objectives, and Task Analysis

Educational Goals

Educational goals are statements that describe in general terms the information to be taught. Consider the topic of capital cities of 50 states in the United States. Before deciding how to present this information, the teacher must determine whether it is appropriate for the students—that is, whether they already know the names of the capital cities or whether this topic would be too advanced for them.

Instructional Objectives

Once the educational goal is written, you can generate more specific instructional objectives. An instructional objective is a very specific statement that identifies the information, skill, or attitude to be learned, and sometimes the means of measuring whether the information is learned. In other words, instructional objectives identify the specific behavior that students will perform. Researchers also use the term *behavioral objective*, but today *instructional objective* is used most often.

Developing objectives helps teachers think through educational goals, organize lessons in a logical manner, develop appropriate instruction, and create useful evaluations. Sharing objectives with students is recommended because it makes students aware of the purpose of the lesson and the teacher's expectations.

Instructional objectives should be as specific as possible. Action verbs such as read, write, recite, compare, laugh, and build should be used. Words that represent actions that are difficult to see such as know, understand, appreciate, and enjoy should be avoided. Two examples of instructional objectives are:

1. The student will recite all 100 multiplication facts in 2 minutes.

2. After 5 minutes of warm-up in the school gym, the student will dribble a basketball with one hand for 20 seconds.

The three parts to each objective state (1) how the behavior will be assessed (after 5 minutes of warm-up), (2) what the student will do—usually stated with an action verb (recite, dribble), and (3) the criterion for success (in 2 minutes, one hand for 20 seconds). In general, a behavioral objective specifies that given a specific condition, a specific behavior will be performed at a specific criterion level.

Task Analysis: Robert Gagné

As mentioned previously, teachers often begin with a general educational goal, for example, to teach fifth-grade math students to work with decimals. Teachers must then develop instructional objectives from the general goals. To generate the specific objectives, they can use task analysis, a process advocated by Robert Gagné (1916–). Task analysis (Gagné, 1977) is the process of breaking down tasks into simpler components called *subtasks*. Instructional objectives can then be written for each subtask. Task analysis can also be used to break down instructional objectives into a hierarchy of skills to determine which subskills need to be taught. There are three steps in a task analysis.

1. *Identify prerequisite skills.* In this step the teacher specifies which skills must be mastered before the student will be able to learn the new task. For example, to be able to run, a physical education student must first be able to walk with proper balance and coordination.

2. *Identify component skills.* In this step the teacher specifies the individual skills that will be taught as part of the new skill. For example, component skills in the running task are proper breathing, relaxed arm movement, and appropriate strides. The teacher may develop instructional objectives for each of these components and decide to teach each component separately.

3. *Determine how to integrate the component skills into the complete task.* In this step the teacher specifies how the complete task will be taught, assuming that each component skill is mastered. For example, once students demonstrate proper breathing and arm movement, they will walk around the track, and then walk more quickly around the track after showing appropriate strides, proper breathing, and arm movement, and so on until they are running.

As an example of task analysis, first consider a high-level intellectual task, learning cognitive strategies. There are several subtasks that students must be skilled in before they will be able to learn cognitive strategies. Robert Gagné has identified these subtasks as a hierarchy of intellectual skills. Each skill in the hierarchy is a prerequisite for mastery of the next skill; students must be able to (1) discriminate among symbols, (2) form concepts, (3) relate the concepts by developing rules, and (4) combine several rules into more complex, higher-order rules. To learn cognitive strategies (the highest level of intellectual skills), therefore, students learn to process information by attending to it, select information to be learned, work with that information, and determine how that information will be retrieved later when it is needed. If your educational goal is to teach students to use cognitive strategies, a task analysis of this goal indicates that you should first teach students to attend to information, then to select relevant information, and finally to work with that information.

Taxonomy of Educational Objectives: Benjamin Bloom

Benjamin Bloom (1913–) and some of his colleagues (1956) classified general educational objectives (cognitive objectives) into a six-level hierarchy of increasing complexity known as the taxonomy of educational objectives.

1. *Knowledge*—At this level information can be recalled. Examples are memorizing facts and formulas and conjugating verbs.

2. *Comprehension*—At this level information can be interpreted and translated. Information is understood and used. Examples are interpreting a diagram and predicting what will happen next in a story.

3. *Application*—At this level information is used to solve problems. An example is calculating how much it will cost to drive from New York to Houston given the distance between the two cities, the average cost of a gallon of gas, and the expected miles per gallon of the automobile.

4. *Analysis*—At this level information can be broken into parts and the relationships between the parts understood. Examples are understanding the similarities between video and audio cassette players and figuring out the plot in a short story.

5. *Synthesis*—At this level information can be used to create novel

Table 9.1

Example of Behavior Content Matrix	
Educational objective	**Example: Story plot**
Knowledge	Define "plot"
Comprehension	Explain how to find the plot in a story
Application	Not applicable
Analysis	Read a new story and identify the plot
Synthesis	Write a new story based on a specified plot
Evaluation	Evaluate the plot in an existing story

information. Examples are writing a short story and designing an experiment.

6. *Evaluation*—At this level information can be compared, contrasted, and judged against a given criterion. An example is comparing the efficiency and maintainability for carburetor and fuel-injection systems.

Classroom Applications of Bloom's Taxonomy

Bloom's taxonomy includes the various levels at which information can be learned. After mastering pertinent facts, students need to learn to analyze, synthesize, and evaluate them. Bloom's taxonomy can be a useful instructional tool, reminding you to build into your instructional objectives each of these important categories.

A systematic way to cover each level of learning and information processing in the taxonomy is to develop a *behavior content matrix* (Gage and Berliner, 1984). A behavior content matrix (see Table 9.1) is a chart showing the type of objective (knowledge, comprehension, application, analysis, synthesis, evaluation) in the left-hand column and the material to be taught at each level on the right. Each level of

Bloom's taxonomy will not necessarily have a corresponding content area, and some material will not be appropriate for all levels in the taxonomy. The teacher should consider both material content and student population when deciding which content areas are covered at each taxonomy level.

The behavior content matrix is a convenient guide for teachers to use in deciding which instruction is appropriate for a given topic and also in constructing their own tests. The first levels, using multiple-choice and fill-in-the-blank questions, are the easiest to test. However, it is also important to test whether students can synthesize and apply what they have learned. These abilities are more difficult to test. Evaluation and test development are discussed in Chapter 11.

Other Taxonomy Proposals

In addition to the taxonomy of educational (i.e., cognitive) objectives proposed by Bloom, Krathwohl et al. (1964) proposed a taxonomy of affective (attitudes and values) objectives and Simpson (1972) proposed a taxonomy of psychomotor (skills) objectives.

Lesson Plans and Lesson Development

After using task analysis to develop specific instructional objectives from educational goals, the teacher must plan how to deliver the instruction and evaluate achievement. The teacher creates *lesson plans*, which specify the content of a lesson, the method of delivery, the amount and nature of practice exercises, and the evaluation strategy. Lesson plans also indicate how much time will be used to deliver the lesson (e.g., six 30-minute presentations) and how students of different ability levels will be accommodated.

Components of An Effective Lesson

Researchers generally agree that there are seven components in an effective lesson.

1. *Provide an orientation, stating the learning objective and explaining why this lesson is important to the students.* Orientation helps students establish a positive *mental set*, an interest in the

material. Intriguing questions, humor, and drama can be used to establish the mental set and prepare students to learn. The orientation should also state what the students should have learned when the lesson is complete.

2. *Ensure that students know the prerequisites.* Review the information that students need to know in order to understand this lesson (or acquire a new skill). This step is an appropriate time to relate the coming information to existing knowledge and to present advance organizers (see "Reception Learning: David Ausubel," p. 163).

3. *Present the new information.* Organization of the lecture or demonstration is important. Point out significant information by saying "The important point here is . . ." or "Remember that . . ." or "This is noteworthy because . . ." Use examples and, as much as possible, demonstrations to get students involved. For most students, information presented visually is remembered better than information that is only heard (Gagné and Briggs, 1979). Utilize humor and drama to add variety to your presentations. These techniques, when not overused, help maintain the students' attention.

4. *Question students.* Briefly check to see whether students have understood what you presented. This brief check, called a *learning probe,* consists of questions that can be answered verbally or written or physical exercises. When you ask questions, wait at least three seconds for students to respond. Research has demonstrated a tendency for teachers to give up too soon on low achievers (e.g., Rowe, 1974). Be careful to provide an adequate wait-time before assuming that the students do not understand or have comments. Present more information or examples as needed to clarify problem areas.

5. *Have students practice.* At this point, have students practice new skills or work with the new information for about 10 minutes. Students should try to complete this work independently, so be sure they have the necessary skills to complete the work before it is assigned. All students should participate in the practice exercises.

6. *Assess performance and provide feedback.* After students complete independent work, assess their performance and give them

feedback on it. Specify how well they performed and what their strengths and weaknesses are. Reteach the problem areas if necessary.

7. *Provide follow-up reviews and additional work.* Have students practice their new skills in a distributed manner, meaning at regular intervals over time. Provide additional review of the important points and relate that information to subsequent lessons.

Design of Lessons

In addition to those seven components, the kind of learning that is to occur should be considered in the design of lessons. Robert Gagné categorized what people can learn into five types of learning outcomes: attitudes, motor skills, verbal information, intellectual skills, and cognitive strategies (e.g., Gagné, 1974). The method you use to teach should depend somewhat on the kind of learning outcome you want to achieve. According to Gagné, attitudes are learned through modeling others and also through one's own positive and negative experiences. A student in junior high school whose friends enjoy basketball will probably learn to enjoy basketball. Learning motor skills involves knowing what steps to perform and making a smooth transition between the steps; learning verbal information involves learning facts and characteristics; and learning intellectual skills involves developing reasoning ability such as solving problems and using symbols. When you design lessons, identify the desired learning outcome, and use that to help you decide how to present the lesson.

Instructional Models and Theories

Several researchers have developed models of instruction that specify general approaches to teaching. A *model* is a proposed concept of the relation between variables and/or a graphic representation of the way something works. Some models are theoretical, meaning that the concepts have not been tested in a real-world situation. Other models are practical models, developed from measures taken in a real-world setting, for example, a classroom. Models are developed to help researchers study complex phenomena, such as classroom learning.

Important Influences on Educational Psychology		
Contributor	Place of Study	Contribution(s)
Robert Gagné (1916-)	Yale and Brown universities	Researched learning outcomes
Benjamin Bloom (1913-)	University of Chicago	Developed taxonomy of educational objectives; created mastery learning as approach to teaching
Jerome Bruner (1915-)	Duke and Harvard universities	Advocated discovery learning; helped establish Harvard University's Center for Cognitive Studies, which laid the groundwork for cognitive psychology in America
David Ausubel (1918-)	Columbia University	Developed concept of advance organizers

Models describe relationships; they do not explain them. Ultimately, educational psychologists want to explain relationships and predict performance. To explain relationships, theories are needed. A *theory* is a set of related statements that explain a given phenomenon and synthesize existing data concerning the phenomenon. Theories also allow one to predict performance in situations where data have not been collected. The goal of educational psychologists, then, is to develop theories of instruction that will describe learning and predict achievement under a variety of circumstances. Models are used to guide the collection of information about a phenomenon and serve as important building blocks for theory development.

A full discussion of instructional theories is beyond the scope of this chapter; however, a brief introduction to these theories is appropriate here. Jerome Bruner, for example, developed a theory of instruction that describes four principles of learning: motivation, structure, sequence, and reinforcement. Bruner's goal is to develop a theory that prescribes how to best teach any given subject. The interested reader should consult Bruner (1966) for detailed information about his theory, and Chapter 6 in this book for information on noncognitive learning theories.

Several models of instruction are presented next. Some models may be more appropriate for teaching a particular topic than others, and you may become more comfortable implementing some models than others.

The Discovery Approach: Jerome Bruner

Jerome Bruner (1915–) believes that teachers should begin lessons with specific examples and stimulate the students to discover the general principles from the examples and details (e.g., Bruner, 1966).

Inductive Reasoning

Generally, this type of learning or reasoning is called inductive reasoning. A related phrase psychologists use is *bottom-up processing*, meaning that you begin with the details, the data, and move toward the discovery of principles that describe how the data are related. A third name for this type of approach is the *EG-rule method* because one uses examples and generates rules.

Structure and Coding

Bruner maintains that teachers should present problem situations and allow students to discover the structure of those situations. Bruner uses *structure* to mean relationships and patterns. To understand the structure, students may use a coding scheme to organize information. A *coding scheme* is essentially a hierarchy of related ideas or concepts. Using a coding scheme helps students organize information to understand the relationships. Bruner believes that when students are presented with a sufficient number of examples, they will be able to determine the rules, relationships, or properties of the items being studied.

Guided Discovery

Because students learn by doing, Bruner's approach is called discovery learning. However, discovery learning in which students are allowed to work for the most part on their own should be differentiated from guided discovery, in which the teacher provides some direction. Guided discovery is generally preferred. The teacher guides the learning by setting up problems and asking key questions. Bruner's approach is consistent with cognitive-Gestalt psychologists, who emphasized learning global concepts and developing generalizations.

Classroom Applications of the Discovery Approach

To implement the discovery approach, teachers begin by introducing problem situations and examples, presenting questions and encouraging the students to answer them and make intuitive guesses when needed. The teacher uses more questions, examples, nonexamples, and coding systems to help students discover the pertinent relationships and solve the problems. While creative thinking should be encouraged, it is important to provide nonexamples so that the students do not overgeneralize.

Generally, this kind of teaching design is considered an inductive model. Some potential shortcomings of the discovery approach are that some children may lack the necessary cognitive skills, and teacher preparation for this kind of presentation can require careful and thorough thinking. Additionally, some children will have difficulty completing work in the time provided.

Reception Learning: David Ausubel

David Ausubel (1918–) believes that teachers should present organized, meaningful, and complete information first, and then move to the more specific examples (e.g., Ausubel, 1963). This approach is generally called *expository teaching*. In contrast to Bruner's approach, Ausubel believes that people learn primarily by reception rather than discovery and that lessons should be organized and focused to facilitate reception learning.

Meaningful Verbal Learning

Ausubel also advocates meaningful verbal learning, which means that information and relationships are presented together in a meaningful manner. Rote memorization is not meaningful learning because information is not related to existing knowledge.

Deductive Reasoning

Ausubel refers to the presentation of general concepts at the beginning of the lesson and the subsequent presentation of additional information and examples as new learning being *subsumed* under existing knowledge. This is also known as *deductive reasoning*, moving from the general to the specific. The related concept in psychology, contrasted with bottom-up processing, is *top-down processing*, meaning that one begins with the general relationships and searches for the data (information).

Advance Organizers

One of the best-known aspects of Ausubel's approach is the specification for advance organizers, that is, a statement used to introduce the material and provide a bridge between what the students already know and what is to be learned. These organizers are used to remind students what they already know, direct attention to what is to be learned, and point out important relationships in the new information. There are two kinds of advance organizers: comparative and expository. *Comparative organizers* activate schemata, bringing information from long-term memory (permanent storage) into working memory (limited-capacity, short-term storage). (Refer to Chapter 7 for more information about human memory.) *Expository organizers* do not activate old information, but provide new information that will be needed to understand the lesson.

Classroom Applications of Reception Learning

To use Ausubel's approach, the teacher begins by presenting the major ideas and organization, and the students submit ideas and responses throughout the lesson. There is considerable interaction between the students and the teacher. The lessons are presented deductively, from the general to the specific, and the information is presented in a sequenced, stepwise manner. Similar to Bruner's discovery approach, Ausubel's expository approach encourages the use of examples and focuses on relationships such as similarities and differences in information.

Generally, this teaching model considers the teacher a transmitter of knowledge. Expository teaching seems most appropriate when students have some knowledge of the material and the purpose of the lesson is to identify relationships or expand existing knowledge. Because students have to be able to work with relationships, the expository approach is most appropriate for students in upper elementary grades and higher.

A Model of School Learning: John Carroll

John Carroll (1963) developed an influential model of school learning. According to Carroll, there are five elements that contribute to effective instruction:

1. *Aptitude*—the general ability to learn. The higher the aptitude for learning, the less instruction time is needed.

2. *Ability to understand the instruction*—the readiness to learn. A combination of general intelligence and verbal ability.

3. *Perseverance*—the amount of time the learner is willing to spend on a task.

4. *Opportunity*—the amount of time the student spends paying attention and trying to learn.

5. *Quality of instruction*—the effectiveness of the presentation of the material, the sequence of instruction, the material used, and the extent to which material is adapted to meet the students' needs.

Carroll discussed the trade-offs between each of these factors and the amount of time needed to learn the material and time available for learning. For example, the higher the student aptitude, the less time would be needed for instruction. The better the quality of instruction, the less time should be needed to master the topic. One feature of this model is that it combines factors that the teacher can control (numbers 4 and 5) with factors the teacher cannot control (numbers 1, 2, and 3).

The QAIT Model of Effective Instruction: Robert Slavin

A more recent model, the QAIT model, proposed by Robert Slavin (1984), concentrates on the aspects of Carroll's model that the teacher can control. There are four elements in Slavin's model: quality of instruction, appropriate levels of instruction, incentive, and time. According to Slavin, all four elements must be adequate to create effective instruction.

1. *Quality of instruction*–the extent to which information is presented in a manner (lecturing, discussing, tutoring, etc.) that helps students, especially whether it makes sense to them. Key activities are organizing the information, using examples, and presenting information at an appropriate pace.

2. *Appropriate levels of instruction*–presenting information that students are ready to learn because they have the prerequisite knowledge or skills. This element is difficult to ensure because students in a class are most often at different skill and ability levels. Teachers can utilize techniques such as peer tutoring, individualized instruction, and self-paced instruction to help provide appropriate instruction to all students.

3. *Incentive*–the degree to which students are motivated to work on the lessons the teacher is delivering. Incentive will vary among students. Lessons that are not inherently interesting can sometimes be made relevant to students' lives or otherwise more appealing. When this is not feasible, reinforcement techniques such as praise, points, prizes, or free time can be used to increase incentive.

4. *Time*–the extent to which the teacher provides adequate time for students to work with the material. Time can be viewed in two parts: time allocated to present the material and time students actually spend working on a subsequent assignment. Advance planning, classroom management skills, and unusual interruptions are most likely to affect this element.

To reiterate, according to Slavin, a lesson is most likely to be effective when the quality of instruction is high, when adequate time is allocated to the lesson, and when students are interested and have the prerequisite skills for learning the material.

Instructional Strategies

This section describes several instructional strategies, which are ways to approach teaching under varying conditions.

Transfer of Learning

One of the fundamental purposes of education is to teach students information and skills that can be utilized later in life. Transfer of learning is the application of information learned in one context to solve a problem in another context. Transfer is most likely to occur when the two skills are highly similar.

Research Findings

Research on transfer of learning has had great impact on twentieth-century education. Over 60 years ago Brolyer et al. (1927) investigated whether learning certain subjects, such as Latin, actually helped students increase their mental abilities. At that time people thought studying Latin and mathematics increased thinking and reasoning skills that would affect learning other subjects. In other words, people associated the study of Latin with increased mental discipline. Brolyer and his colleagues (including E. L. Thorndike) determined that there was no general transfer from Latin and mathematics to other areas. Learning Latin helped students learn more Latin and maybe some English vocabulary, but learning Latin did not facilitate their learning of other subjects. The implication of this work is that students need not study specific courses to develop mental discipline. Over the years high school curricula and graduation requirements have changed in accordance with this finding.

Categories of Transfer

There are several categories of transfer:

Specific transfer–occurs when information learned in one situation is applied in a similar situation. This usually means applying facts, rules, or skills in the new situation.

General transfer–occurs when information learned in one situation is applied to new problems or novel situations. This usually means application of general principles or attitudes in the new situation.

Positive transfer–occurs when information learned in one situation aids learning new information. For example, a student learns about vectors in a mathematics class and uses that knowledge to solve a physics problem.

Negative transfer–occurs when information learned in one situation interferes with learning new information (or applying information). *Proactive interference* (previous information interfering with learning new information) and *retroactive interference* (new learning interfering with previously learned information) are examples of negative transfer. Negative transfer occurs when a student misspells an English word after learning the correct spelling for that word in French.

Zero transfer–occurs when information learned in one situation has no effect on acquisition of (or application of) subsequent information. For example, learning how to swim does not affect learning how to spell.

Vertical transfer–occurs when information learned in one situation aids learning more complex information. For example, learning about different kinds of transfer helps student teachers learn about the more complex teaching process.

Lateral transfer–occurs when previously learned skills are applied in new contexts. For example, a student identifies the plot of one story and later identifies the plot of another story.

Classroom Applications of Learning Transfer

Teaching for transfer can be maximized by using the following techniques:

1. Ensure that students have basic skills before teaching new information.

2. Present information in a thorough, well-organized manner and make it meaningful to students. These aspects facilitate storage of information in long-term memory and retrieval of the information when it is needed.

3. Ensure overlapping of information by relating new information to existing knowledge and to future needs.

4. Give students practice solving problems. Teach them problem-solving skills. (See Chapter 13.)

5. Get students actively involved in the learning process, both during class and in subsequent study sessions. Encourage good study skills. Teach students about note-taking, underlining, summarizing, the PQ4R study method (explained in subsequent section), and similar techniques.

6. Continue presenting information until it is overlearned, meaning that students have practiced a skill or worked with information past the point of mastery.

Mastery Learning

Mastery learning, proposed by Benjamin Bloom (1968), can be an effective strategy for teaching students with different abilities. Bloom's work was based on earlier work by John Carroll (1963). Mastery learning is an instructional approach requiring an established level of performance (mastery) on a given skill before students can progress to a subsequent skill. Instructional objectives are sequenced and accept-able levels of performance, *mastery criteria*, are specified. Students learn the objectives in sequence and do not progress to the next objective until the specified level of acceptable performance is attained.

When adequate time is provided and skills are carefully sequenced, then students succeed. When performance is not acceptable, *corrective instruction*, utilizing another teaching strategy, is provided; generally, however, most students will attain the specified levels of performance and the class tends to progress as a unit. Some students require extra time to attain that specified level of performance, and enrichment activities and other means of occupying the higher-ability students are also needed. Mastery learning can help raise a student's self-concept.

Block and Anderson's Approach

Block and Anderson (1975) developed a mastery approach that provides class time for all instruction. Using this approach, lower-ability students do not have to finish work during recess or at home, but they are given additional instructional time. Block and Anderson specified eight elements in their approach.

1. Define the objective.

2. Develop two tests to measure learning of the objective and specify the criterion (acceptable level of performance).

3. Introduce the objective to the students. State the criterion (acceptable level of performance). Let your students know that you expect all of them to learn the objective.

4. Present the lesson.

5. Give the first test, a formative test. Score the tests. Provide enrichment activities to all students who met the criterion or let them help students who did not.

6. Provide a corrective lesson, using a different strategy from the original presentation, to students who did meet the criterion on the formative test.

7. Give the second test, a summative test, to the students who received the corrective lesson.

8. Score the summative tests and assign grades. Students who met the criterion on either the formative or the summative test receive an A.

The Hunter Program

A well-known mastery program is Madeline Hunter's (1982) mastery teaching program. This program uses a direct instruction format (discussed in a subsequent section) and is summarized below in four steps.

1. Prepare students to learn by reviewing previous material, creating an *anticipatory set* (mind set, or attitude), and stating the objective of the lesson.

2. Present and model the information in a logical sequence both verbally (including examples) and by using diagrams and models. This approach utilizes both hemispheres of the brain.

3. Check students' understanding of the material and give them feedback.

4. After students demonstrate a basic understanding of the material, give them brief, independent practice exercises, and check the exercises as soon as possible.

The Keller Plan

The Keller Plan (Keller, 1968) is another approach to mastery learning. It was developed and first used by Fred Keller to teach a course in psychology and is also referred to as the *personalized system of instruction* (PSI). The PSI provides individual units of instruction that students work through on a self-paced basis. As it is generally implemented, the Keller plan incorporates mastery learning with self-paced instruction and peer-tutoring.

Keller's original plan is as follows. After a student completed one unit and prepared for the test, the student took a test on the material. A proctor (a student who previously earned an A in the course) immediately graded the test. If an answer was marginally correct, the proctor asked the student to elaborate on the answer. A student who met a specified criterion level of performance was allowed to proceed to the next unit. Students who missed the criterion by a few points received a few minutes to study those questions and were retested. Students who missed the criterion by a substantial amount were told to reread and study the unit. Students who passed a certain number of units by a given date were invited to attend a presentation. All students took a final exam at the end of the course.

Direct Instruction

The direct instruction approach is a focused, teacher-directed method. Barak Rosenshine (1930–) is an advocate of this teaching method; refer to Rosenshine (1979) for a summary of this approach. Direct instruction is a structured approach by which students are made aware of the goals, instruction is comprehensive, performance is monitored, and feedback is given. Direct instruction has also been referred to as *explicit teaching* (Rosenshine, 1986) and *active teaching* by Tom Good (Good & Brophy, 1973).

Conditions for Direct Instruction

From a scientific perspective, does direct instruction make sense? Yes, this strategy is consistent with Ausubel's (1963) model of reception learning and belief that people learn by reception. To facilitate reception, teachers should be well organized and focused. Additionally, there should be a lot of interaction between the students and teachers. A direct instruction strategy implements these ideas.

Classroom Applications of Direct Instruction

Direct instruction can be used for mastery learning. The teacher specifies the instructional objectives, clarifies goals for the students, and paces the presentation of material. The teacher may encourage discussion within the scope of the instructional objectives. The teacher provides immediate feedback to students and generally controls classroom events. Direct instruction is an appropriate approach for teaching computational mathematics, reading, and foreign languages. Other approaches, including the discovery approach, may be more appropriate for conceptual material such as science and social studies.

Direct instruction seems particularly well suited for helping students learn basic skills. Rosenshine and Stevens (1986) identified six teaching functions that could be used whenever necessary as a framework for teaching basic skills: (1) review and check the previous day's work, (2) present new material, (3) provide guided practice, (4) provide feedback, (5) provide independent practice, and (6) review periodically (weekly and monthly).

For instruction in high-level skills (not the basics), other teaching methods are recommended. The research on these strategies encourage you to include discussion, questioning, in-depth analysis, and more independent work. In general, Good (1982) provided these guidelines: as students mature and develop affectively, problem-solving or critical thinking is needed. At that time teaching should become less direct. However, do not infer that there is never a need for direct instruction with high-level students. When you are teaching high-level students facts (the "who" and the "when"), it may be appropriate to use direct instruction, even though you often will use other approaches.

Individualized Instruction

Individualized instruction is the process of tailoring instruction to the needs of an individual student. The content and the pace of the material are chosen on the basis of the student's level of knowledge and progress. When a student learns quickly, the instruction is paced quickly. When the student learns slowly, the instruction slows down.

Individualized instruction is consistent with behavioral learning principles (e.g., Skinner, 1984). For example, this form of instruction utilizes shaping to begin at the student's current level of knowledge and reinforcement to increase the level of knowledge. This strategy has been implemented in various forms since the 1960s.

Ways to Implement Individualized Instruction

There are primarily three ways to implement individualized instruction: tutoring, programmed instruction, and more recently computer-aided instruction.

1. Tutoring can be provided by other students (*peer tutoring*) or by adults (*adult tutoring*). Peer tutoring may be implemented by same-age tutors or by cross-age tutors. Cross-age tutoring, especially when the tutor is a few grades above the student, is generally recommended. Peer tutoring is generally beneficial to both the tutor and the student. Peer tutoring is recommended as a supplement to, not a replacement for, classroom instruction. Adult tutors constitute one of the most effective instructional methods known, but can be quite expensive. For any students who need private tutoring, consider seeking adult volunteers from the community.

2. Programmed instruction is a self-paced, self-instructional method. Students use materials that are designed to teach mostly without the aid of the teacher. This method has not been demonstrated to be very effective and is used primarily for students in special education.

3. Computer-aided instruction (CAI) utilizes computers to present, drill, and assess student performance. There are many kinds of CAI programs available, most of which are modeled on programmed instruction methods and behavioral learning theories. CAI can be used to tutor students, provide drill and practice, simulate new or complex information, or provide games. (See Chapter 14 for more information.) A major advantage of CAI as an instructional tool is the ability to branch to alternative lessons on the basis of a student's current level of performance. Research has demonstrated that CAI is an effective supplement to classroom instruction, with greatest achievement gains for low- ability students (e.g., Kulik et al., 1984).

Classroom Applications of Individualized Instruction

Individualized instruction can be an effective instructional technique, sometimes more effective than whole-class instruction, but it can be expensive and resource-demanding. Utilizing other teaching methods in combination with individualized instruction is important. Individualized instruction used alone has not been as effective as desired. Especially at the elementary and secondary school levels, most students should not be left on their own for extended periods of time.

Teaching Students to Teach Themselves

Another aspect of instructional design is teaching students about learning. A few suggestions are presented in this section.

PQ4R Method to Enhance Learning

The PQ4R method was developed by Thomas and Robinson (1972) to help students remember what they read. It is most appropriate for students in the fifth grades and above. This method encourages students to work with information piecemeal, in segments, rather than absorb it all at once and helps them process the material more thoroughly than they would from reading it through all at once. The acronym stands for the following:

Preview–Familiarize yourself with the material by reading through the contents pages, the chapter headings, the keywords, and other relevant material like a study guide.

Question–For each major section, generate questions related to the material. As you read through the material you will try to find the answers to your questions.

Read–Read through the material and look for the answers to your questions. Focus on main headings and important concepts. Adjust your reading speed to the difficulty of the material.

Reflect–While you read, think about the material. Generate examples that are not presented in the book. Relate the information you are reading to things you already know.

Recite–After each major topic ask yourself questions and try to answer them without referring to the book. If you cannot answer them (or cannot generate questions), you may have been distracted, reading at an inappropriate rate, or not understanding what you were reading. Also try to answer your original questions about the material.

Review–Conduct cumulative periodic reviews of the material. This means asking questions that you answered earlier and seeing whether you still remember the answers. This also means rereading the material. You may want to do both, but asking review questions is more effective for getting the information into your long-term memory.

Underlining and Notetaking

Underlining and notetaking are methods used by many students to facilitate learning. If you encourage students to underline information, stress the importance of being selective about what they underline.

Most students underline too much material. Underlining only the important or salient points can help students retain the information.

Notetaking should be used as an adjunct to underlining. After underlining material, students should summarize the main points and write them in their own words. Having students work with the information, by underlining it and/or paraphrasing, may help them to process the information at a deeper level than reading alone. This recommendation is consistent with the information processing model that attributes improved recall to deeper levels of processing (e.g., Craik & Lockhart, 1972). Another suggestion is to have students first *scan* through the material to become familiar with it. Scanning can be accomplished fairly quickly and may help them identify the key ideas.

Open Education

Open education is a concept that originated in England, inspired to a great extent by Piaget's recommendation that children be permitted to interact with objects and one another to encourage learning. The concept was implemented in America in the late 1960s and early 1970s.

Effectiveness of Open Education

Open education has been interpreted as programs in physically open areas, as programs with humanistic teaching practices, and as programs with both open areas and special teaching practices. In fact, the various ways it has been implemented has been one problem with open education. Research on the effectiveness of open education compared to traditional instruction has found minor achievement gains in traditional environments and minor affective gains for open environments.

Features of Open Education

Giaconia and Hedges (1982) analyzed approaches to open education and summarized seven features as follows:

1. *The physical space is open and divided into separate learning areas.* Seating arrangements are flexible.

2. *A wide variety of materials are available for students to manipulate,* including arts and crafts supplies and audiovisual equipment.

3. *Students of different age groups work together.* Peer tutoring can be implemented.

4. *Students make choices about what they want to learn* and are active learners.

5. *Instruction is individualized.* Presentations are sometimes given to small groups rather than the entire class.

6. *Teachers evaluate students' work samples (rather than traditional tests) and provide feedback.* Students receive periodic diagnostic evaluations for determining how much has been learned and what grades should be assigned.

7. *Two or more teachers may share planning, instruction, and evaluation tasks.* This is called *team teaching.* When two or more teachers work together, each teacher can provide specific expertise to many students. Additionally, teachers may integrate their areas of expertise to enhance lesson content. For example, a teacher with an American history background and a teacher with a music literature background might work together to determine whether trends in music in the United States have reflected national historical events. Teachers involved in this team approach often advocate it, but there is little research support to validate the success of this method over traditional teaching methods.

These features are listed as options; seldom are all of them incorporated in the same program.

Learning Centers

Learning centers (also called *learning stations*) are areas around the classroom that are used for special projects and activities. For example, one learning center on creative writing could house a different mystery object each week. Students might use the learning center to explore the mystery object and then write a creative story about it. Another learning center might be for music appreciation with a record or cassette player and headphones. Students could take music appreciation when other work is complete. Another learning center might be a computer program on the five senses. Typically, students choose the times they use learning centers. It is possible to generate instructional objectives for material at learning centers. When learning centers are used in open education, students will probably be expected to master certain objectives at each center. In traditional classrooms learning centers are useful for enrichment activities and reward for other completed work.

Physical Layout of the Classroom

In addition to utilizing appropriate instructional methods, the physical layout of the classroom is an important aspect of instructional design.

Ease of Communication

The teacher should be able to see and hear all the students and the students should be able to clearly see and hear the teacher and the material being presented (chalkboard, filmstrips, etc.). Students with visual or auditory disorders may need special seating assignments.

Facilitation of Traffic Flow

The layout should be designed to permit students to walk freely to and from the restrooms, the teacher's desk, the work areas, and so on without disturbing other students. Teachers should spend time orienting students to the classroom, as well as to halls, restrooms, cafeteria, library, bus and automobile loading areas, and other common areas in the school. Supplies and frequently used materials should be within easy reach of the students.

Personalization of Environment

The learning environment should be personalized as much as possible with posters and other decorative and instructional items (e.g., Marland, 1975). Students should be encouraged to provide some of these items and teachers should try to display class projects. Personalizing the environment stimulates attention, pleases the eye, and provides social reinforcement for good work.

Developing effective instruction begins with instructional objectives that state the material to be learned, the performance criteria, and how performance will be assessed. Researchers have provided taxonomies of cognitive, affective, and psychomotor objectives. Several instructional models were discussed. Bruner's discovery approach emphasizes inductive reasoning and learning by doing. Ausubel's reception learning emphasizes deductive reasoning and the importance of organized presentations. Most instructional models recommend orienting students to the material, ensuring that they have prerequisite knowledge, giving presentations that include examples and demonstrations, allowing students time to work with the new information, administering tests, and providing the students feedback on their performance.

Methods of instruction were also discussed. It is important to design lessons that will teach transfer of learning, that is, teach students how to apply the information they have learned. Other instructional methods are the mastery approach, directive teaching, and individualized teaching. Methods of self-instruction for students were also presented. Teachers may want to spend some class time on how to study and take notes. Finally, the point is made that the physical layout of classrooms is an important aspect of instructional design.

Recommended Reading

Block, J. H., and L. W. Anderson. (1975). *Mastery Learning in Classroom Instruction.* New York: Macmillan. (Short book discussing the philosophy and implementation of mastery approaches.)

Bruner, J. S. (1960). *The Process of Education.* New York: Vintage Books. (Discusses the importance of helping students gain a general understanding and relate things and of confronting students with problems to resolve.)

Bruner, J. S. (1966). *Toward a Theory of Instruction.* New York: Norton. (Presents the four major principles of Bruner's theory of instruction and a discussion of discovery learning.)

Eggen, P. D., D. P. Kavchak, and R. J. Harder. (1979). *Strategies for Teachers: Information Processing Models in the Classroom.* Englewood Cliffs, N.J.: Prentice-Hall. (Discusses five practical instructional models.)

Fenker, R. (1981). *Stop Studying-Start Learning: Or How to Jump Start Your*

Brain. Fort Worth, Tex.: Tangram. (An entertaining guide to becoming an expert student.)

Gagné, R. M., L. J. Briggs, and W. W. Wager. (1988). *Principles of Instructional Design,* (3d Ed.). New York: Holt, Rinehart, & Winston. (A revision of a classic text on instructional design.)

Gall, M. D. (1970). The Use of Questions in Teaching, *Review of Educational Research, 40,* 707-721. (Discusses the effective use of questions.)

Gronlund, N. E. (1978). *Stating Objectives for Classroom Instruction* (2d Ed.). New York: Macmillan. (Describes differences between general objectives and specific learning outcomes and lists phrases that can be used.)

Holt, J. (1967). *How Children Learn.* New York: Pitman. (Describes effective learning.)

Joyce, B., and M. Weil. (1980). *Models of Teaching.* Englewood Cliffs, N.J.: Prentice-Hall. (Compilation of many teaching models with discussion of psychological foundations, research, and outcomes.)

Mager, R. F. (1975). *Preparing Instructional Objectives* (2d Ed.). Palo Alto, Calif.: Fearon. (Provides many suggestions for developing objectives.)

Pauk, W. (1974). *How to Study in College.* Boston: Houghton- Mifflin. (A classic book geared for college students but applicable to secondary students as well.)

References

Ausubel, D. P. (1963). *The Psychology of Meaningful Verbal Learning.* New York: Grune & Stratton.

Block, J. H., and L. W. Anderson. (1975). *Mastery Learning in Classroom Instruction.* New York: Macmillan.

Bloom, B. S. (1968). Learning for Mastery, *Evaluation Comment, 1.* Los Angeles: University of California, Center for the Study of Evaluation of Instructional Programs.

Bloom, B. S., M. B. Englehart, E. J. Furst, W. H. Hill, and O. R. Krathwohl. (1956). *Taxonomy of Educational Objectives: The Classification of Educational Goals. Handbook 1: The Cognitive Domain.* New York: Longman.

Brolyer, C. R., E. L. Thorndike, and E. R. Woodyard. (1927). A Second Study of Mental Discipline in High School Students, *Journal of Educational Psychology, 18,* 377-404.

Bruner, J. (1966). *Toward a Theory of Instruction.* New York: Norton.

Carroll, J. B. (1963). A Model of School Learning, *Teachers College Record, 64,* 723-733.

Craik, F. I. M., and R. S. Lockhart. (1972). Levels of Processing: A Framework for Memory Research, *Journal of Verbal Learning and Verbal Behavior, 11,* 671-684.

Gage, N. L., and D. C. Berliner. (1984). *Educational Psychology* (3d Ed.). Boston: Houghton Mifflin.

Gagné, R. M. (1974). *Essentials of Learning for Instruction.* Hinsdale, Ill.: Dryden Press.

Gagné, R. M. (1977). *The Conditions of Learning* (3d Ed.). New York: Holt, Rinehart, & Winston.

Gagné, R., and L. Briggs. (1979). *Principles of Instructional Design* (2d Ed.). New York: Holt, Rinehart, & Winston.

Giaconia, R. M., and L. V. Hedges. (1982). Identifying Features of Effective Open Education *Review of Educational Research, 52,* 579-602.

Good, T. (1982). *Classroom Research: What We Know and What We Need to Know.* Research and Development Report No. 9018. Austin: Research and Development Center for Teacher Education, University of Texas.

Good, T., and J. E. Brophy. (1973). *Looking in Classrooms.* New York: Harper & Row.

Hunter, M. (1982). *Mastery Teaching.* El Segundo, Calif.: TIP Publications.

Keller, F. S. (1968). "Good-bye, Teacher. . ." *Journal of Applied Behavior Analysis, 1,* 78-89.

Krathwohl, D. R., B. S. Bloom, and B. B. Masia,. (1964). *Taxonomy of Educational Objectives. Handbook II: Affective Domain.* New York: McKay.

Kulik, C., J. Kulik, J., and R. L. Bangert-Drowns. (1984). Effects of Computer-Based Education on Elementary School Pupils. Paper presented at the annual convention of the American Eductional Research Association, New Orleans.

Marland, M. (1975). *The Craft of the Classroom: A Survival Guide to Classroom Management at the Secondary School.* London: Heinemann Educational Books.

Rosenshine, B. (1979). The Third Cycle of Research on Teacher Effects: Content Covered, Academic Engaged Time, and Direct Instruction. In P. L.

Peterson and H. J. Walberg, (Eds.). *Research on Teaching: Concepts, Findings, and Implications*. Berkeley, Calif.: McCutchan.

Rosenshine, B. (1986). Synthesis of Research on Explicit Teaching. *Educational Leadership, 43* (7), 60- 69.

Rosenshine, B., and R. Stevens. (1986). Teaching Functions. In M. Wittrock, (Ed.). *Handbook of Research on Teaching*. (3d Ed.). New York: Macmillan. pp. 376-391.

Rowe, M. B. (1974). Wait Time and Rewards as Instructional Variables, Their Influence on Language, Logic, and Fate Control. I: Wait Time. *Journal of Research in Science Teaching, 11*, 81- 94.

Simpson, E. J. (1972). *The Classification of Educational Objectives: Psychomotor Domain*. Urbana, Ill.: University of Illinois Press.

Skinner, B. F. (1984). The Shame of American Education. *American Psychologist, 39*, 947-954.

Slavin, R. E. (1984). *Research Methods in Education: A Practical Guide*. Englewood Cliffs, N.J.: Prentice-Hall.

Thomas, E. J., and H. A. Robinson. (1972). *Improving Reading in Every Class: A Source Book for Teachers*. Boston: Allyn & Bacon.

CHAPTER 10

Intelligence and Individual Differences

Measures of intelligence provide an indication of an individual's overall ability to adapt to the environment.

While attempting to define and measure intelligence, researchers have identified differences in cognitive ability between people; these variations are known as individual differences in intelligence. Research has been under way for over a century to understand the contributions of hereditary and environmental factors responsible for those differences.

In the classroom, an understanding of the existence and causes of individual differences is essential if the teacher is to design instructional objectives that will optimize the learning and performance of the students. Some students may excel in several areas of cognitive ability (academic areas—mathematics, history, etc.), while others may excel in only one area or may perform below class average in most or all areas, finding academic work quite difficult and laborious.

This chapter describes the history of intelligence testing and the types of tests currently used in most schools, as well as the various aspects of intelligence.

History of Intelligence Testing

During the past century several methods of measuring intelligence have been attempted. For example, early researchers thought intelligence could be determined by measuring vision, hearing, muscular strength, and other sensorimotor functions; subsequent researchers tried to measure intelligence by evaluating cranial features, facial features, and handwriting; and most current researchers determine intelligence by measuring verbal skills (e.g., judgment, reasoning, reading comprehension), spatial skills (arranging blocks, ordering pictures in sequence), and other cognitive abilities. Even today, there is much disagreement about what intelligence is and how it can be measured. Generally, psychologists agree that intelligence is an indication of how well an individual can adapt to the environment. However, they are trying to determine whether intelligence is one general ability, many specific abilities, or both general and specific abilities. If intelligence is many abilities, then how many are there, and what are they?

An important difference between intelligence research in the late 1900s and earlier research is an emphasis on *individual differences*. Individual differences are variabilities between people. While early researchers considered individual differences an inconvenience and ignored them, current researchers study these differences with great concern. Researchers want to know how individuals differ and why some people excel or have deficits in cognitive abilities. Researchers try to determine how hereditary (genetic makeup) and environmental (e.g., socioeconomic status and number of siblings in the family) factors influence these differences. If heredity were the sole factor determining intelligence, teachers would have relatively little impact on students' learning and performance. The view that heredity is the sole determinant of intelligence has now been largely refuted; a number of researchers have demonstrated that the environment also influences intelligence.

Some of the most prominent contributors to the field of intelligence testing are listed in the table on page 185 and described in the text that follows.

Important Influences on Educational Psychology		
Contributor	**Place of Study**	**Contribution(s)**
Sir Francis Galton (1822-1911)	King's and Trinity colleges, University of Cambridge	Emphasized importance of heredity to intelligence; father of intelligence testing
Alfred Binet (1857-1911)	Studied under Jean Charcot	Developed famous intelligence test, which is still used; introduced concept of mental age
Lewis Terman (1877-1956)	Indiana and Clark universities	Constructed first group IQ test; adapted Binet intelligence test for use in America; coined term "IQ"; conducted longitudinal study of gifted children
David Wechsler (1896-1981)	Columbia University	Developed intelligence tests still in use today; promoted idea that intelligence consists of emotional, motivational, and intellectual factors
Charles Spearman (1863-1945)	Leamington College and Leipzig	Provided perspective that mental tests measure general and specific abilities; corrected correlation coefficient for attenuation
Louis Thurstone (1887-1955)	Cornell and University of Chicago	Provided perspective that people have several primary mental abilities; contributed much to measurement theory
J. Paul Guilford (1897-1987)	Nebraska State University and Cornell	Developed structure-of-intellect model; researched nature of creativity

Sir Francis Galton: Heredity and Individual Differences

Sir Francis Galton (1822–1911), an English biologist who was Charles Darwin's cousin, became interested in measuring intelligence in the late 1800s. In 1869 Galton published *Hereditary Genius* and became the first person to record the idea that human intellectual abilities could be accurately measured. He believed that intelligence could be determined psychophysically, by measuring vision, hearing, reaction time, and other perceptual abilities. In 1882 he set up a booth in a museum in London in which he charged admission and measured perceptual abilities. His most important observation was the significant variability between people in performance on sensorimotor tasks. This variability is known today as individual differences.

Alfred Binet: Individual IQ Test

Alfred Binet (1857-1911) studied under the French neurologist Jean Charcot. In 1904 the Minister of Public Instruction in Paris appointed Binet to a special commission to determine how mentally retarded children should be educated. The commission decided that these children should be educated in separate schools from other children and that a test for identifying mentally retarded children should be devised. Binet and a colleague, Theodore Simon, developed intelligence tests specifically for this purpose. Binet believed that intelligence was the ability to make sound judgments and was, therefore, best measured by verbal and reasoning tasks, not sensorimotor tasks that Galton used. Binet designed several intellectual (i.e., cognitive) tasks and ordered them from easiest to most difficult. He then determined how many tasks children of each age (e.g., the average 7-year-old) could answer. He used the concept of *mental age* to score the tests. Therefore, any child who passed the same number of tasks as the average 7-year-old, for example, would be assigned a mental age of 7. Binet's test was effective in predicting students' academic performance. After continuous revisions and additions, Binet published new versions of the test in 1908 and 1911. The tests were individual *intelligence tests*, administered to one child at a time.

Lewis Terman: Group IQ Test

Lewis Terman (1877-1956) published an American version of the Binet test in 1916. Terman developed this test while working at Stanford University and thus named the test the *Stanford-Binet*. This test, which included a number of additional items, was standardized on American children and, like the original Binet, was an individual intelligence test.

Intelligence Quotient

Terman introduced the concept intelligence quotient (IQ), which had previously been used by William Stern, a German psychologist. IQ is calculated by dividing the mental age (the level of mental development as determined by test performance) by the chronological age (the number of years since birth) and multiplying by 100. For example, a 12-year-old child who scores a mental age of 10 has an IQ of 10/12 x 100 = 83. When the IQ is calculated using this method, it is called a *ratio IQ*. One problem with this method is that the rate of increase of mental age generally slows during the teenage and adult years. For example, mental age of teenagers does not increase as quickly as mental age of young children. Therefore, the ratio does not work well for persons over 13 (approximately).

Revisions of IQ Test

The Stanford-Binet test was revised in 1937, 1960, 1972, and 1986. The 1960 and 1972 versions calculate IQs using the *deviation IQ* method, which is based on the percentage of students in each age group who attain a given score. The 1972 version was restandardized on a sample that included black and other minority children. In the 1986 version the mean IQ is 100 and the standard deviation is 16. Mean and standard deviations are discussed in Chapter 11.

David Wechsler: IQ Test and Emotional Factors

David Wechsler (1896-1981) produced several individual intelligence tests. While working for the army, Wechsler noticed that some enlisted men with high-quality work histories scored poorly on the intelligence tests that were administered. Wechsler decided that intelligence tests should measure performance in addition to verbal ability and be administered to adults as well as children. (Binet's tests were designed exclusively for children.) While Wechsler was chief psychologist at New York's Bellevue Hospital, he developed a new intelligence test.

WAIS

In 1939, after determining the norms (test performance for a representative group) on an adult sample, Wechsler published his first intelligence test, the *Wechsler-Bellevue*. He revised the test in 1955, renaming it the *Wechsler Adult Intelligence Scale* (WAIS), and again in 1981, renaming it the WAIS-R (WAIS revised).

Unlike the early Stanford-Binet test, Wechsler's tests include a nonverbal component. (A recent version of the Binet does include a nonverbal component.) The WAIS produces three IQ scores: a verbal IQ, a performance IQ, and a full-scale IQ. The Wechsler full-scale IQ score tends to be very similar to the Stanford-Binet IQ score. Like the Stanford-Binet, the WAIS-R uses deviation IQ scores. The mean score for the WAIS-R is 100 and the standard deviation is 15. For a discussion of mean and standard deviation, see Chapter 11.

Verbal Component

The verbal subscore of the WAIS is based on six subtests:

1. *Information*—29 items regarding general and world knowledge

2. *Comprehension*—14 questions concerning practical information and ability to use existing knowledge

3. *Arithmetic*—14 questions testing arithmetic reasoning

4. *Digit span*—test of short-term memory in which the experimenter recites a series of digits and the subject repeats them

5. *Similarities*—13 items that the test participant compares

6. *Vocabulary*—40 words that the test participant defines

The performance subscore of the WAIS is based on five subtests:

1. *Picture arrangement*—Seven pictures are ordered to tell a story. This task measures ability to understand a situation.

2. *Picture completion*—The subject specifies the missing part in an incomplete picture. This task measures visual recognition.

3. *Block design*—Small blocks are manipulated until the design on the blocks matches a picture. This task measures perceptual analysis and visual-motor coordination.

4. *Digit symbol*—Symbols are assigned to digits. Digits are specified and symbols must be written to parallel the sequence of digits. This task measures memory and speed.

5. *Object assembly*—Puzzle pieces are manipulated to form an object. This test measures manual dexterity and recognition.

Wechsler's Tests for Children

In addition to the adult scales, Wechsler published the Wechsler Intelligence Scale for Children (WISC) in 1949, and a revised edition, the WISC-R in 1974. He also introduced the Wechsler Preschool and Primary Scale of Intelligence (WPPSI) in 1963.

Current Views on Intelligence

Most researchers today would agree that *intelligence* is the extent to which someone is capable of adapting to the environment and that measures of intelligence indicate the level of social functioning as well as a specific level of attained knowledge. P. E. Vernon (1969) summarized the concept of intelligence as basically involving (1) genetic capacity—that intelligence is part of genetic equipment, (2) observed behavior—that intelligence results from both hereditary and environmental factors, and (3) a test score—that intelligence is the construct measured by an intelligence test.

Donald Hebb has referred to these same three meanings as Intelligence A, genotypic form; Intelligence B, phenotypic form, and Intelligence C, intelligence as a test score. Intelligence C is the most controversial of the three meanings because performance on an intelligence test is dependent on the subject's motivation during the test and familiarity with the testing environment, the clarity of the instructions, and other situational factors. Moreover, the social impact of the test score can be tremendous. For these reasons, it is important to understand what the intelligence test is designed to measure and how the results should be interpreted and applied. These issues are presented later in the chapter.

Researchers continue to debate whether intelligence is one general ability, many specific abilities, or a combination of both general and specific abilities. Because performance varies on different mental tasks it is difficult to support the concept of intelligence as one general ability. For example, a student who scores well on a vocabulary test may score average on a reading comprehension task. Concepts of intelligence that have been developed to identify general and specific intelligence and to explain the variability in performance are described below.

Charles Spearman: The g Factor

Charles Spearman (1863-1945) believed that intelligence was a function of general ability (*the g factor*) plus specific abilities (*s factors*). The g factor represents general intelligence, believed to be an inherited factor, which activates the s factors.   Spearman (1927) believed that performance of a mental task was determined by both the g factor and the person's specific ability for that kind of task.

Louis Thurstone: Seven Primary Mental Abilities

Louis Thurstone (1887-1955) criticized Spearman's proposal, believing that there was more than one primary mental ability (Thurstone, 1938). Thurstone maintained that intelligence is a composite of seven factors that he considered primary mental abilities: verbal comprehension, memory, reasoning, ability to visualize spatial relationships, numerical ability, word fluency, and perceptual speed. This concept has been criticized because there appears to be a strong correlation between measures of these abilities; for example, persons who score highly on the reasoning component also tend to score highly in a test of spatial relations.

J. Paul Guilford: Structure of Intellect

J. Paul Guilford (1897-1987), one of the foremost researchers in this area, believed that intelligence is a function of multiple cognitive abilities (Guilford, 1967). Guilford proposed three basic dimensions (abilities) of intellect:

1. *Mental operations, which are thinking processes*—cognition, convergent thinking, divergent thinking, evaluation, and memory

2. *Content, which is what people are thinking about*—visual figures, word meanings, symbols, and behaviors

3. *Products, which are the end result of thinking*—units, classes, relations, systems, transformations, and implications

Guilford believed that completing a cognitive task means performing a mental operation on some content and ending up with a product. Guilford maintained that there are at least $5 \times 4 \times 6 = 120$ possible kinds of cognitive tasks and a separate mental ability for each task. Guilford's concept of intelligence is useful because it incorporates abilities such as divergent thinking that had not been included in previous theories. However, Guilford's concept has the same disadvantage as Thurstone's concept because performance measures on these "separate" abilities is often correlated.

Howard Gardner: Theory of Multiple Intelligence

Howard Gardner (1943–) proposed (1983) a theory of multiple intelligence that identifies seven separate kinds of intelligence: linguistic (verbal), logical-mathematical, spatial, musical, bodily or kinesthetic, knowledge of self (intrapersonal), and knowledge of others (interpersonal). Interestingly, Gardner noted that some people excelled in one of these abilities but scored average on the remaining abilities. Gardner believes that a problem with traditional intelligence tests is that they measure only two kinds of intelligence—linguistic and logical-mathematical. Gardner admits that traditional intelligence scores are accurate predictors of academic success but has argued for discontinuation of the tests because of the possible negative social consequences of low scores.

Robert Sternberg: Triarchic Theory (Components View)

Robert Sternberg (1949–) has provided a modern approach to the study of intelligence that he termed the triarchic theory of intelligence (Sternberg, 1985). Mental processes are investigated in terms of three levels of components, which are basic processes classified by function and generality.

1. *Metacomponents*—processes involved in higher-order functions, such as planning and strategy selection (also known as metacognitive functions)

2. *Performance components*—processes that execute selected strategies, and perceive and store information

3. *Knowledge-acquisition components*—processes used to acquire new information and separate important from irrelevant information

According to Sternberg's theory, metacomponents are similar to Spearman's g factor in that they may affect performance on any task. For example, individuals with successful metacomponents such as problem-solving skills may perform well on several tasks because they select appropriate problem-solving strategies and show persistence. People with weak metacomponents may have difficulty with several tasks. In summary, Sternberg's triarchic theory provides a way to relate mental abilities to underlying basic processes.

General Theories of Intelligence and Intelligence Testing

Group versus Individual Intelligence Tests

Individually administered intelligence tests may allow an examiner to learn how a person handles stress and approaches problems. In addition to producing an IQ, a number, the examiner learns about the person. Individual IQ tests are costly and time-consuming to administer, however, and results may vary depending on the examiner's experience and the rapport established between the subject and the examiner. For these reasons, it has been necessary to devise intelligence tests that can be administered to large groups of people. During World War I there was a need for large-scale and efficient testing of enlisted personnel. Terman was responsible for developing two group intelligence tests for use by the armed services in 1917: the Army Alpha Test, designed for those who could read; and the Army Beta Test, designed for illiterates and non-English-speaking personnel. These tests, especially the former, were considered successful and other group tests were subsequently developed. Some of the more widely used group tests today are the California Test of Mental Maturity (published by McGraw-Hill), the Otis-Lennon Mental Abilities Test (published by Harcourt Brace Jovanovich), and the Lorge-Thorndike Intelligence Test (published by Houghton-Mifflin).

Group tests tend to be paper-and-pencil tests requiring multiple-choice answers. Specific directions are given and the administration is usually timed. Some researchers, particularly Hebb (1978), believe that group intelligence tests are not appropriate in school settings because there is too little control of the test environment during test administration, results are misinterpreted and misused, and only limited information is obtained.

What Do IQ Tests Predict?

Many research studies have been conducted to determine what IQ tests predict. Binet's and subsequent intelligence tests were used to predict academic success. Prediction is not 100% accurate, but there seems to be a substantive correlation between IQ and school grades.

Terman's Study of Gifted Children

In 1922 Louis Terman began a longitudinal study of over 1000 schoolchildren from southern California to investigate the lives of intellectually gifted children—specifically to ascertain whether these gifted children were healthier, happier, more successful, or otherwise different from persons with average or below-average intelligence. Each child in this study had an IQ of 140 or greater and was tested and interviewed every few years to enable researchers to learn about their lifestyles. When Terman died in 1956, his students continued this work and published some of the results (Terman and Oden, 1959).

Before Terman's study, many people believed in a stereotype of the genius child, a skinny, unpopular, awkward, uncoordinated person wearing glasses. Terman's work has demonstrated that this stereotype is, for the most part, invalid. Terman found that bright children are not physically fragile or smaller than average-intelligence children of the same age. In fact, he found the bright children to be above average in a number of physical characteristics, including general health and development, and also in early development (e.g., walking and talking a couple of months sooner than average children). The bright children were more likely to make high grades in school, be leaders, and be emotionally and socially well-adjusted. When they became adults, these former bright children were more likely than the average person to earn more money, have a managerial job, and make scientific or literary contributions. They were less likely than the average to get a divorce.

IQ Tests as Predictors

These findings are interesting, but should not be construed to imply that a high IQ guarantees this type of success. Some persons with high IQs will not fare as well. Additionally, having an average IQ score certainly does not rule out the possibility that a person will be above average physically or earn above average income.

The Influence of Heredity and Environment on IQ

A major research issue is whether intelligence is the result of heredity—and is, therefore, innately limited—or environmental influences, and is, therefore, potentially improvable. Anne Anastasi (1958) argued that researchers should concentrate on understanding the impact of both heredity and environment on intelligence rather than be concerned with which factor weighed more heavily—in other words, that researchers should ask "how," not "which."

Studies of Twins

Much of the research conducted to address this nature/nurture issue compares the intelligence scores of twins, some raised together and others raised in separate environments. Identical twins share all (100 percent of) their genetic makeup, fraternal twins and other siblings share half (50 percent of) their genetic makeup, and unrelated individuals share no genetic makeup. Research indicates that identical twins raised in the same environment have similar intelligence scores. If heredity heavily determines intelligence, then identical twins raised in different environments should also have similar intelligence scores. If environment contributes significantly, then identical twins raised in different environments (not similarly enriched) should show substantively different intelligence scores, in spite of shared genetic makeup. Additionally, if environment is a major factor in determining intelligence, then siblings, and even strangers, raised in the same environment should have similar intelligence scores (IQ).

Research Findings. A review of much of this literature was conducted by Erlenmeyer-Kimling and Jarvik (1963). Results indicated that identical twins raised together have very similar IQs, identical twins raised apart have similar IQs (not as similar as those raised together), siblings raised together have fairly related IQs (not as similar as those of identical twins raised apart or together), unrelated children raised together have somewhat similar IQs, and unrelated children raised apart do not have similar IQs. These results considered aggregately suggest that both heredity and environment influence intelligence, but that heredity seems to have the greatest impact.

Limitations of Research. One problem with these studies is that researchers seldom know much about the environment of identical twins raised separately as the twins have often been adopted. Adoption agencies try to place children in the optimum environments; thus the identical twins raised apart may be raised in enriched and similar, though separate, environments. Therefore, the contribution of environment to intelligence may be more significant than initially believed; research continues on this issue.

Classroom Applications of Heredity and Environmental Factors

Examples of environmental factors generally believed to influence intelligence are books and other learning materials in the home, parental reinforcement and expectations for school success, adequate nutrition, and appropriate mental stimulation. The influence of environmental factors seems to be most important when children are young, up to 8 years old. When environmentally deprived children are placed in enriched environments, academic achievement and IQ scores may increase dramatically; however, longitudinal follow-up studies indicate that these increases have not been maintained later in life. One question related to this heredity/environment issue concerns the extent of a teacher's influence on a student's IQ score and intelligence per se. Do students come to the classroom with a certain "amount" of intelligence, or can teachers work to influence intelligence scores? It seems that teachers can potentially influence these scores, although the extent of this influence is unclear.

Gender Differences

For infants and preschool children most research indicates no gender differential for IQ scores. Older boys may score differently from older girls on certain subtests, but not on the full-scale scores. Maccoby and Jacklin (1974) reported females excelling in verbal ability and males excelling in visual, spatial, and mathematical tasks; however these results have provoked some controversy. The results beg the next question as to whether the results are due to environmental or hereditary influences. Boys tend to be encouraged in mathematical, visual, and spatial tasks, and they tend to take more math courses than females do. When girls are encouraged to take courses and apply themselves in these areas, there is no measured difference between males' and females' performance. Irrespective of average differences between males and females, all males will not be superior to all females, nor will all females be superior to all males on performance of a given task. In your class, for example, certain girls will outperform boys on math exams and some boys will outperform some of the girls on verbal exams. These findings imply, therefore, that all subject areas should be presented and emphasized equally to males and females.

Racial Differences

Arthur Jensen (1969) noted differences in IQ test scores between whites and blacks. He attributed the differences in scores (which were lower for black children) primarily to heredity. However, his conclusion is based on correlational data, that is, information that was not directly controlled by an experimenter. Therefore, it is unclear whether the differences in scores were caused by hereditary factors. In fact, researchers may never be able to control relevant factors sufficiently to corroborate Jensen's conclusion. It is important to consider plausible alternative explanations. For example, the majority of experimenters are white and may be somewhat biased in their expectations for certain children or be unable to establish rapport with black children as well as with white children. Another factor is the environment in which the black children were raised, which was generally less affluent than that of white children and less conducive to academic success (fewer incentives offered and less parental help with schoolwork). This environmental factor could contribute to lower IQ scores.

One way to investigate this issue is to test black children raised by white parents in an environment that encourages academic achievement. Scarr and Weinberg (1976) conducted studies within this framework. The black children they tested eventually demonstrated an average IQ of 106, which is significantly higher than the national average for blacks. Scarr also noted even higher IQ scores for the black children who were adopted as infants and hence exposed to an enriched environment during the critical development years.

Culture-Fair Tests

Jensen's work points out a critical, complicated issue in intelligence testing. Are intelligence tests designed primarily for middle-class white students and, therefore, unfair to minority students? On one hand, intelligence scores are relatively accurate predictors of academic success—students who score poorly on the tests are not likely to do well in school and vice versa; on the other hand, intelligence tests may accurately reflect problems in school environments. Thus, researchers have argued that tests should be designed to be culture-fair (i.e., culture-free, or non-culture-specific). Such tests would accurately measure the intelligence of persons of any ethnic or cultural background, and that person's cultural background would not affect test results. For example, a student from Greece who was not fluent in English would theoretically score the same on the IQ test as someone fluent in English and of the same underlying intelligence. The fact that the person is not fluent in English would not adversely affect the intelligence score. These tests would measure cognitive abilities and not be affected by a person's cultural background.

R. B. Cattell has discussed the two basic kinds of intelligence: inherited and acquired. Cattell (1963) argues that intelligence tests could be used to accurately measure intelligence that is inherited, irrespective of a person's cultural background. The application of prior knowledge to new information, termed *crystallized general ability,* is highly valuable and influenced by cultural values. Examples of crystallized intelligence are reading comprehension, balancing a checkbook, and social etiquette. Students apply crystallized general ability when they take math and achievement tests. Contemporary intelligence tests measure crystallized general ability. The ability to adapt to new situations, termed *fluid general ability,* is not dependent on formal education. Examples of fluid general abilities are reasoning and dealing with abstractions and the ability to solve problems that do not require special training. Fluid ability, according to Cattell, is primarily inherited. Cattell argues that intelligence tests should measure fluid general abilities. Cattell (1957) designed a test, *Cattell's Culture-Fair Test,* to measure fluid general ability. Despite Cattell's design, this test is likely to be easier for students who are accustomed to working with paper and pencil and are motivated to perform well on a test.

Classroom Applications of Test Scores

When tests reveal that some students perform below others, it is important to provide appropriate education to those students irrespective of the underlying cause of the differences. Teachers should share this attitude and utilize test scores as information that can be used to design appropriate instruction, not overgeneralize about underlying abilities of different groups of students.

Intelligence Testing and
Implications for Instruction

Applying Results of Intelligence Tests

To effectively interpret and utilize intelligence test scores, determine whether the score was obtained from a group or an individual test. If a group test was used, you have only a small portion of the whole picture. Group tests provide limited information and should be interpreted cautiously. If an individual test was used, look for more than a test score. Read the test administrator's comments and be willing to request more information. When you try to make sense of the IQ, the score number, remember that it is a composite of performance on many tasks. It may indicate superior performance in some areas, but inadequate performance in other areas or consistent performance across all areas. The number is only a general index of learning ability and is subject to error. Therefore, do not interpret the number as an absolute indicator of someone's ability.

Intelligence is not a simple concept. One test score (or even two or three scores) cannot provide a comprehensive analysis of a person's overall intellectual abilities. This problem is compounded by the fact that researchers are still trying to define intelligence and determine and measure its causative factors. Thus, teachers must not place too much emphasis on a single test score. There is a general tendency among educators, students, and others to place undue faith in individual numeric test scores. The results of an intelligence test should be used in conjunction with other evaluations, such as teacher observation, results of achievement tests, measures of social skills, and input from parents. Numbers are useful in context but are neither invincible nor all-telling. Your expectations of a student who seems to do well in your class should not alter if the student scores low on an IQ test. Be especially careful when interpreting scores of minority students because there might be language barriers or other situational problems, resulting in scores lower than what they should be. As a final point, if you are comparing scores among different students, ignore small differences in the numbers because they might not be meaningful.

Some of the problems with intelligence testing received attention in the 1960s. The publication of Hoffman's (1963) *The Tyranny of Testing* and Black's (1963) *They Shall Not Pass*, helped to increase public awareness of the important issues and limitations in testing.

Individual Differences

As you read above, one of Sir Francis Galton's early observations was the striking variability between people (Galton, 1869). He noticed this phenomenon specifically in regard to sensorimotor abilities, but other researchers have documented this finding for academic abilities. The general term used for this phenomenon is individual differences.

Factors in Individual Differences

Individual differences are a function of many factors, the most influential being heredity, socioeconomic status (SES), culture, and birth-order (whether the child is the youngest, oldest, etc. among family siblings). Other recently suggested factors are divorce, child abuse, and working mothers (e.g., latchkey situations in which children come home after school and are in the home alone).

Teaching Strategies

There are important implications here for teaching strategies, including the formation of special groups and ways of dealing with individual differences.

Grouping Methods. A fundamental question is how to group children for instructional purposes. There are two major methods: (1) ability grouping by class or track, placing students at different levels in separate classes, and (2) forming special work groups within a class. Ability grouping is used most often in junior and senior high schools. However, there are a few problems with this method. The low-ability students tend to cause the most behavior problems and have few or no achievement-oriented peer models. They also tend to receive lower quality instruction and are subject to negative attitudes from other students. High-ability students tend to benefit from segregated classes. Teachers are generally more enthusiastic when dealing with these students and assign more creative problems.

Grouping students within a class is used most often in elementary schools, typically in reading and math. This method works well. Teachers using this method should conduct periodic assessments to ensure that students are in groups appropriate for their current functional level. Teachers should also discourage children comparing groups.

Aptitude Treatment Interaction. In addition to forming special groups, teachers can modify the way they present information to accommodate different students. The term aptitude-treatment interaction (ATI) is used to indicate that individuals react differently to various teaching methods. For example, some students benefit from direct instruction, others benefit from independent work, and still others are challenged by open-ended questions and discussions. A particular benefit to individualized instruction is that lessons can be paced to fit the particular student's learning abilities. For more information about ATI and different teaching methods, refer to Chapters 2 and 9.

Teaching to Meet Particular Needs. Schools today have implemented many methods of dealing with individual differences. Ability grouping is sometimes implemented. For example, above-average high-school math students are grouped for instructional purposes. These students are exposed to more advanced, college-preparatory topics than are average students. Special full-time and part-time programs have been developed for students who demonstrate above-average intelligence. These programs are geared to provide stimulating enrichment activities beyond the regular academic curriculum. Occasionally parents do not want their children separated from "regular" students. When special programs do not exist or parents do not want their children to participate, the regular classroom teacher can usually find ways to enhance the student's learning, such as allowing the student to complete extra reading assignments, undertake special library projects, or serve as a tutor for lower-ability students. As mentioned previously, teachers may implement individualized instruction for students needing special help. The teacher might provide the instruction, other students might be used as tutors, computer programs might be used to instruct or drill students, or students might be asked to attend other classes. Other teachers may implement teaching methods that will work for a particular child and might also be able to demonstrate positive expectations and develop rapport. Special-education classes are also available to meet exceptional needs. In short, there are many ways that classroom teachers can deal with the individual differences of students. Managing these differences helps students develop intelligence and meet their potential.

Teacher Expectations

Teacher expectations can have an important impact on students' intelligence scores. Rosenthal and Jacobson (1968) conducted a test on all children in one school during the spring of 1964. Most of those students were of lower socioeconomic backgrounds. The researchers told teachers that the tests indicated which students were "late bloomers." The researchers then selected several children at random and informed the teachers that those students would make large academic gains. The students selected were not actually different from the students not selected, but the teachers thought they were. The researchers revisited the schools a few times and assessed the intellectual gains of the students. The students whom teachers expected to achieve large gains actually did so. The teachers had not spent more time with these students but had a positive attitude toward them. That attitude affected the students' intellectual gains. This finding argues for demonstrating positive attitudes and expectations to all students.

Definitions of intelligence and methods of intelligence testing were discussed in this chapter. Most psychologists agree that intelligence is the ability to learn and to adapt to one's environment. Recent research suggests that it may also indicate the extent of acquired knowledge. Originally, intelligence was considered a unidimensional characteristic. In the early 1920s Spearman introduced the idea that intelligence may be a function of a general ability plus abilities specific to certain tasks. Subsequent psychologists postulate multiple abilities. Thurstone and Gardner both suggested there are seven primary abilities, and Guilford proposed 120 separate abilities. Most recently Robert Sternberg developed a triarchic theory of intelligence that relates mental processes to underlying basic processes.

Popular means of measuring intelligence are group tests and individual tests. Group tests have limited use, but can be efficiently administered. Individual tests, such as the Stanford-Binet and the WAIS, provide useful information but are costly to administer.

Intelligence seems to be a function of both heredity and environmental stimulation. Intelligence test scores, IQs, are generally quite

*accurate predictors of school success, but caution should be exercised
in the interpretation and use of these numbers.*

Recommended Reading

Black, H. (1963). *They Shall Not Pass.* New York: Morrow. (A candid look at
the use of testing in public schools.)

Corno, L., and R. E. Snow. (1986). Adapting Teaching to Individual Differences in Learners, In M. Wittrock, (Ed.). Handbook of Research on Teaching, 3d
ed. New York: Macmillan. (A thorough discussion of research on teaching and
individual differences.)

Gardner, H. (1983). *Frames of Mind: The Theory of Multiple Intelligences.* New
York: Basic Books. (Gardner presents his theory as a way to conceptualize
human cognitive abilities.)

Guilford, J. P. (1967). *The Nature of Human Intelligence.* New York: McGraw-
Hill. (Presents a history of the study of intelligence and provides a theoretical
foundation for present studies.)

Hoffman, B. (1963). *The Tyranny of Testing.* New York: Collier Press. (Elo-
quent review of problems in testing.)

Jensen, A. R. (1985). *Behavioral and Brain Sciences,* 8, "The Nature of the
Black-White Difference on Various Psychometric Tests: Spearman's
Hypothesis." 193- 263. (Describes the heritability of intelligence and responses
of leading researchers in the field to Jensen's work.)

Phi Delta Kappan. (March 1986). Women in Education. (Deals with several
topics on sexism and education.)

Spearman, C. (1927). *The Abilities of Man: Their Nature and Measurement.*
New York: Macmillan. (Describes general and specific intellectual abilities.)

Sternberg, R. (1985). *Beyond IQ: A Triarchic Theory of Human Intelligence.*
New York: Cambridge University Press. (Relates information-processing to
intelligence.)

Sternberg, R. J. (1986). *Intelligence Applied: Understanding and Increasing
Your Own Intellectual Skills.* New York: Harcourt Brace Jovanovich. (A
simplification of material from Sternberg's 1985 book; presents a program for
training intellectual skills.)

References

Anastasi, A. (1958). *Heredity, Environment, and The Question "How?"* Psychological Review, 65, 197-208.

Black, H. (1963). *They Shall Not Pass.* New York: Morrow.

Cattell, R. B. (1957). *Culture-Fair Intelligence Test.* Champaigne, Ill.: Institute for Personality and Ability Testing.

Cattell, R. B. (1963). The Fluid and Crystallized Intelligence: A Critical Experiment, *Journal of Educational Psychology, 54,* 1-22.

Erlenmeyer-Kimling, L., and L. F. Jarvik. (1963). Genetics and Intelligence: A Review. *Science, 207,* 1323-1328.

Galton, F. (1869). *Hereditary Genius.* London: Macmillan.

Gardner, H. (1983). *Frames of Mind: The Theory of Multiple Intelligences.* New York: Basic Books.

Guilford, J. P. (1967). *The Nature of Human Intelligence.* New York: McGraw-Hill.

Hebb, D. O. (1978). Open Letter: To a Friend Who Thinks the IQ Is a Social Evil, *American Psychologist, 33,* 1143-1144.

Hoffman, B. (1963). *The Tyranny of Testing.* New York: Collier Press.

Jensen, A. R. (1969). How Much Can We Boost IQ and Scholastic Achievement? *Harvard Educational Review, 39,* 1-123.

Maccoby, E. E., and C. N. Jacklin. (1974). *The Psychology of Sex Differences.* Stanford, Calif.: Stanford University Press.

Rosenthal, R., and L. Jacobson. (1968). *Pygmalion in the Classroom.* New York: Holt, Rinehart, & Winston.

Scarr, S., and R. Weinberg. (1976). IQ Test Performance of Black Children Adopted by White Families. *American Psychologist, 31,* 726-739.

Spearman, C. (1927). *The Abilities of Man: Their Nature and Measurement.* New York: Macmillan.

Sternberg, R. (1985). *Beyond IQ: A Triarchic Theory of Human Intelligence.* New York: Cambridge University Press.

Terman, L., and M. Oden,. (1959). *Genetic Studies of Genius: The Gifted Group at Mid-life. Thirty-five Years' Follow-up of the Superior Child.* Stanford, Calif.: Stanford University Press.

Thurstone, L. L. (1938). Primary Mental Abilities. *Psychometric Monographs, No. 1.*

Vernon, P. E. (1969). *Intelligence and Cultural Environment.* London: Methuen.

CHAPTER 11

Measurement, Testing, and Evaluation

Basic measurement concepts, testing, and evaluation are discussed in this chapter. Probably the most common way to measure learning is to give a test. The most useful tests produce valid and reliable scores. Standardized tests, are developed by psychologists or other professionals trained in test construction, are administered to all students in a controlled manner so that all students who take the test do so under similar conditions. Nonstandardized tests, which are typically developed by teachers to evaluate performance with respect to specific learning objectives, tend to be administered in a less controlled manner. Several types of tests and the scores they yield are discussed in this chapter. A discussion of some alternative ways to evaluate students without giving tests is also presented.

Differences between Measurement, Testing, and Evaluation

Measurement, testing, and evaluation indicate how much a student has learned and what subsequent instruction should emphasize. *Measurement* is the quantitative (i.e., numerical) assessment of performance. For example, a measurement of student performance is 45 out of 50 correct math problems, or 90 percent. Measurement can be used to compare performance between students and to indicate one student's strengths and weaknesses. *Tests* are instruments used to measure performance, that is, to provide an indication of a student's level of performance. In educational settings, tests are used to help teachers and other school personnel make decisions regarding instruction. Tests can be developed by teachers or by professional test developers and produced by publishing companies. *Evaluation* can be either quantitative or qualitative appraisal of performance and includes value judgments. Evaluation, then, goes beyond—or adds insight to—measurement. An example of evaluation is: "John's most recent math score was 95 percent correct; therefore, he is making good progress in math." Unlike measurement, evaluation does not need to be quantitative; an example of this would be "Mary's social skills seem to be improving." Evaluation can be made on individual students, entire classes, schools, school districts, and so on. Evaluations made on entire classes are usually called *program evaluation* and evaluations made on schools, *school evaluation*.

Basic Measurement Concepts

Measurement is a way of quantifying (assigning numbers to) an evaluation. The utility of the measures is largely a function of their reliability and validity. *Reliable measures* provide consistent results because performance is measured consistently over time and in specific situations. If an intelligence test given to the same student on two consecutive days indicates that the student shows above-average intelligence day 1, but below-average intelligence on day 2, these inconsistent results are not useful (unless the reasons for the substantively different performances can be accounted for by the testing environment (e.g., the test administrator frightened the student, or the student did not feel well on day 2). *Valid measures* are true indicators of whatever the test is intended to measure, because performance in the designated domain is accurately assessed. If a test designed to measure intelligence included only reading comprehension questions, it would not be a true indicator of intelligence because intelligence is generally defined as more than an ability to comprehend reading passages. Therefore, this "intelligence test" would not produce valid measures of intelligence. Measurements that are not valid and reliable are not useful to educators and researchers because they do not consistently and accurately describe performance. Because these concepts are so important in test interpretation, they are discussed in more detail below.

Reliability

Reliability is a measure of the consistency of scores when the same person takes the same test on different occasions or takes an equivalent form of the test under different conditions. There are four types of reliability: test-retest, alternate form, split-half, and interrater.

1. *Test-retest reliability*—measured when the identical test is given to the same student on two occasions. This form of reliability shows how generalizable the test scores are over different occasions (which may mean over time or over two situations). The higher the reliability, the less the test is affected by daily changes in the person taking the test. For example, if an individual takes the same intelligence test on Monday and then a week later, on the following Monday, the scores obtained on the two administrations should be very similar. If the scores are very similar, the test has high test-retest reliability.

2. *Alternate form reliability*—measured when the same person is given two forms of the test. Performances on the first and second forms are compared. This type of reliability indicates the degree of generalizability of test scores (over time and in different situations), and similarity between the two forms. There are several forms of the SAT. The alternate forms were designed to produce similar results.

If one student takes the test twice, using alternate forms of the test, scores on both forms should be very similar. If scores are similar, the test has high alternate form reliability.

3. *Split-half reliability*—measured when items from one test are divided in two groups and a correlation is generated between performance on items in the two groups. An effective way to split the items is odd-numbered items belong to one group and even-numbered items belong to another group. This form of reliability does not indicate generalizability over time, but does measure consistency of the items within the test. A major advantage of this type of reliability is that it only necessitates one administration of the test. For instance, a teacher who administers a spelling test of 50 words, and then scores the odd-numbered words separately from the even-numbered words, can compare performance on the two halves of the test. If scores on the two halves are similar, then the test has high split-half reliability.

4. *Interrater reliability*—measured when two scorers grade the same test independently. The extent to which the independently derived scores are similar indicates consistency between scorers. This form of reliability is important on essay tests and other subjective evaluations, but not on objective tests. If two different examiners give the same student the same intelligence test and then score it, the scores will probably be quite similar. If the scores generated by both examiners are similar, the intelligence test has high interrater reliability.

Validity

Validity is the extent to which a test measures what it purports to measure. The validity of a math aptitude test is the extent to which the test actually predicts math performance (not reading performance, interest in math, or anything else that it is not intended to predict). There are three types of validity: content validity, construct validity, and criterion-related validity.

1. *Content validity*—the extent to which a test covers the material representatively. If there are 10 learning objectives in a unit, are all 10 objectives covered on the test? Content validity is especially

important for achievement tests. For example, consider developing a test to measure how well students learned spelling words over a 1-year period. Students were assigned 300 spelling words. Because you do not have time to administer a test on all 300 words, you develop a test of 30 representative words. The 30 words you select represent each of the spelling rules students had to learn. Some of those rules were "i before e," "oo versus ou," "ai versus ei," and "es versus s." The point is that you do not select the first or the last 30 words the students learned, or any arbitrary list. Instead, to ensure high content validity, you select words that represent what the students were suppose to learn over the year, that is, all the spelling rules.

2. *Construct validity*—the extent to which the test measures a theoretical construct. Intelligence tests are intended to measure the theoretical construct of intelligence. The extent to which intelligence tests measure (i.e., quantify) intelligence determines the construct validity of the test. For example, you would not expect to see personality-type questions on a test designed to measure intelligence. An intelligence test that includes questions such as "What do you think about your mother?" or "Who is your favorite actor?" would probably have low construct validity.

3. *Criterion-related validity*—the extent to which test scores can be used to predict performance in specific situations. To measure criterion-related validity, performance on the test is compared to a criterion, that is, an independent measure of what the test is intended to predict. For example, Scholastic Aptitude Test (SAT) scores and grade-point average (GPA) in high school have high criterion-related validity for academic performance in college. Persons who score well on the SAT and persons who have high GPAs tend to receive good grades in college.

In addition to these three types of validity, you will also see references to *face validity*. Although face validity is not considered a major type of validity, it is the extent to which a test appears to measure what it is intended to measure. When you read the questions on a test, do they seem comprehensively representative of the material and appropriate for the age and education of the persons taking the test?

Standardization

Standardization, another important measurement concept, implies that a test is administered and scored using a specified set of procedures. Testing directions are specified in the test manual and read verbatim by the administrator, the amount of time students can spend working on the test may be predefined, the way to answer student questions may be discussed in the test manual, and so on. Most published tests that are professionally developed include specific instructions to ensure that the test is administered and scored in a standard way.

Administration of Tests

Teacher-made tests should also be administered in a standardized (i.e., predefined, regulated) manner if possible. For example, when you give an in- class test to students, maintain a calm and quiet environment, and allow them only 30 minutes to take the test. A student who is absent for the in-class test takes a make-up test the following day. The same 30-minute time limit should be imposed and a similar testing environment should be provided. For example, the make-up test should not be administered in class if the other students (those not taking the test) are moving around and making noise in the classroom because the noise and distraction would create a different testing environment than the one maintained during the original test.

Norms

Another important aspect of standardization is establishing norms. Norms indicate average (i.e., normal) performance. Standardized tests provide normative data that are used for comparing performance. When a test is standardized, it is administered to a large group of people (the *norming sample*) who are similar to those for whom the test is designed. The performance levels for this large group of people establish the norms. When your students take the test, their raw scores are converted to standardized scores and compared with performance of persons in the norming sample. A subsequent section, "Commonly Reported Scores," describes several ways to convert raw scores to standardized scores.

Descriptive Statistics

Descriptive statistics are used to summarize and organize data. The scores, measurements, and distributions presented in this section are some of the most common ones used to describe data from educational and psychological studies.

Raw Score

The simplest measurement is a raw score, typically the number of correct responses. On a math test with 50 questions, for instance, a student who correctly answers 45 questions receives a raw score of 45. Raw scores are easy to calculate, but they do not mean very much to someone interpreting test scores. The raw score does not indicate how well the person performed in comparison to other students or whether the student has mastered the instructional objectives. More useful information is obtained by converting the raw score to other measures, called *derived scores*.

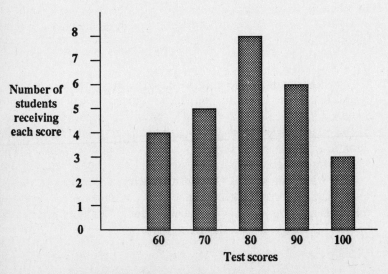

Fig. 11.1 Histogram of a Frequency Distribution

The following measures are used to assess a student's performance and compare it with that of other students.

Frequency Distribution

Frequency distribution indicates the distribution of test scores, in other words, how many people received each score. To simplify graphing and reporting scores, individual scores are usually grouped into sets. For example, all scores between 90 and 94 might be graphed at 90, all scores between 85 and 89 might be graphed at 85, and all scores between 80 and 84 might be graphed at 80. Frequency distributions are often graphed on bar charts called *histograms*. For example, the histogram shown in Fig. 11.1 illustrates that three students scored near 100, six students scored around 90, eight students scored near 80, five students scored about 70, and four students scored around 60.

Range

Range is the separation (i.e., the distance) between the lowest and the highest score. If scores on one test were 25, 30, 44, 48, 68, 72, 74, 98, and 99, then the range of scores for that test would be 25 to 99. Another way to express that range would be to say there was a 74-point spread in the scores ($99 - 25 = 74$). If the range of scores on a particular test is large, then the teacher has some indication that more instruction is needed.

Measures of Central Tendency

Measures of central tendency indicate the typical score for the group of people who took the test. The most commonly used measure of central tendency is the arithmetical average, called the *mean*. The mean is very useful for comparison of one student's performance with the class as a whole. If an individual's score is 95 and the mean is 90, you know the individual scored better than average (but you do not know whether that difference is meaningful). There are three measures of central tendency: the mean, the median, and the mode. In a normal distribution, the mean, median, and mode are the same number.

1. *Mean*—the arithmetic average of the scores. To calculate the mean, add each score and then divide that sum by the number of scores. For example, to obtain the mean of 22, 24, 26, 28, 30, 31, 31, 33, 37, and 38, perform the following calculations:

Add: $22 + 24 + 26 + 28 + 30 + 31 + 31 + 33 + 37 + 38 = 300$

Divide: $300/10 = 30$

The calculation of the mean is denoted $\Sigma X/N$ and the resulting number is denoted $\overline{X}$.

2. *Median*—the middle score in the distribution. Half the scores are higher and the other half are lower than the median. For the scores listed above, the median is 30.5. To obtain the middle score, arrange the numbers in ascending or descending order (from smallest to largest or largest to smallest). If the number of scores is even, the median is the average of the two middle scores. Add the two middle scores together and divide by 2. In this example, the two middle scores are 30 and 31, and the average of those numbers is 30.5. When the number of scores is odd, the median is the middle score. For example, the median of 3, 4, 5, 6, and 7 is the middle number, 5. In this example, there are two numbers lower than 5 and two numbers higher than 5. The median is most often used when there are a few scores at the extremes of the distribution and one does not want the extreme scores (called *outliers*) to have a large affect on the average. For example, you might expect two exceptionally bright students in your class to score very high on a particular test. If you are interested in how the whole class scored on the test and you do not want those two high scorers to influence the average, you might use the median rather than the mean as a measure of central tendency.

3. *Mode*—the score that occurs most frequently in the distribution. For the scores listed above, the number occurring most frequently is 31. Because it occurs twice, 31 is the mode for this set of scores. Occasionally, a distribution may have two scores that occur frequently; this special distribution is called a *bimodal frequency distribution*. The mode is not reported very often in educational and psychological research.

Standard Deviation and Variance

Standard deviation indicates how far the scores are spread out from the mean. It is an indication of the amount of variability in scores.

Variability in scores is not inherently favorable or unfavorable; it is simply a number that helps describe the distribution of scores. Two sets of scores might have the same mean, but the distribution of scores could be very different. For example, consider these two sets of scores:

1. 48, 49, 50, 51, 52: mean = 50; SD = 1.41.

2. 10, 30, 50, 70, 90: mean = 50; SD = 28.3.

Although the average score in either set is 50, there is more variability in the second set of scores. The variability indicates a wide range in the amount of learning that occurred—some students performed well, others did not. When teachers identify variability in a set of scores, there may be implications for further instruction. Perhaps some of the students did not have appropriate background or were inattentive. The variability in performance could also be due to the type of test used. Perhaps students were required to give verbal responses aloud, and this made some students nervous. Test-related anxiety or other factors may have contributed to the variability, and the teacher should investigate as needed.

The teacher should utilize the standard deviation when interpreting test scores because it helps put scores in perspective. For example, consider the following descriptions of two sets of scores:

1. Mean = 50; SD = 10; Robyn's score = 41 (average)

2. Mean = 50; SD = 4; Robyn's score = 41 (poor)

In description 1, Robyn's score is within 1 standard deviation of the mean and is considered an average score. Referring to the diagram of the normal distribution (Fig. 11.2), note that 68 percent of the scores are expected to fall between +1 and − 1 standard deviations from the mean. However, in the second description, Robyn's score falls below 2 standard deviations from the mean. This time, the score is considered far below average. The normal distribution diagram demonstrates that very few students (about 2.5 percent) are expected to score below 2 standard deviations from the mean. This example illustrates why the teacher needs to consider both the mean and the standard deviation to interpret a test score. (See page 216 for more on normal distribution.)

To calculate the standard deviation, use the following steps:

1. Determine the mean. The mean is calculated as $\Sigma X/N$ and denoted as $\overline{X}$.

2. Subtract the mean from each raw score. This is calculated as $(X - \overline{X})$ and is termed a *difference score*.

3. Square each of those difference scores. This is calculated as $(X - \overline{X})^2$ and is called a *squared difference score*.

4. Add together the squared difference scores. This is calculated as $\Sigma (X - \overline{X})^2$ and is referred to as the *sum of the squared difference scores*.

5. Divide that sum by the number of original scores. This is calculated as $\Sigma (X - \overline{X})^2/N$ and is called *variance*.

6. Take the square root of the variance. This is calculated as $\sqrt{\Sigma (X - \overline{X})^2/N}$ and is termed the *standard deviation*, which is sometimes abbreviated SD.

The standard deviation and the variance are closely related measures. Variance is important because it allows researchers to predict which factors are influencing performance, but a complete discussion of variance is beyond the scope of this book. For interpretation of test scores, the standard deviation is the measure of importance. The greater the standard deviation, the greater the spread of scores. Similarly, the smaller the standard deviation, the more closely the scores are clustered about the mean.

Table 11.1 illustrates calculation of the mean, the variance, and the standard deviation for a set of test scores. These formulas are appropriate if you have tested the entire population of interest. If you need to estimate scores for students who did not actually take the test, then you would use slightly different formulas, which can be found in a statistics textbook.

Normal Distribution

Normal distribution (see Fig. 11.2, p. 220) is a common distribution of scores that is expected for most educational and psychological variables (when a large number of scores are collected). In a normal

Table 11.1

Calculating the Mean, the Variance, and the Standard Deviation		
Raw Scores X	Difference Scores $(X - \overline{X})$	Squared Difference Scores $(X - \overline{X})^2$
2	$2 - 10 = -8$	64
4	$4 - 10 = -6$	36
6	$6 - 10 = -4$	16
8	$8 - 10 = -2$	4
10	$10 - 10 = 0$	0
11	$11 - 10 = +1$	1
11	$11 - 10 = +1$	1
13	$13 - 10 = +3$	9
17	$17 - 10 = +7$	49
18	$18 - 10 = +8$	64
Mean $= \Sigma X / N = 100/10 = 10.$		
Variance $= \Sigma (X - \overline{X})^2 / N = 244/10 = 24.4.$		
SD $= \sqrt{\Sigma (X - \overline{X})^2 / N} = \sqrt{244/10} = \sqrt{24.4} = 4.9.$		

distribution, test scores (or any measure) are evenly distributed around the mean score (the average). Half of the scores fall above the mean and the other half below the mean. Most scores fall near the mean. Fewer and fewer scores occur as one follows the curve, away from the mean toward the tails of the distribution. An important property of the normal distribution is that the percentage of scores that will occur within each area under the curve is known. Because of its bell-like shape, the normal distribution curve is commonly called the *bell-shaped curve*. When a normal distribution is expressed in standard scores, the distribution is specifically referred to as a standard normal distribution or *z* distribution.

Commonly Reported Scores

In standardized tests, several types of scores are commonly reported. Each score is a slightly different method of understanding an individual's performance relative to that of other students.

Z Scores

Z scores indicate how far the score is from the mean of the distribution, that is, how many standard deviations away from the mean a specific score is. These scores are calculated with a mean of 0 and and standard deviation of 1. Z scores are useful for comparing performance on two or more tests that may have different means and standard deviations.

Use the following steps to calculate a z score:

1. Subtract the mean for an entire set of scores from an individual's score.

2. Divide that difference by the standard deviation for the entire set of scores.

The formula is $z = (X - \overline{X}) / SD$.
Using earlier examples,

1. Mean = 50; SD = 10; Robyn's score = 41 (average)

2. Mean = 50; SD = 4; Robyn's score = 41 (poor)

Robyn's z score for the first set of numbers is $(41–50)/10 = -0.9$

Robyn's z score for the second set of numbers is $(41–50)/4 = -2.25$

The negative sign indicates that the z score fell below the mean; a positive sign would indicate that the z score is above the mean. Consistent with the earlier discussion of standard deviations, the calculation of z scores demonstrates that for the first set of scores, Robyn's performance was less than 1 standard deviation below the mean. For the second set of scores, her performance was more than 2 standard deviations below the mean.

T Scores

T scores, like z scores, indicate how far the score is from the mean of the distribution and are expressed in numerical terms. *T* scores are calculated using a mean of 50 and a standard deviation of 10. The major advantage of using *t* scores is that negative numbers are avoided.

To calculate a *t* score:

1. Multiply the *z* score by 10.

2. Add 50.

The formula is $t = 10$ (*z* score) $+ 50$.
Using earlier examples one obtains:

1. Robyn's *z* score of $- 0.9$ is equivalent to a *t* score of 41; thus, $(- 0.9)(10) + 50 = 41$.

2. Robyn's *z* score of -2.25 is equivalent to a *t* score of 27.5; thus, $(-2.25)(10) + 50 = 27.5$.

Referring to the normal distribution figure, note that a *t* score of 41 is within 1 standard deviation below the mean. Similarly, the *t* score for the second set of scores, 27.5, is more than 2 standard deviations below the mean.

Percentile Scores

A percentile score (also called *percentile rank*) indicates the percentage of students who scored at or below one student's score. A percentile score of 88 means that the individual scored the same as or better than 88 percent of the normative sample. A percentile score does *not* mean the individual correctly answered 88 percent of the questions. Percentile scores are often used in test reports. Take a minute and review the percentile illustration on the normal distribution figure (Fig. 11.2). Note that percentiles near the middle of the graph are closer together than percentiles at the ends of the graph. This means that percentiles near the center of the distribution represent raw scores that are closer together than do percentiles near the ends of the distribution. Consider the following cases:

1. Marie scores in the 90th percentile. Marcus scores in the 99th percentile.

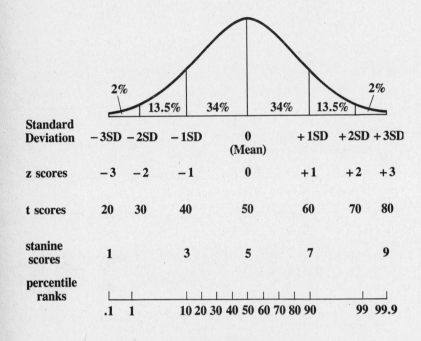

Fig. 11.2 Normal Distribution Diagram

2. Wanda scores in the 40th percentile. William scores in the 49th percentile.

In both cases, there is a difference of 10 percentile points. However, those 10 percentile points indicate greater raw score differences between Marie and Marcus than between Wanda and William. Although the raw scores are not provided, one knows that Wanda's and William's raw scores were closer together than Marie's and Marcus's raw scores.

Stanine Score

Stanine score is a representation of the raw score on a 9-point scale. The stanine scale has a mean of 5 and a standard deviation of 2. The only scores on the stanine scale are the whole numbers 1 through 9.

Table 11.2

	Range of Percentile Scores Assigned to Each Stanine	
Stanine	Range of Percentile Scores Included in Stanine	Number of Percentage Points at Each Stanine
1	0 – 3	4
2	4 – 10	7
3	11 – 22	12
4	23 – 39	17
5	40 – 59	20
6	60 –76	17
7	77 – 88	12
8	89 – 95	7
9	96 – 99	4

Stanine stands for "standard nine." Each stanine rank includes a specific range of percentile scores. For example, the lowest 4 percent of scores are assigned to stanine 1, and the next 7 percent of scores are assigned to stanine 2. As an example, a person who scores in the 9th percentile obtains a stanine score of 2. Using the stanine table presented below, and assuming that the obtained scores fit a normal curve, one can convert raw scores to stanine scores quite easily. If 100 students took a test, the four lowest scoring persons belong to stanine of 1, the persons receiving the next seven lowest scores belong to stanine 2, and so forth. If 200 students took a test, then persons with the 8 lowest scores (4 percent of 200 = 8) would belong to stanine 1. Table 11.2 illustrates which percentiles are assigned to each stanine.

Grade-Equivalent Scores

Grade-equivalent scores are raw scores expressed in terms of grade levels. These scores are generally calculated from separate norming samples for each grade. On a particular test, suppose that the raw-score average for all eighth-grade students in the norming sample was 50. Any student who later takes that test and scores 50 is assigned a grade-equivalent score of eighth-grade (irrespective of the student's actual grade). Grade-equivalent scores are reported in whole numbers and decimals (e.g., 5.7, 10.3, 12.0). The whole number represents the grade (e.g., 5 = fifth grade, 10 = tenth grade, 12 = twelfth grade). Although the decimal usually represents tenths of a year, people sometimes interpret the decimals as months. A student who receives a grade-equivalent score of 5.7 on a reading test performed similarly to students in the norming sample who were in fifth grade and 7/10s through the academic year. Understand that a third-grade student who earns a grade-equivalent score of 5.7 should not automatically be promoted to the fifth grade. This one test score does not indicate a student's ability to complete the more advanced work that fifth-graders undertake. The relatively high grade-equivalent score simply indicates mastery of the material covered on the test.

Testing

As mentioned earlier, there are basically two modes of test preparation: standardized (tests constructed and published by professional test developers) and nonstandardized (teacher-made).

There are several reference sources listing tests on various subjects. To determine if a test has been published on a specific topic, you can check *Tests in Print III* (Mitchell, 1983), which is an index to a great many tests. If you would like a professional's review of a specific test, consult the *Ninth Mental Measurements Yearbook* (Mitchell, 1985), which provides critical reviews of all commercially published tests in the English language. To determine if a computerized assessment instrument is available, consult *Psychware Sourcebook* (Krug, 1987), which references computer-based products for educational and psychological assessment.

Objectives of Tests

Teachers use tests to obtain various types of information about students. Most standardized tests are norm-referenced, that is, one student's performance is compared with that of other students. Some tests are designed for comparing performance across classes, schools, states, and so on. Tests that measure student achievement or student aptitude are commonly administered in public schools; these tests are usually norm-referenced tests.

Criterion-referenced tests are used to determine whether a student's performance meets a predetermined criterion level. Although criterion-referenced tests can be standardized tests, many are created by classroom teachers. One special kind of criterion-referenced test is the competency test, which measures basic skills in specific domains and compares performance to a specified criterion.

Other tests are used to diagnose academic and perceptual problem areas. Additionally, special inventories have been developed to determine vocational interests.

Standardized, norm-referenced, and criterion-referenced tests are described in more detail below. These tests are designed to be administered to individual students or large groups of students.

Standardized Tests

Standardized tests are administered under regulated conditions and are scored according to predefined specifications. They are typically published tests constructed by professionals trained in test development. During test construction, items on the test are checked for problems and changed or discarded when necessary. Once a final version of the test is developed, the test is administered to a large group of people, the *norming sample* (see p. 224), who are similar to the people for whom the test was designed. The scores from the norming sample provide a basis (the norms) for comparing later test scores.

There has been controversy concerning possible biases in standardized tests. A *bias* occurs if persons from an identified population are more likely to perform better (or worse) than persons from other populations. Tests should be constructed to be free from bias. Designing tests to be *culture-fair* or *culture-free* means designing tests that are not unfairly difficult for students from families with low socioeconomic status (SES) or minority students. These students tend to score lower than middle-class students on most standardized tests. This disparity may be attributable to any of the following reasons: the language used in the test is different from that used by low SES and minority students; questions included in the test concern experiences more familiar to middle-class students; or low-SES and minority students may not be as motivated as middle-class students to perform well. In addition to being culture-fair, tests should not be biased against one sex or persons from a particular religious background. One goal in test construction is to presuppose only experiences that are common to all persons for whom the test is designed, irrespective of culture, sex, or religion.

Norm-Referenced Tests

Norm-referenced tests provide a means for comparison of each person's level of performance with performance of others who have taken the same test. A person's raw score (number correct) is compared to a norm to determine whether that person performed better, worse, or the same. The norm group (also called the *norming sample*) chosen for comparison depends on the purpose of the comparison. Norm groups can be a particular class, a particular school district, or even all tenth graders in the nation. Norm-referenced tests often are used to determine overall level of academic achievement.

Norm-referenced tests are particularly useful for differentiating various levels of performance (such as top performers, average performers, and poor performers) and measuring cognitive objectives. They are not as effective for measuring affective or psychomotor objectives.

Results from norm-referenced tests do not indicate which objectives have been met and which objectives should be taught next. Additionally, norm-referenced tests tend to encourage competition between students because scores are compared.

Most achievement tests (e.g., the Iowa Test of Basic Skills) report an individual's score and the standing of that individual relative to normative groups. Typical comparisons are the individual relative to other students in that school and the individual relative to other students in the nation.

Criterion-Referenced Tests

Criterion-referenced tests provide a means for comparison of each person's level of performance with a specific criterion. Scores are not compared between students. A person's raw score (number correct) is compared only to the criterion and indicates whether or not the student has successfully mastered a particular learning objective. The mastery criterion is specified before the test is administered and is expressed as a statement of the acceptable level of performance. Such a criterion might be that a student will correctly solve 80 percent of the problems without assistance.

Criterion-referenced tests are particularly useful for identifying exactly what the student can and cannot do. They can be used whenever performance can be broken down and defined in specific objectives. Criterion-referenced tests work well for a number of cognitive, affective, and psychomotor objectives and are useful for determining which students should be grouped together for instructional purposes and whether students have met prerequisite objectives.

One problem with criterion-referenced tests is determining an appropriate mastery criterion. Sometimes the criterion is assigned arbitrarily. Criterion-referenced tests indicate which students can and cannot perform a given objective without specifying which of the passing students performed the best and which of the failing students performed the worst.

Driver's license exams can be considered mastery tests because one must obtain a certain score on a written test, a vision test, and a driving test before a license will be awarded. The examinee has to demonstrate a specific level of competence in knowledge and skill (and visual acuity) to earn a driver's license. Minimum-competency exams are another common criterion-referenced test.   Examinees must demonstrate a specific level of competence in the area being tested.

Group Tests

Group tests are given to several students at the same time. They are very cost-effective and can usually be scored quickly. Test administration is usually a standardized process that does not require a highly trained administrator. Group tests do not provide very much information about the test environment, special circumstances, and other potentially relevant information. Most achievement tests used today are group tests. For example, the Scholastic Aptitude Test is generally administered to a large group of students simultaneously.

Individual Tests

Individual tests are administered to one student at a time. Experienced test administrators can learn interesting details about a student's test-taking style and motivation that cannot be learned from group tests. However, individual tests are relatively expensive to administer and the test score can be greatly influenced by the test administrator and the amount of rapport established between that person and the student. Although group intelligence tests exist, the most common intelligence tests, the Stanford-Binet and the Wechsler Intelligence Scale for Children (WISC), are administered to one individual at a time.

Types of Tests

Achievement Tests

Achievement tests measure how much students have learned in a particular area, such as mathematics, reading comprehension, science, and social studies. Achievement tests are the most common type of standardized test. Several standardized, norm-referenced achievement tests are used in schools today. Examples of group tests are the California Achievement Test (CAT), the Comprehensive Test of Basic Skills (CTBS), the Iowa Test of Basic Skills, the Metropolitan Achievement Test, the SRA Achievement Series, and the Stanford Achievement Test. Examples of individually administered tests are the Wide-Range Achievement Test (WRAT) and the Peabody Individual Achievement Test.

Aptitude Tests

Aptitude tests measure abilities that have been acquired over a long period of time and indicate how well a student is expected to perform in a particular area. Although both achievement tests and aptitude tests measure ability, only aptitude tests are additionally used to predict performance in the future. The intelligence test is probably the best-known aptitude test. This kind of test is discussed in detail in Chapter 10. Another well-known aptitude test is the Scholastic Aptitude Test (SAT), used by college-entrance examiners to predict which students will be successful in college. Vocational-aptitude tests, such as the

Differential Aptitude Test (DAT), are used to measure aptitudes that predict success in various careers. Students take the DAT to determine whether they have the aptitude needed for a career they want to pursue.

Vocational Interest Tests

Vocational interest tests (often called interest inventories) measure career areas in which students might be interested. Typically these tests provide a list of activities (such as reading horror stories, nonfiction, or romances) and ask students to indicate which activities they would most and least prefer. The students' patterns of responses are compared with responses from people working in each career area. These results indicate areas of interest, not ability. Test results from interest inventories should be interpreted with great caution and should not be the sole criterion for choosing a career.

Diagnostic Tests

Diagnostic tests, which measure particular strengths and weaknesses in a student's learning process, are designed to identify problems a student has perceiving, processing, and expressing information. These tests are generally administered at the elementary-school level when a learning problem is indicated. Among other things, diagnostic tests measure how well a student can distinguish sounds, coordinate eye and hand movements, remember words, and distinguish between the foreground and the background in a picture. These tests are usually administered on an individual basis. Common diagnostic tests for diagnosing problems in a variety of areas are the Detroit Test of Learning Aptitude and Part I of the Woodcock-Johnson Psycho- Educational Battery: Tests of Cognitive Ability. Common diagnostic tests used for diagnosing problems in specific domains are the Frostig Developmental Test of Visual Perception and the Wepman Auditory Discrimination Test.

Competence Tests

Competence tests (sometimes called *minimum-competence tests*) are usually criterion-referenced tests used to determine whether students have mastered a designated set of basic skills, for example, reading at sixth grade level, writing a paragraph concisely, and showing proficiency in the four basic mathematical operations. Some school districts have implemented competence testing and require students to pass a test to qualify for graduation from high school or to move from one grade to another. One initial reason for implementing competence testing was a concern over the large number of functionally illiterate teenagers. Today, researchers disagree regarding the potential impact of competence testing.

Truth in Testing

Several organizations have lobbied to make testing procedures more available to the public. Supporters of this truth-in- testing movement want the public to be able to access more information about nationwide tests, such as reliability, validity, and development information. They have also requested that correct answers be made available to persons who have completed a test to enable examinees to verify their test scores. However, providing correct answers increases expenses associated with maintaining reliability and validity of the test because the material must be frequently updated (new items must be added continuously).

New York State passed a truth-in-testing law in 1980 that is applicable to admission tests to most college and professional schools.

Administering Tests

There are several things you can do while administering tests to help ensure the validity and reliability of standardized tests and to increase the likelihood that students will perform their best on all tests.

1. *Know how to administer the test.* Read the instructor's manual before administering the test. Practice giving the test. Be sure to follow instructions, especially time limits.

2. *Make sure that students know how to take the test.* Before administering the test have students practice answering questions in a similar format and marking answer sheets. Instruct students whether they should guess on questions they are unsure about (on the basis of scoring penalties for incorrect answers).

3. *Help students be comfortable during the test.* Tell them an

anecdote or joke just before the test to help relieve some of the tension. Explain that it is important for students to try their best, but do not make it seem that the test is the most important event in the world.

4. *Monitor students during the test.* Be available to answer questions (appropriately), consider restroom breaks, watch (unobtrusively) for cheating, and try to minimize distractions and noise during the test.

5. *Double-check that the test is appropriate for your students.* If several students have similar problems with the test, make a note of this and discuss it with appropriate administrators at your school.

Improving Test-Taking Skills

The following ideas can be presented to students to help them improve their test-taking skills.

1. Review the material the night before the test. Notice the word *review*, not *learn*.

2. Prepare yourself for the test by coming to class well-rested and nourished (get a good night's sleep and eat a good breakfast). Allow time to get to the test without rushing.

3. Take a few minutes to look over the test.

4. Read each question carefully and read through all choices.

5. Answer the easy questions first.

6. Find out whether there is a penalty for guessing on multiple-choice questions. If so, do not guess unless you can eliminate at least one choice; if there is not a penalty, try to eliminate some of the choices and then guess. If there is not a penalty and you are about to run out of time, answer the remaining questions with the same letter.

7. Do not spend too much time pondering one question. If you are unsure, make a note and return to it later.

8. Before you complete a long essay question, briefly outline the major points. Be concise.

Effects of Coaching

In recent years there has been an increase in the advertisement and availability of test preparation courses. Some of these courses are designed specifically to train students for a particular test while other courses are designed to teach students to become better test-takers in general. Researchers have been studying the effects of these programs for many years. A few general conclusions are presented here. For a detailed summary, see Anastasi (1988).

1. There is a difference between education and coaching. Coaching is test-specific and may not carry over to environments beyond the particular test. In orther words coaching may increase test performance without affecting the underlying knowledge domain. Education, on the other hand, is more likely to influence both test performance and subsequent behavior.

2. Coaching is more likely to help students taking achievement tests rather than aptitude tests.

3. Coaching is more likely to help persons with deficit educational backgrounds rather than persons who are already familiar with testing procedures.

4. The amount of test score gain due to coaching is a function of the specificity of the coaching; the greatest gains occur when the preparatory questions are highly similar to the real test questions.

5. Some intensive coaching programs do not produce any increase beyond what students would be expected to achieve after a year of regular classroom instruction. In other words a year of regular classroom instruction can provide the same gain as the intensive coaching programs.

6. A potential value of coaching is to narrow some differences between experienced and inexperienced test-takers by teaching the less experienced what to expect and how to approach the test.

Developing Your Own Tests

Although published tests are generally useful instruments, designed to cover various subject areas comprehensively, at times these tests may be too expensive to administer to a large group, may not measure certain instructional objectives specifically covered in your class, may not be available, or may require specific administration procedures that you cannot provide, and so on. Teacher-developed tests can provide especially useful information because they can be designed to measure specific instructional objectives. There are three basic steps to constructing your own tests: (1) determine which instructional objectives should be measured, (2) determine which type of question is most appropriate for each objective and write the test questions, and (3) ensure that the test is valid and reliable. These steps are discussed below in more detail.

Determining Instructional Objectives

Before constructing your test, determine which instructional objectives should be covered and what type of learning (i.e., knowledge, comprehension, application, analysis, synthesis, evaluation) should be measured for each objective. Ideally, the teacher makes these decisions while planning lessons. A *table of specifications* can be used to list the main topics (or instructional objectives, if you want more detail) and the skill levels to be tested. Each cell in the table specifies the number of test items that should be created for each topic at a given skill level. As specified in the sample table shown as Table 11.3, which is based on topics from this chaper, four test items will be written to measure knowledge about types of evaluation. The teacher should determine the number of test items on the basis of the importance of the topic and the amount of time allocated to cover it. The most important topics and those requiring the most teaching time should receive the most number of test items. Developing a table of specifications compels the teacher to consider the relative importance of each topic and to identify what type of learning is appropriate for each. Additionally, the completed table of specifications is a great test-development tool. The teacher

Table 11.3

Example of Table of Specifications for Topics in Chapter 11					
Topic	Know-ledge	Com-prehen-sion	Ap-plica-tion	Syn-thesis	Total
Chapter concepts	3				3
Measurement con-cepts		10			10
Types of measures	3		5		8
Types of scores	5		5		10
Types of tests	5		5		10
Administering tests			2		2
Test-taking skills		2			2
Developing tests	5			5	10
Alternatives to tests			5		5
Teacher-assigned grades	2				2
Types of evaluation	4				4
Professional ethics			1		1

refers to the table to determine how many questions at each skill level should be developed.

The table of specifications discussed here should not be confused with the behavior content matrix discussed in Chapter 7. The behavior content matrix identifies the specific objectives and desired skill level for a topic or course; the table of specifications identifies the number of test items that should be created for each topic at each skill level.

Determining Type of Question

To determine which types of question are most appropriate, first decide whether an objective test or a subjective test is needed.

Objective tests use true-false, multiple-choice, completion items, and matching. Scoring is straightforward and, for the most part, not open to interpretation. Correct answers are predefined and usually unambiguous. Different persons scoring the same objective test will most likely assign the same scores.

Subjective tests allow the student to elaborate on ideas, thoughts, and responses to a question, thus providing the teacher with more information regarding the student's level of knowledge. Scoring subjective tests generally requires more time and thought than does scoring objective tests. Correct answers are less well defined and subject to interpretation. Different persons scoring the same subjective test may assign different scores.

While writing the test items, the teacher should utilize vocabulary and sentence structure appropriate for the students who will take the test.

True-False Tests

True-false items require students to validate statements. Typically, students evaluate individual sentences as accurate (true) or inaccurate (false). True-false items are used primarily to measure recall of facts but can also be designed to measure higher-level skills, such as the ability to evaluate information. They are also useful for testing students' ability to make comparisons between two items or events (which is more important, larger, etc.). Because true-false items can be read and answered quickly, they can be used to measure learning over many objectives. You may want to use true-false questions if it becomes difficult to generate plausible alternatives to multiple-choice questions.

True-false questions are fairly easy to construct and score. Additionally, they can be scored reliably, because no interpretation is necessary. To help ensure the reliability of scoring, have students write in the words "true" and "false" or circle either word on an answer sheet. Scoring items can be a little more difficult if students write in only "T" or "F," due to individual differences in writing style, and it is easy for students to modify these letters when they receive their scored tests (and then say, "but Ms. Smith, I got this question right and you marked it wrong"). Because there are two responses to each true-false item (true and false), there is a 50 percent probability that the student will guess the item correctly by random chance. Discuss test results with any student whose score falls below 50 percent on a true-false test. Try to determine whether the student was not feeling well, was unmotivated, filled out the answer sheet incorrectly, or did not understand directions.

Use the following guidelines when constructing true-false items:

1. Do not use phrases directly from a textbook or other material presented to students. Students might respond to familiarity with the phrase instead of an understanding of the material. Rephrase the questions. Whenever possible, write questions that cause students to think (apply or synthesize material), not merely rely on memory of facts. For example, suppose you were creating a true-false question to test knowledge of information in this paragraph. You could use the first guideline verbatim as a question, i.e., "Do not use phrases directly from a text or other material presented to students." (True.) However, a better question (from a test-construction perspective) would be a paraphrase of that information instead of the verbatim sentence, such as "Well-designed true-false tests include items that require students to think." (True.)

2. Do not use vague, general expressions and no-exception words, such as "all," "always," and "never." These expressions suggest that the item is probably false, and thus students might answer the item correctly without knowing the material. For example, "All true-false questions are easy to write. (False.)" is a poor question because almost anyone could guess the correct answer.

3. Use statements that are unquestionably true or false. For example, "Cancer is caused by cigarettes" may be true in certain cases, but cancer is also caused by other events. A knowledgeable student would find this question ambiguous. Better wording would be "Smoking is one cause of lung cancer."

4. Try not to use negatively worded questions because they result in greater errors and take more time to answer.

5. Try to use an equal number of true and false questions. A student

who notices that most answers are true may develop a response bias and be more inclined to respond "true" when the answer is unkown.

6. Present only one idea in each statement.

Examples of true-false questions are as follows:

1. True-false questions can measure only recall of facts. (False.)

2. True-false items are an efficient way to assess learning of many objectives. (True.)

3. To have students make comparisons, true-false questions are better than fill-in-the-blank questions. (True.)

Multiple-Choice Tests

Multiple-choice items include a partial statement or question (called the "stem") and several response choices. The response choices include incorrect alternatives (known as "distractors") and a correct choice (known as the "target"). Sometimes more than one correct choice can be designated. Multiple-choice items require students to differentiate between correct choices and distractors. They to do not have to generate the answer. Several researchers have tried to determine the optimum number of distractors (e.g., Lord, 1977), but results have not been conclusive. The optimum number of choices seems to be a function of several variables, including reliability desired, test length, and student ability level. Typically, three or four choices (including the target) are used. With more than four choices, reliability of the test decreases; with fewer than three choices, students are more likely to guess the correct response without understanding the material. One of the most important aspects of developing effective multiple-choice items is to create plausible distractors. Another important aspect in question development is to include relevant information in the partial statements. For example, the stem "Multiple-choice questions are" is not informative and open to many interpretations. A better stem would be "When compared to true-false questions, multiple choice questions are."

Multiple-choice items can be used to measure learning across many subjects and skill levels, from recognition of facts to application of principles.

Use the following guidelines to construct multiple-choice items:

1. Rather than repeat the same words in each choice, include those words only once in the stem.

2. Use parallel syntax for each choice and ensure that all choices are grammatically correct. Distractors should look similar to the target.

3. Do not use global expressions and no-exception words, such as "all," "always," and "never." These expressions clue the student that the item is probably false; therefore, students can answer the item correctly without knowing the material.

4. Do not make the target the longest or shortest choice.

5. Be careful about including "all the above" as a choice. If students can identify one choice as a distractor, then they can eliminate "all the above" also.

6. Use three or four choices (including the target).

7. Do not use one letter position more than others for the correct choice. The correct choice should appear at positions a, b, c, and d an equal number of times (approximately) on the test.

8. Avoid using negative terminology (e.g., "no," "not," and "except") in the stem because it can be confusing. If you must use negative words, highlight them by underlining or capitalizing.

9. As mentioned previously, use plausible distractors. The distractors should be related to the question.

10. Do not include irrelevant information in the stem.

11. Make each item independent of the other items (i.e., do not include the answer to one question in a previous question).

12. Check stems to make sure the grammar will not help students eliminate alternatives.

Examples of multiple-choice questions are as follows:

1. Incorrect alternatives on multiple-choice questions are known as

   a. Deterrents

   b. Distractors

   c. Targets

   d. Choices

(The correct answer is b—distractors. In this example, the stem is a partial statement.)

2. When you develop multiple-choice questions, why should you use at least three choices ?

   a. To provide plausible alternatives

   b. To increase the chance of a correct guess

   c. To reduce the chance of a correct guess

   d. To maximize reliability

(The correct answer is c—to reduce the chance of a correct guess. In this example, the stem is a question.)

3. A z score of –2 is equal to a percentile rank of approximately 4, assuming that which of the following conditions is true:

   a. The mean of all the test scores is 50.

   b. Stanine scores are not assigned.

   c. The assigned test scores are 0 to 100.

   d. The test scores are normally distributed.

(The correct answer is d—the test scores are normally distributed. In this example, the student must think about the item and apply knowledge to determine the correct answer. This item measures higher-level learning, not recognition of facts.

Completion Tests

Completion items (also called *fill-in-the-blank items*) require students to add information to incomplete statements. Typically, there is only one correct answer. Like true-false and multiple-choice items, they can be read and answered quickly, and therefore, used to measure learning covering many objectives. Unlike multiple-choice and true-false items, however, completion items do not give the student a chance to recognize the correct answer. The student must generate the correct answer or an acceptable alternative. Completion items are usually fairly easy to construct. They require a little more time to score than do true-false and multiple-choice items because the teacher must generate a list of acceptable responses in addition to reading each student response. There will be times when the teacher expects one particular word, but the student provides an alternative that may be acceptable. Reliability in scoring is generally high because minimal interpretation is necessary.

When constructing the test, specify the correct answers, including all acceptable alternatives. Before grading the test, scan through the test papers for acceptable answers that were not originally considered and add these to the key (list of correct answers). Then, as the papers are graded, you will be able to identify and count all acceptable answers as correct responses.

Use the following guidelines when constructing completion items:

1. Do not use phrases directly from a text or other material presented to students. Students might answer correctly because they memorized the phrase or term rather than understood the material. Rephrase each statement. Write each statement so that students must think about it (apply or synthesize material), not merely recall facts. For example, *instead of* "Unlike multiple-choice and true-false items, completion items do not give the student a chance to _____ the correct answer" (recognize), *use* "One reason multiple-choice items can be easier to answer than completion items is that the student is only required to _____ the correct answer in a multiple-choice item." (recognize).

2. Provide enough clues so that the student knows what kind of information to provide. Avoid ambiguity. For example, *instead of* "William James died in _____" (Is the student expected to give the date or the place of death?), *use* "William James died in the year _____" (1910).

3. Generally use only one or two blank spaces to minimize ambiguity and misinterpretation.

4. Place the blank space at the end of the sentence so the sentence provides clues before the problem is presented.

5. Avoid grammatical clues.

Examples of completion items are as follows:

1. Completion items, which require students to supply missing information, are also called _____ items. (fill-in-the-blank)

2. To have students make comparisons, _____ items are better than completion items. (true-false)

Matching Tests

Matching items require students to choose statements from one list or column that correspond to (i.e., match) statements from another list or column. Matching items are used primarily to measure recall of facts or concepts. Matching items are effective for assessment of a student's understanding of the interrelationships of several concepts. Items can be scored reliably because minimal or no interpretation is necessary. However, the test can be slightly difficult to score if the students draw lines between items in each list or column. Preferably, assign a letter to each item in the first list or column (list 1) and a letter to each item in the second list or column (list 2). Then ask the students to write the appropriate letter of the item in list 2 next to the item in list 1 that it matches.

Use the following guidelines when constructing matching items:

1. Use more items in list 2 than in list 1. If you use the same number of items, then the last pair can be determined by default (chance), because only one item in each list remains. Also, a student who is confused about one item and misses that pair will automatically miss a second pair.

2. Be careful about adding too many items to either list. Lists with more than six items can be confusing and time-consuming to complete. If you readily create more than six items for one question,

consider making two or more questions from your original question and divide the items between the questions.

3. Specify whether students can match an item in list 2 with more than one item in list 1.

4. Provide instructions that specifically state the basis for matching items.

An example of a matching item might be:
"Match the muscle type on the right with the characteristics on the left. More than one muscle type should be assigned for some of the characteristics."

	Characteristics	Muscle Type
a	multiple nuclei in each motor unit	a. skeletal
b, c	one nucleus per motor unit	b. smooth
a, c	striations present	c. cardiac
b	striations absent	
a	voluntary	
b, c	involuntary	

Essay Questions

Essay questions require students to elaborate on a specified question or statement. Short essay questions may be answered in one paragraph. Other essay questions are designed for answers that require a page or two. Essay questions can be used to assess a student's understanding of important terms; ability to compare and contrast events, items, or concepts; and ability to describe relative advantages and disadvantages of different approaches, procedures, and policies. Essay questions provide an effective means of measuring attainment of higher-level skills, such as the ability to evaluate and synthesize information. Additionally, they can be used to measure creative ability, unique approaches to problems, and imagination, which objective tests (multiple-choice, true-false, fill-in-the-blank, and matching) are not designed to measure. An additional advantage of essay tests is that students cannot provide answers based on recognition of available information because the answers are not provided.

Essay questions are fairly easy to develop, but scoring them can be time-consuming. Because of the subjective scoring procedure usually implemented, the reliability of scores on essay tests is lower than that of objective tests. *Interrater reliability* is particularly low; two teachers scoring the same response are likely to assign different scores. To help increase the reliability of scoring, write down an outline of the optimal answer before you begin grading the tests. Specify information that is required for a good answer and list other information that is optional. Identify how points can be lost. Specify how many points will be gained or lost. When you receive the essays, scan through them thinking about the outline you created. As you scan the essays you may think of other points that should be added to your outline or may notice that none of the student papers mention a particular piece of information that you considered important. Once you have revised your outline as needed, you are ready to score the students' responses. Another potential problem with essay items is that a student's relative ability to organize information and write clearly will influence how difficult the item is to answer (irrespective of how well the student understands the material) and to score. Because answering essay questions is more time-consuming than answering objective questions, they may not be the most efficient way to assess factual learning. Use essay questions when you need to assess higher-level learning or creative abilities.

Use the following guidelines when constructing essay items:

1. Specify how much detail is expected and approximately how long the answer should be. Do not write "Discuss test construction." A better statement is: "In a 100- to 200-word essay, describe four types of objective test items. Include the advantages of each type and specify in general terms the expected reliability of each type." Be sure to indicate whether you are imposing a time limit and if so, specify (10 minutes, 20 minutes, 1 hour, etc.). For timed tests, keep students posted. At regular intervals (e.g., every 15 or 30 minutes) write on the board the amount of time remaining.

2. Write out an optimal answer to each essay item and scan the students' responses before scoring them. Time yourself when you

write the answer. Most students will need three or four times longer than you needed to answer the question. Be sure to allow students that amount of time.

3. Decide before the test is given whether you will deduct points for spelling and grammatical errors and inform the students. If you deduct for mechanical errors (as opposed to content errors), indicate to the students how many points were lost for this reason.

4. Write students' names on the back of the paper, or write identification numbers on the front. This procedure helps minimize grading bias due to teacher expectations.

Examples of essay items are as follows:

1. In 50 words or less, explain two problems with scoring essay questions. (Six-point question.)

Teacher's outline:

1. Interrater reliability is low, so write down expected answers ahead of time. (Up to 3 points credit.)

2. Writing ability and technical errors are factors. (Up to 3 points credit.)

3. It can take a long time to score (Okay, but not the best answer. One point credit.)

4. Take off up to 1 point for technical errors.

2. When scoring essay questions, it can be difficult to distinguish between student's writing ability and knowledge of the content. Imagine that you teach a fifth-grade social studies class. Using 100 to 150 words, explain how you would handle this problem. (15-point question.)

Teacher's outline:

1. Add 5 points for each creative, reasonable idea. Possible ideas include, but are not limited to, use of oral tests, giving unlimited time in class, and allowing students to complete for homework.

2. Add 3 points for "do not count off for technical errors." It is correct, but not original because it was mentioned in class lecture.

Checking Test Validity

After choosing the type of question and writing the test items, try to determine whether the test is valid and reliable. Validity and reliability are important for teacher-made tests as well as published tests. Any useful performance measure will be an accurate and consistent indicator of performance. Most likely, you will not determine the validity and reliability statistically as the test publishers do, but you can conduct informal evaluations.

There are many ways for you to check the validity and reliability of your tests. Consider giving the test to a few students. Find out how much time the students need to complete it and whether they misunderstood or misinterpreted any of the questions. Additionally, have other teachers review the test to determine whether it appears to measure what it is intended to measure. Use a table of specifications to ensure the test covers all appropriate instructional objectives and emphasizes the most important ones.

After giving the test, compare student scores with other indicators (e.g., homework, in-class discussions, special projects, previous grades). If several students did a good job on homework assignments but scored poorly on a related test, you should review the test results to determine where the discrepancies occurred. Perhaps the test covered material that the students had not studied, the questions on the test were confusing, more instruction is needed, or the students were not motivated. If the test requires modification, make needed changes. You may need to eliminate, reword, or reformat some of the questions, or add other questions. This test-development process allows you to have confidence that the performance measures you obtain are true (valid), reliable indicators of learning. Once the tests are scored, check how the scores are distributed. For most tests, scores should approach a normal distribution (unless it is a criterion-referenced test). The majority of scores should fall near the middle of the distribution. If most students score an A, the test was too easy. If most students score an F, the test was too difficult and should be modified. Additional instruction is probably warranted. If you developed a criterion-referenced test, the normal distribution is not applicable. This type of evaluation procedure is discussed in more detail in the next section.

Alternatives to Tests

The focus of this chapter has been the utility of testing for evaluating student performance. Both teacher-made tests and professionally developed, published tests are valuable evaluation instruments. However, testing is not the only means of measuring performance or evaluating students. In fact, there are many times when testing is not an efficient or appropriate data collection procedure. Behavioral measures, such as excessive talking, trips to the pencil sharpener, change in study habits, and time spent reading are difficult to directly measure using tests. There are several alternative evaluation procedures.

Self-Evaluation

Self-evaluation allows students to determine (or at least have some input concerning) the grade that is assigned. Self-evaluation may be used alone or in combination with peer or teacher evaluations. Before students make their evaluations, give them some guidelines. Let them know what kind of performance grade A work is. Be sure they understand your expectations. For example, to evaluate a group project, tell students that factors contributing to the self-evaluation should be how helpful one was to other students, how much responsibility one assumed, and how available one was. The advantage to self-evaluations is that they allow students to feel that they have some control or voice in the grading process. One problem, however, is that some students may overrate their performance. If the teacher disagrees with the self-evaluation, some discussion may be needed. Especially when evaluating performance in group activities, you may learn that a student contributed more work behind the scenes than you realized. For example, a student who spent 8 hours doing library research may not be highly visible, but did make a significant contribution to the team. Also students may evaluate themselves according to criteria that you do not consider relevant or important. For example, Ruth spent 8 hours collecting costumes instead of working with team members. Ruth might consider collecting costumes a significant contribution, but you might not. If you do not agree with Ruth's self-evaluation, give her a chance to justify the evaluation. You can use the discussion to learn more about Ruth's contribution and performance and to reiterate your expectations. Self-evaluations are most equitably used in conjunction with other evaluations.

Contracting

Contracting is used to specify the quality and quantity of work that must be produced. Students contract for a particular grade. When they do, they agree to the required work. For example: To receive an A, the student will attend class regularly, read three chapters, complete three homework exercises, and complete a special project. To receive a B, the student will attend class regularly, read three chapters, and complete three homework exercises. To receive a C, the student will attend class regularly, read two chapters, and complete two homework exercises. To receive a D, the student must read at least one chapter and complete one homework exercise. A student who does not turn in at least one homework assignment will receive an F. One advantage to contracting is reduced anxiety concerning grades. Students know that when the required work is completed (with reasonable quality), then the specified grade will be awarded. One difficult aspect of contracting is determining and communicating to students the quality of work that is expected.

Pass/Fail Approach

A pass/fail or credit/no credit approach is used to encourage learning without the pressure of earning specific grades. Students may still take tests, but the grades are not as important as in a traditional grading system. Any grade average above a D is considered passing or credit. The teacher should be very specific about course requirements, even though a grade is not assigned. For example, if the teacher expects students to attend all lectures, take all exams, hand in homework, and so on, the students should be informed and understand the consequences if they do not. The pass/fail system can be an incentive for students to try courses in subjects that are unfamiliar to them, without risk of failure. Some students are more relaxed with pass/fail grading than letter grade assignments. However, most students perform better when they work for letter grades.

Mastery Approach

The mastery approach is used when most students are expected to meet or exceed a predetermined criterion for a set of objectives. Advocates of this approach believe that given appropriate instruction, most students will master most objectives. Therefore, the normal distribution is inappropriate. Each objective is taught until most students master it. Students do not receive further instruction until they meet criteria at the present skill level. One advantage of the mastery approach is the emphasis on success. All students are expected to be successful, and the instruction is designed to facilitate success because it is presented one objective at a time. However, some students will require more instruction and more time per objective. Maintaining momentum and keeping advanced students from becoming bored and impatient with the slower students can be difficult. This topic is discussed in further detail in Chapter 9.

Classroom Observation

Classroom observation provides information that cannot be assessed on a test. You can observe students' work habits, such as perseverance and frustration level, and behavior problems, such as disruptive conduct. This information can be especially valuable to students who are performing below average. For example, Ben scores poorly on a math test. You observe that he is spending most of the math period talking with a classmate rather than completing math exercises. You discuss this problem with Ben and point out the possible relationship between the talking behavior and the low test grade. You discuss the possibility of moving him to a new location in the classroom.

Consider another example. You observe Michael becoming increasingly frustrated during math exercises. You notice that Melinda has finished the assignment already. After quickly reviewing Melinda's work to make sure that she understands the concepts, you ask her to work with Michael. A few minutes later, Michael is back on track.

Especially when assignments are difficult for students, it is helpful for the teacher to comment on positive work habits. For example, social science projects are particularly difficult for Cynthia. She works very hard to earn a C. However, on a group activity, you observe that Cynthia helps everyone in the group feel at ease and work together. When you evaluate Cynthia's contribution to the social studies project, you assign two grades, one for content and another for effort. You encourage Cynthia to continue working hard in social science and you identify areas of improvement, but you also acknowledge the effort she devoted to the project and her contribution to the effectiveness of the team.

Other Evaluation Sources

Classroom and take-home projects are other sources of evaluation. Homework assignments, special projects, in-class exercises, and participation in class discussion should be averaged with test scores to evaluate student performance. Students should know how important each of these evaluation sources is to the final grade.

Teacher-Assigned Grades

Guidelines

For many students and parents, grades are the bottom-line indicator of performance. Your grading system is important. Use the following guidelines in your grading system:

1. *Make sure students understand the system.* Tell them how much emphasis is placed on tests, homework assignments, in-class participation, and so on. After assigning grades, spend time discussing them with each student. Student-teacher conferences and (or) parent-teacher conferences are important in the evaluation process. Parents and students need to understand how grades are assigned and the student's academic strengths and weaknesses. Parents and students can also provide feedback about your grading system. Ask them

whether it is helpful to them and whether they would like to have further information.

2. *Include both objective and subjective evaluation tools to determine grades.* Tests provide important, objective indicators of performance, but they do not indicate a student's full range of interests and abilities. Include your classroom observations, student effort, student improvement, and classwork as you calculate the final grade. Be able to identify strengths and weaknesses for each student.

3. *Try to avoid bias in grading.* Establish criteria before assigning grades. What kind of performance deserves an A, a B, and so forth? For example, will in-class tests carry more weight than homework assignments? How important is attitude? How important are daily quizzes? The relative importance of each factor should be determined before grades are assigned and should be implemented similarly for all students.

4. *Inform students of their relative rank or position in the class distribution.* Show them how the grades were distributed; if you do not, they will probably try to figure it out, anyway.

5. *Be careful how you decide when to change grades.* If students expect that you are willing to change grades, they will ask. You should be willing to change grades if you made a miscalculation or other mechanical error. If a large number of students miss a question on a test, do not count that question in the final grade. Also, remember to change the question before using the test again.

Absolute and Relative Standards

You can assign grades on the basis of either an absolute or a relative standard (the grading curve).

An *absolute standard* means that a given grade is established by predetermined percentage scores. A common absolute standard is shown in Table 11.4. Criterion-referenced grading can also be based on an absolute standard. For an example, see Table 11.5.

A *relative standard* means that grades are assigned by class rank, that is, students are graded on the curve. A certain percentage of

Table 11.4

| Example of Absolute Standard for Grading ||
Grade	% Correct
A	90-100
B	80-89
C	70-79
D	60-69
F	< 60

Table 11.5

| Example of Absolute Standard for Criterion-Referenced Grading ||
Grade	Criteria
Excellent	20 math problems correct in 10 minutes, no help
Above average	18 math problems correct in 15 minutes, no help
Average	15 math problems correct in 20 minutes, 1 help
Below average	12 math problems correct in 25 minutes, 3 help
No mastery	10 math problems correct in 30 minutes, 4 help

students will receive A's, a certain percentage will receive B's, and so on. The top scorers will receive A's, the next highest scorers will receive B's, and so forth. The teacher decides what percentage of students will receive each grade. This grading system tends to create competition between students because they are vying for a limited number of good grades. Students also feel as if they have minimal or no control over their grades when this system is used because even if they answer most of the questions correctly, they may not earn an A because there are only a few A's available for that class. A common relative standard is shown in Table 11.6. For instance, if there are 30 students in the class, then the two or three highest scorers (7 percent of 30) would receive an A.

Table 11.6

Example of Relative Standard for Grading		
Grade	Percent of Students	Number of Students (if 30 students in class)
A	7	2-3
B	24	7-8
C	38	11-12
D	24	7-8

A variation to the relative grading system is implemented by many teachers. The teachers review the distribution of obtained scores and adjust the scores to assure the correct proportion of students receive an A, a B, and so on. Students appreciate this grading system when scores are adjusted upward. One disadvantage of this system is that teachers adjust scores differently and without specific rules for implementing the adjustments. This process can be difficult to justify.

Evaluation

Evaluation plays an important role in education. Evaluation of students' skills and abilities is used to select students for special programs and to diagnose students' strengths and weaknesses. Evaluation is also used to determine the effectiveness of instruction, the usefulness of special programs or new curricula, and the mastery of certain learning objectives. Evaluation is used to report student progress to parents and is also used by guidance counselors to help students make career decisions. Another important use of student evaluation is for researchers who investigate the effectiveness of different teaching methods.

There are basically four types of evaluation that the classroom teacher can use to learn about the effectiveness of instruction and meet students' needs: formative, summative, placement, and diagnostic.

Formative Evaluation

Formative evaluation occurs during instruction. Results are used to modify the instruction to best meet the students' needs. Formative evaluation can occur through quizzes, homework, or class discussions. Formative evaluation should be used frequently but should probably not be a formal part of a student's grade because its purpose is to help tailor instruction to meet students' needs. Formative evaluations are most often teacher-made tests, but special, customized tests can be ordered from publishers. For example, a high-school biology unit covers four chapters of material. The teacher gives an in-class quiz at the end of each chapter and then reviews the test results to determine which material requires further discussion. The teacher reviews the necessary material. Each in-class quiz provides formative evaluation.

Summative Evaluation

Summative evaluation occurs after instruction. Results are used to determine how well learning objectives were met. Summative evaluation typically occurs through final exams, term papers, and class projects. The basic purpose of summative evaluation is to measure whether and how much the students learned. Continuing the example above, students subsequently take an exam on all four chapters. The score on this exam is recorded. This exam provides summative evaluation.

Placement Evaluation

Placement evaluation occurs before instruction. Results are used to match students with programs, that is, to place students in programs appropriate to their interests and abilities. Placement evaluation occurs by means of standardized tests, teacher observations, and previously administered summative evaluations. For example, before a student is placed in a class for mentally retarded students, an intelligence test will be given. A student who scores below a predefined minimum level will be placed in a special class. Another example of a placement test is the use of reading tests to determine which reading group is most appropriate for each student in a class.

Diagnostic Evaluation

Diagnostic evaluation usually occurs during instruction. Results are used to determine the academic strengths and weaknesses of the students. Diagnostic evaluation typically is determined by using standardized or teacher-made tests. Diagnostic evaluation is often used to determine why a student is having difficulty, such as difficulty in reading. This kind of evaluation might include vision tests, hearing tests, and other tests used to determine how the student approaches a reading assignment (e.g., does the student rely on pictures, sound out words, use context clues, does the student skip over unfamiliar words, etc.).

Program Evaluation

As just exemplified, evaluation is often used to describe performance for an individual student. However, to investigate the effectiveness of teaching methods, new curricula, and other variables, large-scale evaluations are conducted. Researchers conducting these evaluations assess performance of many students on several variables. Such evaluations are generally called *program evaluation* or *school evaluation*. For example, when a new curriculum is developed, formative evaluation data allow the developer to determine the effectiveness of new procedures and the clarity of new material. Evaluation results indicate areas where review or further work is needed. After the new curriculum is revised and implemented, summative evaluation can be used to determine the effectiveness of the new curriculum relative to the old curriculum on specified objectives. This evaluation data allows school administrators to identify strengths and weaknesses in school curriculum.

This information can be quite valuable. For example, on a recent achievement test Jefferson High students scored higher than any other students in their school district on reading comprehension. The principal at Jefferson High created a task force to investigate this finding.

The task force identified three key aspects of the reading program at Jefferson that were believed to produce the high comprehension scores. Subsequently, Jefferson High reading teachers presented a summary of those three aspects to other reading teachers in the school district. The reading teachers at other schools plan to implement those three aspects. The hoped-for result is that next year's reading comprehension scores will be high across the school district.

Program evaluations are conducted to determine the effectiveness of many special programs, such as open education and computer- aided instruction. School evaluations are conducted to determine the effectiveness of diferent types of schools, for instance public versus private schools.

Professional Ethics

A presentation of measurement, testing, and evaluation is not complete without attention to professional ethics. "Ethical Principles of Psychologists," published in 1981 in the *American Psychologist*, discusses the ethical distribution and use of psychological tests in detail. A few key points are itemized:

1. Published tests must be purchased, administered, and interpreted by appropriately trained personnel. The amount and type of training depends on the test. This requirement is intended to protect individuals against the improper use of test results.

2. The examinee should be told the purpose of the test and how the results will be used.

3. The test results cannot be distributed without the examinee's consent.

4. Test results should be communicated to the examinee in understandable, lay terms.

Student performance is evaluated to select students for special programs, diagnose academic and perceptual problem areas, and determine effectiveness of instruction and mastery of learning objectives. Different types of evaluation occur before, during, and after instruction.

Standardized tests, one method of evaluation, are constructed by profes-
sional test developers, generally printed by publishing companies, and
require standard administration and scoring procedures. Some stand-
ardized tests can pose disadvantages for minority students, such as
cultural or language barriers. Standardized scores are used to com-
pare performance across students and tests. The mean is a measure of
central tendency, describing how the students performed on a test
overall. A measure that is particularly important when interpreting
scores is the standard deviation, which indicates the degree of
variability in student performance on the test. Teacher-made tests are
also developed and used to measure classroom learning. Many dif-
ferent types of tests can be developed by teachers or professional test
publishers. Norm-referenced tests provide a basis for comparison of
performance between students. Criterion-referenced tests measure
performance against a predefined criterion. Two major types of test are
achievement and aptitude tests. Achievement tests measure how much
learning has occurred, while aptitude tests measure the potential for
learning a particular area.

For any test to be useful, it must be valid and reliable. A valid test
measures what it purports to measure. A reliable test provides consis-
tent results from one occasion to another.

When administering tests, it is important to be familiar with the
instructions, help the students feel comfortable, and be available to
answer questions during the test.

Recommended Reading

Anastasi, A. (1988). *Psychological Testing* (5th ed.). New York: Macmillan. (Excellent source for in-depth discussion of basic measurement concepts.)

Bond, L. and Glaser, R. (Eds.). Testing: Concepts, Policy, Practice, and Research *American Psychologist*. (October, 1981). (A special issue on testing which covers test bias, coaching, professional ethics, and other topics.)

Mitchell, J. V., Jr., (Ed.). (1985). *Ninth Mental Measurements Yearbook.* Lincoln, Nebr.: University of Nebraska Press. (Critical reviews by professionals of all commercially published tests in English.)

Mitchell, J. V., Jr., (Ed.). (1983). *Tests in Print III.* Lincoln, Nebr.: University of Nebraska Press. (An index to tests, test reviews, and literature on specific tests.)

Gronlund, N. E. (1985). *Measurement and Evaluation in Teaching* (5th ed.). New York: Macmillan. (Another good source for more discussion of basic measurement concepts.)

Krug, S., (Ed.). (1987). *Psychware Sourcebook*, (2d ed.). Champaign, Ill.: MeriTech. (A reference guide to computer-based products for educational and psychological assessment.)

Lyman, H. B. (1986). *Test Scores and What They Mean*, (4th ed.). Englewood Cliffs, N.J.: Prentice-Hall. (An easy-to-read source regarding understanding test scores.)

Millan, J., and W. Pauk. (1969). *How to Take Tests*. New York: McGraw-Hill. (Presents test-taking strategies.)

Standards for Educational and Psychological Testing. (1985). Washington, D.C.: American Psychological Association. (Presents the technical, professional, and administrative standards in testing.)

References

Anastasi, A. (1988). *Psychological Testing* (6th ed.). New York: Macmillan.

Krug, S. (Ed.). (1987). *Psychware Sourcebook* (2d ed.). Champaign, Ill.: MeriTech.

Lord, F. M. (1977). Optimal Number of Choices Per Item—a Comparison of Four Approaches *Journal of Educational Measurement*, 14, 33-38.

Mitchell, J. V., Jr. (Ed.). (1985). *Ninth Mental Measurements Yearbook*. Lincoln, Nebr.: University of Nebraska Press.

Mitchell, J. V., Jr. , ed. (1983). *Tests in Print III*. Lincoln, Neb.: University of Nebraska Press.

CHAPTER 12

Problem Solving and Creativity

Problem solving and creativity in the classroom are discussed in this chapter. Teaching students how to solve problems by applying knowledge or skills they have accrued is one of the ultimate goals of education. Traditional and current concepts in problem solving, including problem-solving techniques that can be taught to your students, are discussed in this chapter.

Creativity is a quality that each student possesses and expresses to some degree. This chapter presents current definitions of creativity and methods of measuring and encouraging creativity in students.

Problem Solving

A historical perspective and definition of problem solving within the education context, as well as strategies for enhancing or encouraging problem-solving abilities in students, are presented in this section.

Definition of Problem Solving

Problem solving involves the application of knowledge or skills to achieve a goal; in broad terms, the transfer of learning to a new situation.

Problem-solving skills are utilized whenever a person is in one situation, but wants or needs to be in another situation. Solving riddles or puzzles, finding the most direct route to a supermarket, and determining an efficient strategy for managing a task are examples of problem-solving behavior.

Research on Problem-Solving Ability: Historical Perspective

For the last nine decades educational psychologists have attempted to determine the fundamentals of problem-solving ability by studying issues such as whether solutions develop immediately or gradually and whether effective problem solving occurs only after progression through specific steps. The conclusions of several well-known educational psychologists are presented below.

Edward L. Thorndike: Trial-and-Error Process

The research of Edward Thorndike (1879-1949) was discussed briefly in Chapter 1. In some of his most famous experiments, Thorndike (1911) placed hungry cats in puzzle boxes with food ouside. The boxes were "puzzles" because the cats had to figure out how to pull out a bolt to get out. Because the cats were hungry and could not get at the food, they were in a problem-solving situation. Thorndike observed the behavior of the cats and recorded it in detail. At first the cats took a long time to open the box, and they appeared to do it only accidentally. When the cats were put back in the boxes time after time, they opened the box more quickly and went to the food. Eventually, when the cats were placed in the box, they would open the box and exit almost immediately. Thorndike referred to this behavior as trial-and-error learning and later argued that humans solve problems in this same manner, meaning that problem solving is incremental and does not require thinking.

John Dewey: Pragmatic Process

In the early 1900s John Dewey (1859-1952) was interested in applying aspects of psychology and education to real-world problems. This sort of interest, characteristic of the functionalists, was popular at the turn of the century. On the basis of extensive observations, Dewey (1933) determined that effective problem solving involves a basic

Important Influences on Educational Psychology		
Contribution	Place of Study	Contribution(s)
Edward Thorndike (1874-1949)	Columbia University, Teachers College	Wrote the textbook *Educational Psychology;* used controlled laboratory studies; discussed trial-and-error learning; documented the law of effect; believed problem solving is incremental and does not require thinking
John Dewey (1859-1952)	Johns Hopkins University	Believed in ecological concept; advocated learning by doing; wanted classroom to be interactive; determined that effective problem solvers follow 5 basic steps
Wolfgang Köhler (1887-1967)	Berlin	Cofounder of Gestalt psychology movement; believed problem-solving behavior was insightful, not trial-and-error
J. Paul Guilford (1897-1987)	Nebraska State University, Cornell University	Developed structure-of-intellect model; researched nature of creativity; distinguished between convergent and divergent thinking
Ellis Paul Torrance (1915-)	Mercer University, University of Minnesota	Developed several tests for assessing creativity; identified three components of creativity

five-step process. Programs designed to teach problem-solving skills often incorporate these five steps.

1. *The problem is presented.* There is no need for a problem-solving strategy if there is no problem. When there is a problem, it should be clearly presented.

2. *The problem is defined.* Problem-solving strategies stress the importance of defining the problem in as many ways as possible. Each problem definition will most likely lead to a different solution. For example, a student has searched for a summer job, but has not been hired. Has the student realistically identified potential employers? Has the student dressed appropriately and communicated a positive attitude while interviewing with potential employers? Each of these problem definitions warrants different problem-solving behaviors. In the first case the student may need to look for different kinds of employment. In the second case the student may need to continue applying for the same type of job, but devote more effort to improving appearance and interview skills.

3. *Several hypotheses are developed.* Hypotheses are alternative ways of solving the problem. Generally, the more hypotheses are generated, the more likely it is that one will solve the problem.

4. *Several hypotheses are tested.* Once the hypotheses are generated, the relative advantages and disadvantages of each hypothesis must be evaluated.

5. *The best hypothesis is chosen.* In this final step, the problem solver weighs the relative advantages and disadvantages of each hypothesis and chooses the one expected to have the greatest overall benefit.

Wolfgang Köhler: Insight Process

Wolfgang Köhler (1887-1967), a cofounder of Gestalt psychology, held ideas regarding problem solving that differed from those of Thorndike and Dewey. Köhler (1925) conducted several problem-solving experiments with apes. He placed fruit outside the normal reach of the apes, sometimes outside the cage and sometimes suspended from the cage's roof. To solve the "problem" of reaching the fruit, the apes discovered how to use poles to reach the fruit outside and to stand on boxes to reach fruit hanging from the roof. After observing this behavior, Köhler argued that problem-solving behavior is not a trial-and-error process; rather, problem-solving behavior is insightful. Apes (and people) think about the problem, consider the entire situation, and then have sudden *insight* that allows them to resolve the problem. According to Köhler's view, there are no intermediate steps in the problem-solving process.

Brief Comparison of Thorndike, Dewey, and Köhler

All three psychologists believed that the initial stage in the problem-solving process was the presentation or recognition of a problem state. Unlike Thorndike, Dewey and Köhler described a step in which hypotheses were generated or the problem was carefully deliberated. Again, unlike Thorndike, Köhler (and, to some extent, Dewey) believed that the solution was generated suddenly, during a period of insight. In contrast, Thorndike believed the solution developed over a period of several trials.

Current Approach to Problem Solving

Today, the most popular approach to problem solving utilizes an information-processing perspective. Psychologists have developed computer models of the human problem-solving process to work through a problem and develop a solution, and thereby have learned a great deal about this process.

Problem Representation

Information-processing psychologists (e.g., Bransford and Stein, 1984) stress the importance of the problem representation in the problem-solving process. To construct a problem representation, one must understand several aspects of the situation:

1. The *initial state* occurs when the problem is recognized.

2. The *intermediate state* occurs when the person begins to solve the problem. *Operators* are the actions the person can take to bring about the goal state. Some operators are governed by rules; that is, the actions one can take are sometimes limited. It is important to ascertain the limitations and to incorporate them in the problem-solving strategy.

3. The *goal state* is the outcome the person desires. Once the problem representation is developed, the solution paths can be deter-

mined. *Solution paths* connect the initial state with the goal state and are used to solve the problem. All possible paths that one considers create one's *problem space*. An individual's problem space on a given problem may include paths that do not lead to the solution, lead only to the solution path, or lead to the solution path plus other paths. Because individuals represent problems differently and create different problem spaces, different solutions to problems are generated.

Much of the research on problem solving investigates how people progress through the problem space. Because there can be so many paths to explore, it is important to utilize efficient problem-solving techniques. Researchers try to determine how different people solve problems.

Problem-Solving Methods

There are several categories of problem-solving methods. From least to most efficient, these categories are random search, heuristics, and algorithms.

Random Search

A random search is the least efficient means of problem solving because only chance determines when the correct solution, the goal state, will be reached. Random searches are conducted without any prior information or knowledge of the most expedient means of reaching the solution. Randomly looking through the pages in an educational psychology textbook for a definition of educational psychology is an example of a random-search procedure. This will probably not be an efficient way to locate the definition. The only way to improve a random search is to be systematic so as to avoid searching the same path twice.

Algorithms

Algorithms are rules guaranteed to result in the correct solution to a problem. When an algorithm can be used to solve the problem, the solution will be found in the most efficient manner. An algorithm for producing soft-boiled eggs includes the following steps: place eggs in saucepan; add water to 1 inch above eggs; heat to boiling; remove from heat; cover; let stand for 3 minutes; cool in cold water; then break shell and eat.

Heuristics

Heuristics are rules of thumb involving some application of knowledge of the problem that sometimes expedite problem solving and may lead to the correct solution. As a general rule, for example, you would expect a definition of educational psychology to appear near the beginning of the textbook. Applying that heuristic, you would search through the first few pages of the book for the definition. If the heuristic holds true, then this approach will be more efficient than the random search. As a second example, suppose that you are lost and ask someone for directions. As a general rule, the directions you receive will help you arrive at the desired location. If the directions are misleading, however, this approach is not efficient.

The methods described below are within the category of heuristics.

Difference Reduction. Difference reduction is an attempt to reduce the difference between the initial problem state and the goal state. This method generally attempts to render the problem state increasingly similar to the goal state. Often, the difference-reduction method utilizes *proximity searches* to achieve this effect. A very common proximity search is the "hot-and-cold" game where one person tries to find a hidden object. As the person gets close to the object, someone says "hotter." If the person moves away from the hidden object, someone says "colder." Using the verbal hints of hot and cold, the person is able to move closer and closer to the hidden object, the goal state.

Sometimes the difference between the problem state and goal state must be increased rather than reduced, and persons trying only to increase the similarity will not be able to achieve the goal state. Interested readers can consult Atwood and Polson (1976) for an example of this problem.

Means-Ends Analysis. In means-ends analysis, the goal state can be broken down into several problems, each of which is solved in turn, often with the use of proximity searches. The goal state is eventually reached when the final problem is solved. A classic example of means-ends analysis is the tower of Hanoi problem (Fig. 12.1).

Three posts and three rings are shown in the diagram. The three

Initial State

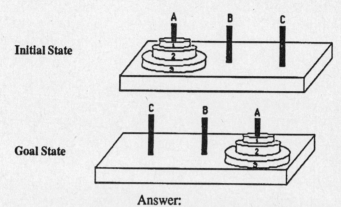

Goal State

Answer:

Move disc 1 to peg C; disc 2 to peg B; disc 1 to peg B; disc 3 to peg C; disc 1 to peg A; disc 2 to peg C; disc 1 to peg C.

Fig. 12.1 Tower of Hanoi

rings are of different sizes. The three rings should appear on the last (rightmost) post with the smallest ring on top and the largest ring on the bottom: this is the goal state. The rings can be moved to any post, but only the top ring on a post can be moved first, and a larger ring can never be placed on a smaller ring. The rings must be moved one at a time and must always be placed on a post.

To accomplish the goal state, the problem might be subdivided into several subtasks. An example of one subtask might be to get the largest ring over to the last post. It might be helpful to break that subtask into smaller problems. How many subtasks can you generate?

Working Backward. Working backward is essentially means-ends analysis in reverse, involving reasoning backward from the goal to subgoal to subgoal and finally finding a subgoal that is easy to achieve or prove. This method is often used to find mathematical proofs, such as proving that an object is a rectangle (this would be the goal) by showing that it contains congruent triangles and, therefore, parallel sides of equal length. This method often works well but may present difficulties if the subgoals are not independent of each other.

Pattern Matching. Pattern matching is an attempt to match two objects, for example, a pattern in memory and a current problem. If a match exists, then a solution that worked before might be tried on the current problem. In other words, after identifying the problem and goal states, one tries to remember a similar situation. If a similar situation is found in memory, one may apply the solution that previously worked. Chess players utilize pattern matching to determine some of their moves. They remember patterns from previous games and pictures in magazines and use those patterns when a similar problem arises.

Analogies. Analogies can be used to guide the solution of novel problems when similar problems have already been solved. A person uses the solution to a known and similar problem to guide the problem-solving process for the novel problem. If you were a physician pioneering radiation treatment to kill cancer cells, how would you approach this problem? There are many possible ways to administer the radiation treatments. Perhaps you would think of a famous battle in history. You remember that invading troops were subdivided into small groups and attacked the enemy from several locations. Although the territory on which the battle took place suffered minor damage at several locations, there was no major damage. On the basis of this analogy, you investigate the possibility of administering treatments in small doses from several locations. The success of your approach will depend to some extent on the validity of your analogy. Obviously, in a situation such as this, it is important to investigate systematically the feasibility and utility of the approach. Reasoning by analogy seems to be an important problem solving method, but few people are adept at it. One obstacle is in identifying an appropriate analogous situation.

Models. Models can be used to guide problem solving. A person will set up a model similar to the real problem and work through the solution to the model. This method is especially useful for expensive or time-consuming problem solving. Consider an architect designing a 32-story building. Rather than use building materials to test ideas, which is impractical, the architect will use paper, pencil, and small-scale design aids to experiment. The architect can show a completed model to electricians, carpenters, and clients. The model can be modified as needed, and subsequently the 32-story building can be created.

Abstraction. Abstraction can be used when a problem seems too complex to solve. Simplify the complex problem and concentrate on the solving the simpler problem. When that solution is found, an analogy may be applied to the original problem so that it can be solved. For example, to solve a six-disk tower of Hanoi problem, one might first determine a solution to a three-disk problem.

Expert versus Novice Problem Solvers

A growing area of research centers on differences between expert and novice problem solvers. Do experts employ different problem-solving methods, do they have more domain-specific knowledge (i.e., knowledge in their area of expertise), or do they organize information differently from novices? If researchers can identify the differences, there are implications for teaching novices to become better problem-solvers. Chess players, musicians, and computer programmers are typically investigated in expert-versus-novice studies.

One might expect expert chess players (chess masters) to use problem-solving methods different from those of novices, but they do not appear to do so (e.g., Chase and Simon, 1973). For common configurations, chess masters typically make quick decisions about the next move, on the basis of patterns of the pieces on the board. Novices take much longer and carefully deliberate which possible move will take them closer to the win. However, if an unusual configuration appears on the chessboard, the novice and the chess master both use a means-ends approach to determine the next move. Chess masters do not have better memory, per se, and they do not have better problem-solving strategies. What they seem to have is more domain-specific knowledge than do novices, and they have that information well organized in long-term memory, allowing them to efficiently search for solutions.

Experts are generally not born experts; most people work hard for years to achieve expertise in a given field. In addition, someone who is an expert in one field is likely to be an average performer in other fields. Some general results of the expert-versus-novice studies indicate that experts better remember information that is involved in solving the problem. For example, expert chess players remember board patterns with more pieces than novices do. They also remember the consequences of those patterns. Experts also learn to represent the problem in more abstract ways than do novices and they tend to organize the information in ways that will facilitate problem solving.

Factors Influencing Problem Solving

Several factors can influence the problem-solving process regardless of the method employed. Assuming that the problem has been well identified and defined, the following factors are important.

Representation of the Problem

Representation of the problem can significantly influence the problem-solving process. Some persons represent a problem with more detail than is needed to solve the problem; others represent only the relevant points. Some persons prefer visual representations, while others prefer auditory representations, and so on. Without accurate representation, the problem has little chance of being resolved. For example, sometimes it is important to represent problems on paper rather than holding all of the information in memory. Consider a mathematics equation with 15 steps. Even if you have the ability to solve the problem, you may not be able to do so unless you write it down.

Functional Fixedness

Functional fixedness occurs when the problem solver is determined to represent an object in its traditional way. If the problem solution depends on representation of an object in a novel way, then the problem-solving process is hampered. A classic example was presented by Maier in 1931. Among other objects, Maier presented the subjects with the following: a chair, a pair of pliers, and two strings suspended from the ceiling. The problem was to tie the two strings together. The problem is difficult because the two strings are far enough apart that the subject cannot reach both strings at the same time. Less than 40 percent of the subjects in Maier's experiment were able to solve the problem within 10 minutes. The solution was to tie the pliers to one of the suspended strings and swing that string like a pendulum. The string with the pliers would then swing close enough to the second string so both could be grasped and tied. The difficulty in solving this problem was that subjects did not think of the pliers as a weight that could be used to construct a pendulum. In other words, the subjects were fixed on representing the pliers in a traditional manner, rather than in a novel way that was needed to derive a solution.

Response Set Effects

Response set effects occur when the problem solver becomes set (i.e., determined or biased) on certain operators on the basis of previous experiences. This kind of response is also called a *set effect*. A classic example of the set effect was presented in Luchins's (1942) water-jug experiments. In these experiments, Luchins gave the subjects water jugs of various capacities and an unlimited supply of water. For example, a subject was given three jugs: *A* with a 5-cup capacity, *B* with a 40-cup capacity, and *C* with an 18-cup capacity. At the end of the experiment, the subject was to have exactly 28 cups of water. Initially the water jugs were empty and the subject could fill and empty them as many times as needed. Before reading further, try to solve this problem.

To solve the problem, the subject could fill *A* and pour it into *B*, then fill *A* again and pour it into *B*, and then fill *C* and pour it into *B*. This would provide $5 + 5 + 18$ cups = 28 cups of water. The solution was $2A + C$. Luchins demonstrated that a set effect occurs when several problems are presented each of which requires the same response solution. If you successfully solved five problems with a $2A + C$ response and then you were given a sixth problem to solve, you would most likely try the same $2A + C$ response on the sixth problem. If that sixth problem could not be solved with the $2A + C$ response, it would be difficult for you to solve it. Someone who had not seen the first five problems, and thus had not developed a response bias of $2A + C$, would most likely have an easier time than you would solving problem six. Response set effects that are interfering with effective problem solving can often be interrupted with a brief break and a reminder to look for a different kind of solution.

Response set effects can also facilitate problem solving. For example, a list of anagrams (scrambled words) that are semantically related, like parts of a car or types of pasta, can generally be solved more quickly than can a list of anagrams that are not semantically related.

Incubation Effects

Incubation effects occur when someone has worked unsuccessfully on a problem for a long time, puts it away for a few hours, days, or weeks, and on returning to the problem, finds the solution almost immediately. Incubation effects seem to be related to set effects. A person begins thinking about a solution that will not work and reaches an impasse with that line of thinking. After leaving the situation for a while, the person is able to consider alternative approaches, one of which will solve the problem. For example, while writing this book, it was difficult to think of appropriate examples to include in each section. After most of the book was written, the author thought of many examples while walking around, driving, or talking to colleagues.

Interruptions and time for a fresh look at the problem help most when a single insight is needed. Solutions of other types of problems, such as a long-division math problem, are not facilitated by an interruption. Those problems require continuous work so that the problem solver will not lose track of the process and have to begin again.

Planning

Planning is extremely important in the problem-solving process. Once the problem is recognized and clearly defined, the planning process allows you to try out different hypotheses. With minimal effort you can think through your alternatives and determine whether the strategy chosen is likely to work. Many professionals, such as architects, graphic designers, and teachers, develop plans as an integral part of the problem-solving process. Analogies and abstractions are used to develop plans.

Teaching Problem-Solving Skills

There are several things you can do to help students improve their problem-solving ability.

1. *Provide an accepting climate.* You should encourage students to view problems creatively and allow time for incubation. If students feel that their creative ideas will be carefully considered and have merit, they will be more likely to participate. Therefore, it is

important that you establish an accepting environment and be sensitive to individual differences.

2. *Teach students to carefully define the problem.* Students must understand the problem before attempting to solve it. Check that students understand the problem state, the goal state, the operators, and any restrictions on the operators. You might have students practice verbally defining problems for you.

3. *Show students how to analyze a problem.* Teach students to sort out the important and unimportant information. Have them write and think about the materials they have to work with. What specific problems are they confronted with, and how could the materials be used to solve each of those problems? In other words, what's the plan?

4. *Teach students to generate hypotheses.* Teach students to *brainstorm.* This process (Osborn, 1963) encourages two or more people to generate as many alternatives as possible without judging the value of the alternative. Judgment is suspended until another session. The emphasis is on developing creative alternatives for later review. Quantity, not quality, is important. Brainstorming is intended to prevent people from focusing on one solution prematurely.

5. *Teach students to evaluate the merits of each hypothesis.* Teach them to think through or write down the implications of several hypotheses. Show them that this process helps them determine the best hypothesis and that their first choice is not necessarily the best. The point here is to teach students not to jump to conclusions. Sometimes several hypotheses may be plausible, but one of those may generate a less costly solution. Teach students to incorporate the value of time, money, and morality in choosing a solution.

6. *Teach students about factors that influence problem solving.* Is it a response effect? Do they need to put the problem away for a while? Do they have requisite knowledge? Have they identified the key elements? Is the problem well defined? Teach students about the factors that affect problem solving. Let them know that it is normal to run into these obstacles and that they will be especially good

problem solvers when they learn to recognize and overcome these obstacles.

7. *Teach students to use analogies*. When successful solutions to similar problems exist, they can be used to reduce the number of errors and the time needed to solve a "new" problem.

8. *Give students the opportunity to practice problem solving and provide feedback*. Start a notebook of problems. You can find puzzle books and math books with problems and solutions. Check the "Recommended Reading" list at the end of this chapter for sources. You can introduce real-world problems from your own experiences and share them. You can encourage the students and their parents to contribute problems for the class to ponder. Consider setting up a learning center of problems. Include a bonus problem-solving question on quizzes. The purpose is to encourage students to think by exposing them to problems. It is also very important that you provide feedback to them. If students are unable to solve a problem, determine what obstacles they are encountering.

9. *Encourage students to be IDEAL problem solvers*. Bransford and Stein (1984) stress these five steps in problem solving:

a. *I*dentify the problem.

b. *D*efine and represent the problem.

c. *E*xplore possible strategies.

d. *A*ct on the strategies.

e. *L*ook back and evaluate the effects.

Creativity

Definition of Creativity

Creative behaviors are unusual or surprising and also have value according to certain established conventions or norms of behavior. Behaviors are creative when you, your peer group, or society considers them creative. Although value is a relative attribute, it is important in the definition of creativity. Without it, driving a car on a sidewalk and standing in a classroom screaming at the top of one's lungs might be considered creative behaviors.

Creative behavior is characterized by originality of thought and execution. Creativity is involved in certain kinds of problem solving. According to Hayes (1978), problem solving is usually judged to be creative when most people would not have arrived at the solution and the solution is valid.

Be careful to formulate a general definition of creativity that includes behaviors in addition to the visual and performing arts. Writing and painting can be creative behaviors that have aesthetic value. However, designing bridges, developing psychological experiments, and researching new cancer treatments are also considered creative behaviors.

Historical Perspective

Early investigation of creativity is credited to Sir Francis Galton in the late 1870s. Contemporary work includes that of J. Paul Guilford and Ellis Paul Torrance.

Francis Galton

Galton studied family histories of famous people, including scientists, musicians, and poets, to determine whether genius is hereditary (Galton, 1870). Galton included his now well-known cousin, Charles Darwin, in the study. Galton noticed that one's likelihood of becoming notable is higher if one has a creative relative. In the book *Hereditary Genius,* Galton concluded that genius is hereditary. Today, researchers realize that persons who are related are likely to share not only a common genetic makeup but also wealth, values, and experiences. This evidence essentially discredits Galton's conclusion because we cannot separate the effects of genetic makeup, wealth, values, and experience to determine how much of each factor contributes to genius.

Stages in the Creative Process

Traditionally, researchers (e.g., Wallas, 1921) identified four stages in the creative process that are similar to steps in the problem-solving process described earlier in the chapter. This traditional view of creativity provides a general description of the creative process. The four steps are as follows:

1. *Preparation.* During preparation, the person collects relevant information and investigates the problem. Contrary to popular thought, creativity often involves development of knowledge and skills. Consider the situation when a basketball player throws the ball from midcourt, with 1 second remaining, and the ball goes through the basket winning the game. An enthusiastic fan is likely to shout, "Wow, what a lucky shot!" On the contrary, the "luck" is attributable in great part to many years of practice.

2. *Incubation.* During incubation, the person is not consciously thinking about the problem. A term borrowed from the computer industry and gaining popularity today is "background processing," meaning that work is ongoing, but is not immediately apparent.

3. *Illumination.* During illumination, the person realizes a possible way to solve the problem. Illumination is similar to insight, discussed previously.

4. *Verification.* During verification, the solution is implemented.

Today researchers believe that incubation occurs only during certain creative processes. They also believe that illumination is an occasional phenomenon; that other times the solution is derived in a gradual fashion.

J. Paul Guilford

Contemporary work in creativity was initiated by J. Paul Guilford (1897-1987) in the 1950s and 1960s (e.g., Guilford, 1950). Guilford distinguished between two kinds of thinking: convergent and divergent. In the context of creativity, *convergent thinking* produces problem solutions that will be generally accepted. *Divergent thinking* produces several problem solutions, some of which may be novel and not necessarily readily accepted. The emphasis in divergent thinking is on variety and quantity. According to Guilford, divergent thinking is the process primarily involved in creativity.

Ellis Paul Torrance

Ellis Paul Torrance (1915-) built on Guilford's work and has provided the most influential work in this area (e.g., Torrance, 1965). Torrance identified three components of creativity: fluency, flexibility, and originality.

1. *Fluency.* The more alternatives one can generate for a given problem, the greater one's fluency is for that particular problem. Fluency is important because the more alternatives a person generates, the more likely it is that one of the alternatives will provide a solution (assuming that some of the alternatives are plausible).

2. *Flexibility.* Flexibility goes beyond fluency in considering the nature of the alternatives. The more different kinds of alternatives the person generates for a given problem, the more flexible the person is for that particular problem. For example, two students are asked what they could do with a ball. Aileen says she could kick it, bounce it, roll it, and throw it in the air. Donna says she could throw it, sit on it, paint it, and use it as a paper weight. Both students would get fluency scores of 4 because they each generated 4 responses. Aileen would get a flexibility score of 1 and Donna would get a flexibility score of 4. Aileen's responses were of the same nature. Donna's responses were of different kinds.

3. *Originality.* The third and perhaps most important component of creativity is originality, the extent to which the idea is unique or uncommon. In the preceding example, Donna's idea of sitting on the ball was uncommon, and therefore, more creative than Aileen's ideas.

Assessing Creativity

Torrance developed the instruments that are most often used to assess creativity. He constructed two types of test: verbal and graphic. On *verbal tests,* the subject is asked to list as many uses as possible for a specified object. On *graphic tests,* the subject is shown a diagram, for example vertical lines, and asked to create drawings from the lines. The list or the drawings generated are scored for fluency, flexibility, and originality. Fluency is the number of responses, and flexibility is the number of categories of response. Points for originality are calculated if that subject's response matches less than 10 percent of the responses of the previous test subjects. Of all of Torrance's tests, the one most commonly used is Thinking Creatively with Words (Torrance, 1974; Torrance and Ball, 1984).

Creative People

Superior intelligence is not necessarily a prerequisite for creativity. Generally, it seems that average intelligence is needed for people to demonstrate creativity. There are no conclusive results beyond that finding. Some highly intelligent people are also very creative and some are not. Similarly, some persons with average intelligence are very creative and some are not.

Contrary to somewhat popular belief, creativity is not generally considered a personality type. Creativity seems to result from an approach, a process that some people follow, and not a particular personality type.

Studies have been conducted to find common characteristics among highly creative persons. These studies suggest that highly creative persons tend to have a strong sense of humor, are good at entertaining themselves, are persistent in tasks they undertake, deal well with lack of structure, and have rich fantasy lives. As you might predict, highly creative persons tend to approach problems in novel or unusual ways.

Teaching for Creativity

You can do several things to encourage and foster creativity in your students. There is empirical evidence that creativity training procedures can be used to increase scores on creativity tests.

1. *Establish a classroom atmosphere that is receptive to novel ideas.* Allow children to explore novel approaches and new ideas without fear of failure or harsh judgment. When a novel idea is way off target, show why it is not likely to work, but reward the thought that produced the idea. Find something positive in all novel ideas. Work with interesting and unusual questions; do not dismiss them as

unimportant or off the track. Model creativity yourself, and reward it in your students.

2. *Encourage students to touch, feel, and otherwise explore things in the environment.* Let children spend time closing their eyes and feeling the classroom desks, walls, floor, other children, paper, and other objects. Ask students to describe interesting things they heard, saw, felt, or smelled on their way to school. Have children look at one small area and describe it in intricate detail.

3. *Dedicate time to encouraging creativity.* Establish learning centers on creativity. Have whole-class or small-group creative activities at which time you introduce problems that necessitate creative thinking. Teach children to brainstorm. Let them know that you expect them to be creative during special activities and during regular classroom activities.

4. *Encourage students to take interest in many fields.* Introduce them to new activities; take them on field trips; have guest speakers; and have older students speak to, read to, or entertain your class.

5. *Teach students that everyone can be creative to some extent.* Teach students that few artists or scientists developed masterpieces or major breakthroughs on the first attempt. Reward attempts and improvements.

6. *Teach students the components of creativity.* Teach them that creativity is determined by the number, originality, and types of alternatives generated. This training procedure can help increase creativity. Training students in the problem-solving process can also be useful.

7. *Encourage students to acquire knowledge in a particular field.* Although specific knowledge is not always needed, it does enhance the creative process. Specific knowledge can be used to create plausible alternatives, generate appropriate analogies, and make inferences.

Educational Programs that Teach Thinking

At the root of both problem solving and creativity is thinking. Students need to be able to think clearly, critically, and efficiently to be effective and creative problem solvers. The educational system needs to help students acquire this ability. In many ways students develop thinking skills indirectly during the educational process. For example, math teachers typically demand methodical, systematic work and philosophy teachers expose students to theories of some of the greatest thinkers in history. In the last 20 years, however, there have been frequent complaints that high-school graduates do not have the requisite thinking skills for college and that math students do not really understand the problems they solve.

Training programs have been developed specifically to increase thinking skills. In these programs, obtaining better thinking skills is the objective, not a by-product. Research on educational psychology, cognition, metacognition, problem solving, and decision making provides the foundation for these programs. Empirical evidence supporting the effectiveness of these programs, especially long-term results, is inconclusive. In some instances performance on mental abilities tests has improved on exposure to these training programs. There are concerns that the design of these programs does not ensure transfer of the thinking skills to real-world problems and that the programs will not prove to have long-lasting effects. Additionally, there is no consensus as to which specific skills will lead to better thinkers. Two programs are briefly described below. For more detail, refer to Nickerson et al. (1985) or Sternberg (1984).

Instrumental Enrichment

Instrumental Enrichment (Feuerstein et al., 1980) utilizes paper-and-pencil activities to help students identify and practice basic principles of thinking. This program was designed for mildly retarded and learning-disabled adolescents but can be used with all students. There are 14 exercises of different complexities. Students participate in this program 3 to 5 hours per week (optimally for a couple of years). Students usually work alone, but there are some group activities. A typical activity includes the presentation and discussion of the exercise, time to complete the exercise, discussion of solutions, and a final step in which students try to generate the principle from which the exercise was designed.

This approach emphasizes a construct that Feuerstein calls *mediated learning experience* (MLE), which uses adults to discuss and demonstrate how problems can be solved and information interpreted. Students will increase their cognitive skills by learning from the adults and the environment. Teachers are specially trained to relate the principles practiced in the exercises to subject areas. Some of the exercises include "organization of dots" (connecting dots), "numerical progressions," and "syllogisms."

Philosophy for Children

Philosophy for Children (Lipman et al., 1980) encourages discussions about topics related to thinking, such as the process of inquiry, generalizations, and cause-effect relationships. This program is generally used with fifth- through twelfth-graders and taught during the school year. To begin each lesson, students read an excerpt from a novel. The excerpts include characters who engage in some reasoning process and then discover principles that are applicable to the students' lives. Students discuss the principles and relate them to class activities. Students are encouraged to analyze their own problem-solving strategies and to carefully define problems.

Computer Programming

Teaching students to write computer programs is another way to train thinking skills. Because programming involves important cognitive tasks of planning, hypothesis generation, hypothesis testing, and decision-making, some researchers believe it can be used to improve thinking skills, including divergent thinking abilities. LOGO (Papert, 1980) is a graphics-oriented programming language designed specifically for children (even primary-age children). Students actually use LOGO to learn mathematics by instructing (i.e., programming) a "turtle" (a small triangle on the computer screen) to draw figures. The turtle leaves traces of its path around the screen. Among other programming tasks, students can program the turtle to move up, down, left, or right. To program the computer, students must determine how the task can be accomplished. While doing this, the students learn about their own thinking processes. Preliminary studies (e.g., Clements and Gullo, 1984) indicate that training students to program computers can increase problem-solving skills. As Clements and Gullo state, the gain is made specifically when students learn to program computers. Merely using computers (as in computer-assisted instruction) does not necessarily affect problem-solving skills.

Teaching students effective problem-solving skills is an integral part of the educational process. Problem solving involves defining a problem, generating and testing hypotheses, and choosing the optimal alternative. Heuristics—rules of thumb—can be used to help solve problems. Common problem-solving methods are difference-reduction, means-end analysis, working backward, and pattern matching. Factors that influence problem solving are representation of the problem, functional fixedness, set effects, incubation effects, and planning. To improve the problem-solving ability of students, teachers should expose them to problem situations, help them define problems, generate hypotheses, and carefully analyze problems, and explain to them which factors influence problem solving.

Creative behaviors, in addition to being unusual or surprising, have some value to an individual or society. Creative behaviors are often assessed on the basis of fluency, flexibility, and originality. E. Paul Torrance developed several tests for assessing creativity. To encourage students to be creative, teachers should provide an accepting atmosphere, encourage exploration, allocate class time to projects that develop creativity, and teach students about the aspects and definition of creativity.

Recommended Reading

Bransford, J. D., and B. S. Stein. (1984). *The IDEAL Problem Solver*. San Francisco: Freeman. (Provides ideas for improving one's own problem-solving skills.)

Bruner, J. (1986). *Actual Minds, Possible Worlds.* Cambridge, Mass.: Harvard University Press. (A collection of essays on the mind and imagination.)

Dewey, J. (1933). *How We Think.* New York: Heath. (A classic book on problem-solving training procedures.)

Gardner, H. (1983). *Frames of Mind.* New York: Basic Books. (Provides a summary of Piaget's theories on children's thinking.)

Gardner, M. (1978). *aha! Insight.* San Francisco: Freeman. (A collection of illustrated problems with general guidelines a solutions.

Gilhooly, K. J. (1982). *Thinking: Directed, Undirected, and Creative.* New York: Academic Press. (Includes two excellent chapters on problem-solving and one excellent chapter on creative thinking.)

Glover, J. A. (1980). *Becoming a More Creative Person.* Englewood-Cliffs, N. J.: Prentice-Hall. (Presents theoretically based suggestions for enhancing creativity.)

Guilford, J. P. (1950). Creativity. *American Psychologist,* 5, 444-454. (This article essentially founded the current study of creativity.)

Hayes, J. R. (1981). *The Complete Problem Solver.* Philadelphia: The Franklin Institute. (Discusses the psychology of problem-solving and skills that enhance this ability; presents many examples.)

Krulik, S., and J. Rudnick. (1980). *Problem Solving: A Handbook for Teachers.* Boston: Allyn & Bacon. (An introduction to problem-solving including a large collection of problems; intended to help teach problem-solving.)

Mayer, R. E. (1983). *Thinking, Problem Solving, and Cognition.* San Francisco: Freeman. (A popular text regarding cognition and problem-solving.)

Newell, A., and H. A. Simon. (1972). *Human Problem Solving.* Englewood-Cliffs, N.J.: Prentice-Hall. (Probably the most influential book on problem solving since Dewey's.)

Segal, J. W., and S. F. Chipman. (1985). *Thinking and Learning Skills.* Hillsdale, N.J.: Erlbaum. (Contains advanced readings in problem-solving and other intellectual skills.)

Torrance, E. P. (1983). *Creativity in the Classroom.* Washington, D. C. : National Education Association. (A classic book providing numerous ideas for encouraging creativity in the classroom.)

Wickelgren, W. A. (1974). *How to Solve Problems.* San Francisco: Freeman. (A classic book on solving college-level math and science problems.)

References

Atwood, M. E., and P. G. Polson. (1976). A Process Model for Water Jug Problems. *Cognitive Psychology*, 8, 191-216.

Bransford, J. D., and B. S. Stein. (1984). *The IDEAL Problem Solver*. San Francisco: Freeman.

Chase, W. G., and H. A. Simon. (1973). The Mind's Eye in Chess. in W. G. Chase, (Ed.). *Visual Information Processing*. New York: Academic Press.

Clements, D. H., and D. F. Gullo. (1984). Effects of Computer Programming on Young Children's Cognition. *Journal of Educational Psychology*, 76, 1051-1058.

Dewey, J. (1933). *How We Think*. New York: Heath.

Feuerstein, R., Y. Rand, M. B. Hoffman, and R. Miller. (1980). *Instrumental Enrichment: An Intervention Program for Cognitive Modifiabilty*. Baltimore: University Park Press.

Galton, F. (1870). *Hereditary Genius*. New York: Appleton.

Guilford, J. P. (1950). Creativity. *American Psychologist*, 5, 444-454.

Hayes, J. R. (1978). *Cognitive Psychology: Thinking and Creating*. Homewood, Ill.: Dorsey.

Köhler, A. (1925). *The Mentality of Apes*. New York: Harcourt Brace.

Lipman, M., A. M. Sharp, and F. Oscanyan. (1980). *Philosophy in the Classroom*. Philadelphia: Temple University Press.

Luchins, A. S. (1942). Mechanization in Problem Solving. *Psychological Monographs*, 54, No. 248.

Maier, N. R. F. (1931). Reasoning in Humans: II. The Solution of a Problem and Its Appearance in Consciousness. *Journal of Comparative Psychology*, 12, 181-194.

Nickerson, R. S., D. N. Perkins, and E. E. Smith. (1985). *Teaching Thinking*. Hillsdale, N.J.: Erlbaum.

Osborn, A. F. (1963). *Applied Imagination*. (3d Ed.). New York: Scribner's.

Papert, S. (1980). *Mindstorms*. New York: Basic Books.

Sternberg, R. (1984). How Can We Teach Intelligence? *Educational Leadership*, 42, 38-48.

Thorndike, E. L. (1911). *Animal Intelligence*. New York: Macmillan.

Torrance, E. P. (1965). *Creativity in the Classroom*. Englewood Cliffs, N.J.: Prentice-Hall.

Torrance, E. P. (1974). *Torrance Test of Creative Thinking*. Lexington, Mass.: Ginn.

Torrance, E. P., and O. E. Ball. (1984). *Torrance Test of Creative Thinking*. New York: Scholastic Testing Service.

Wallas, G. (1921). *The Art of Thought*. New York: Harcourt, Brace, & World.

CHAPTER 13

Teaching Exceptional, Disadvantaged, and Bilingual Students

This chapter describes the characteristics and educational needs of exceptional, disadvantaged, and bilingual students.

The classification "exceptional" includes children who are perceptually or physically impaired, physically or learning-disabled, emotionally disturbed, mentally retarded, and highly gifted. Most teachers work with exceptional children at some time or other. Identifying children who may be exceptional is essential so that they can receive specialized instruction.

Disadvantaged children typically come from low-income families and have not had many of the learning-conducive experiences outside school that other students have had.

Bilingual students are children from non-English-speaking homes who may encounter language barriers or difficulties in regular coursework and classroom activities. The classifications exceptional, disadvantaged, and bilingual are separate; thus, a bilingual student is not necessarily exceptional or disadvantaged, and vice versa.

Exceptional Students

Exceptional students include both handicapped and gifted students. The U.S. Department of Education has identified major categories of handicapped students. The characteristics of exceptional children in each of the major categories are discussed in this chapter.

Roughly 11 percent of the public school population are handicapped students. In 1986, public schools served more than 4,317,000 handicapped students, approximately 70 percent of whom were taught in regular (mainstream) classes, approximately 25 percent in separate classes, and 5 percent in other settings (e.g., special schools and private homes).

Learning Disabilities

In 1986 there were more than 1,800,000 learning disabled students enrolled in the public schools in the United States, representing approximately 43 percent of the total U. S. public-school handicapped student population for that year.

Characteristics

Students with a learning disability may have near-average to above-average intelligence and difficulty on certain academic tasks such as reading, language skills, or math. A learning disabled student's intellectual development may be high in some areas but below average in the problem area(s). The key to identifying a student with a learning disability is that performance in the problem area must be markedly lower than that in other areas. Problems commonly associated with learning disabilities are hyperactivity (excessive physical activity); difficulty concentrating, remembering, and interacting with other children; irritability and impulsiveness; clumsiness; poor sense of direction or time; immaturity; and a need for immediate reward.

Classroom Strategies

Teaching students with learning disabilities requires both patience and creativity. There are two major challenges for the teacher working with these students. The first challenge is to communicate information in alternative ways to enable the student to participate and learn. For example, a student who has difficulty encoding auditory information may benefit from presentation of the material using a visual medium. The second challenge is to help students overcome the disability. Using the same example, the teacher would teach the student how to learn from auditory information. This challenge is generally undertaken by persons specifically trained in teaching learning disabled students.

To help a student with a learning disability in the regular (mainstream) class, the classroom teacher can break a task into smaller parts, sequence these subtasks, and provide frequent feedback. Breaking the task into smaller parts provides the student with more opportunities for success and makes it easier for the teacher to monitor progress and identify problem areas. The teacher can also provide special projects for a student to work on to help overcome a specific disability. Peer tutoring can be an effective means of providing practice on specific problem areas, but this requires careful selection of peer tutors and definition of specific projects for the "team." The classroom teacher can also use multimedia equipment such as computers, which have great potential for drill and practice that the learning disabled students need. Additionally, computers can display stimulating graphics, animated images, and synthesize sounds, any of which may provide an effective means of communication with the learning-disabled student. Video and audio presentations can also be used to supplement or substitute for regular classroom presentations. With young children, teachers try to involve the kinesthetic sense, in addition to seeing and hearing. For example, a student who has difficulty recognizing letters may be shown how to draw the letter in sand or tactilely feel a letter made of sandpaper.

There are many kinds and levels of learning disability. This particular handicap can be extremely frustrating for an otherwise average student. Flexibility in strategy is important for the teacher—if one approach does not work, try another. It can also be helpful to talk with a student's previous teachers and other colleagues for ideas. Special-education teachers may be able to offer specific techniques. When you find an approach that works with a particular student, make a note of it so that the information can be used by the student's next teacher.

Speech Impairment

In 1986 students with speech impairment represented approximately 26 percent of the U. S. handicapped public school population. Students with speech impairment lisp, stutter, reverse words or sounds, or speak with a nasal tone. Students are identified as speech-impaired when speech production deviates from the norm to the extent that it calls attention to itself or interferes with communication.

Categories

Speech disorders can be categorized as articulation, voice, or stuttering disorders. *Articulation disorders* involve modification of speech sounds, usually by adding, omitting, substituting, or distorting sounds. *Voice disorders* involve problems with voice quality, pitch, or loudness. *Stuttering* involves prolongation or repetition of sounds or hesitation. Students may receive speech therapy during school by a speech pathologist.

Classroom Strategies

Speech impairment can cause learning problems because the development of language and cognitions are affected by the ability to speak. In other words, speech impairment can represent much more than a cosmetic problem.

To accommodate students with speech impairment the classroom teacher can model appropriate speech and provide reinforcement for the use of language. The classroom teacher can ask a speech therapist for additional activities that can be practiced in the classroom. Students with speech or language disorders may need help developing positive self-concepts.

Mental Retardation

In 1986 mentally retarded students represented approximately 15 percent of the U. S. handicapped public-school population. Students with mental retardation have below-average intelligence. By definition, mentally retarded persons have IQ scores below 70, had the onset of the retardation prior to adulthood, and have below-average adaptive behavior. *Adaptive behaviors* are sensorimotor and social skills. These students lag behind students of average intelligence in academic, language, and social skills development.

Categories

There are three categories of mental retardation.

Mildly or educably mentally retarded–IQ scores between 69 and 55. Most retarded persons have this level of functioning. Some students within this category may be placed in regular classrooms; however, without special assistance, these students will most likely have great difficulty.

Moderately or trainably mentally retarded–IQ scores between 54 and 40. Students within this category are not likely to be placed in a regular classroom.

Severely or profoundly mentally retarded—IQ scores below 40. These students are generally trained in special training institutions or special public-school classes.

Classroom Strategies

To accommodate educably mentally retarded students, the classroom teacher should plan lessons to ensure success. Break tasks into smaller parts and cue or otherwise prompt students for appropriate answers. Limit the number of possible choices. When a student is successful, provide positive feedback so the student recognizes that the correct response was made. Provide more exercises for these students than for average students. Overlearning is important to ensure that the task is mastered. When moving to new tasks, proceed in very small steps. When introducing new material, associate one stimulus with a single response and consistently use that association when rehearsing the material. To teach the concept of one, show the student one item (e.g., one car). Continue to show one item until the concept is well learned. Do not show different items at various times, for instance, one car on Monday, one boat on Tuesday, and one coat on Wednesday. After the concept is learned, help the student generalize to other situations. Show one car, for example, and say "This is one car"; then show one boat and say "This is one boat." Then work until the student can say "one" for the car or the boat.

While working with educably mentally retarded students, concentrate on developing competence with basic reading and writing skills, good hygiene practices, and appropriate social skills. Acquisition of these skills will prepare students to function and think independently. Development of occupational skills is also important. Special-education programs for mentally retarded persons are beginning to emphasize vocational education, which prepares students for employment following high school. These programs help students acquire marketable skills and secure employment (Hasazi et al., 1985).

Behavior or Emotional Disorders

The terms behavior disorder and emotional disorder are generally used interchangeably. In 1986 students with behavioral or emotional disorders represented approximately 9 percent of the U. S. handicapped public-school population.

Characteristics

Students with behavioral or emotional disorders may be aggressive, impulsive, disruptive, withdrawn, isolated, extremely fearful, or self-mutilating. These students exhibit such behaviors over a long period of time. By definition, these students have at least average or near-average intelligence.

Classroom Strategies

To accommodate students with behavioral or emotional disturbance, the classroom teacher should utilize behavior management programs. For information on behavior modification and classroom management, refer to Chapter 3. Preventive planning is an important concept when working with these students. Once a problem arises, it tends to escalate. As mentioned in Chapter 3, the most effective management techniques include identification and prevention of potential behavior problems

The classroom teacher can also help these students develop appropriate behaviors. The student and teacher can develop a "contract" in which the student pledges to learn to control behavior and is rewarded for doing so. While helping a student improve control, the teacher might want to be tolerant of times when the limits are exceeded and provide gentle reminders of the original expectations.

Classroom teachers may need to learn how to interrupt a student from self-mutilating behaviors such as biting one's arm and banging one's head against a wall, floor, or desk. Teachers must know how to intervene to stop such behaviors to protect students. Special quiet areas can be provided in the classroom for students to have a place to go when they anticipate a problem.

Students with extremely short attention spans, frequent impulsive behaviors, and excessive activity levels are sometimes diagnosed as *hyperactive*. It is not uncommon to find students with both hyperactivity and learning disabilities. *Drug therapy* is recommended by some psychiatrists to help control excessive and disruptive behavior. The drug Ritalin (generic name of methylphenidate) is commonly used to control hyperactivity. Drug therapy is also used to control other emotional and behavior disorders. Ritalin, like all drugs, should be used cautiously. Teachers should be aware of possible side effects from the drug and should watch for and report significant changes in student behavior. Students undergoing drug therapy should be evaluated on a regular basis by a qualified physician.

Physical Handicaps

In 1986 students with physical handicaps (including both orthopedic impaired and health impaired) represented approximately 2.6 percent of the U. S. handicapped public-school population. Most students with physical handicaps are identified and diagnosed as handicapped by physicians.

Categories

Common physical handicaps include orthopedic diseases such as arthritis and impairments such as missing or malformed arms and legs; neurological disorders such as epilepsy and cerebral palsy; endocrine disorders such as diabetes; and vascular or respiratory disorders such as heart problems and asthma. Students with these handicaps have a variety of special needs. Some students need special equipment to help them communicate, others need special chairs or walkers; and others may need help taking medication, eating, or using the restroom.

Classroom Strategies

Teachers may need to rearrange furniture in the classroom to remove obstacles and facilitate movement within the room. To accommodate students with physical impairments, teachers should familiarize themselves with the medical condition and the physician-prescribed care of each of these students (e.g., use of prosthetic devices, some of which require periodic maintenance). Teachers should also be familiar with and competent in administering emergency medical procedures such as injecting insulin and handling seizures. To plan for medical emergencies, the teacher might assign students special roles, such as asking one student to summon the school nurse, another to contact a school administrator, another to bring water and a first-aid kit. The teacher should help all students in the class become familiar with special devices and emergency procedures. Modeling a confident, calm approach to special needs and emergency situations will go a long way toward helping students deal with special circumstances. A teacher who runs out of the classroom during an emergency screaming "Morton just fell out of his chair—help!" will have a classroom of hysterical students to deal with later.

Students with physical impairments may have a poor or low self-concept. The classroom teacher should try to counteract this by planning special projects and other learning incentives to help these students develop a more positive self-concept. Many students with physical impairments will be highly motivated and capable students. For this reason they are potentially good peer tutors.

Hearing Impairment

In 1986 students with auditory impairments represented approximately 1.5 percent of the U. S. handicapped public-school population.

Characteristics and Categories

Students with hearing (auditory) impairments ask for instructions to be repeated, turn their heads to try to hear better, speak in monotones, watch others' lips instead of their eyes, have poor speech production, demonstrate lack of attention, and cannot locate sounds.

There are two categories of auditory impairment: *hard of hearing* and *deaf*. Hard-of-hearing students have partial hearing. Some students with partial hearing have difficulty with faint sounds, while others have trouble perceiving conversations and louder sounds. Deaf students have no functional hearing.

Classroom Strategies

To accommodate students with auditory impairments in the classroom, you can arrange the physical layout of the classroom to place these students in optimal locations. You should face these students when giving instructions. Because students with hearing impairments miss instructions and explanations, you need to check to make sure that they understand. Create special signals the students can use when they think they missed important information. When you repeat information, reword it rather than simply repeat it verbatim.

When presenting lessons, plan to incorporate visual descriptions and instructions. Dramatizing events and using video productions with captions will help meet the needs of hearing-impaired students and also entertain the whole class. To accommodate deaf students and students with severe hearing impairment, a special interpreter may be needed. The school district will provide for this expertise. However, for day-to-day communications, encourage all students to face hearing-impaired students and learn sign language when it is necessary. You may provide learning centers or special activities in sign language (or refer students to places where such projects are offered).

Remember to plan for emergencies such as fire alarms. Arrange for a special visual signal and possibly a buddy system so that someone will communicate special instructions to these students in the event of an emergency. Practice implementing these signals. For example, when an auditory fire alarm is activated, point to the bell or use sign language. Because it is sometimes difficult to attract a student's attention from the front of the room, you may plan to have a special student indicate to the hearing-impaired student(s) that a fire alarm has been activated. Planning ahead for emergencies can prevent unnecessary confusion and panic.

As a final note about hearing-impaired students, it is critically important to identify students at an early age so that they can benefit from special speech and language training. Preschool and elementary classroom teachers are in an excellent position to help identify children who may have hearing impairments.

Visual Impairments

In 1986 students with visual impairments represented approximately 0.6 percent of the U. S. handicapped public-school population.

Characteristics and Categories

Students with visual impairments tend to hold books extremely close or far away, tilt their heads at peculiar angles when looking at objects, complain about visual problems, and rub their eyes. When glasses or contact lenses will not adequately correct the vision problem *and* special materials or procedures are needed by a student, that student is considered visually impaired.

There are two categories of visual impairment: *partially impaired* and *blind*. Some students who are blind have no functional vision; others are legally blind. Persons who are legally blind need to be 20 feet from letters that normal-sighted people can read from 200 feet away (20/200 vision), but they can perceive objects, colors, and shadows in the environment. There are many degrees of partial visual impairment.

Classroom Strategies

To accommodate students with visual impairments you could arrange the physical layout of the classroom to place these students in optimal locations; perhaps with help and suggestions from these students themselves. Think of which learning tasks are vision-oriented; examples are reading math formulas from the blackboard, watching filmstrips, and reading maps. Sometime when you can work with the visually-impaired student(s) without attention from the rest of the class, ask the student to sit in different seats around the room to determine which provides the best viewing angle. You might also plan lessons with an auditory or tactile format rather than a visual presentation.

Especially if students have difficulty reading, you could tape-record assignments, word problems, answers to problems, stories, and so on. Oral presentations can be less frustrating, more efficient, and more entertaining for visually-impaired students. If you do not have time to prepare the auditory or tactile material yourself, ask students to help. Students in your class or other classes may enjoy preparing the tapes. Consider having your librarian maintain a tape library that all teachers can contribute to and borrow from. Also, you may find auditory materials that can be borrowed from special-education teachers in your school or school district. Some public libraries or special libraries for visually impaired adults stock additional cassettes and large-print books. You may need to order special books and classroom materials in braille or large-print depending on the degree of impairment. Talking calculators, talking books, embossed maps, specially designed lamps, and other classroom aids are available for these students.

In addition to accommodating these students during class lessons, think about free time and learning center materials that are appropriate. Keep large-print books, auditory tapes, and tactile projects around the classroom so that visually-impaired (and regular students) can continue to explore and learn in their free time.

When developing lesson plans to incorporate the needs of visually impaired students, provide hands-on projects because these students "observe" the environment by touching, listening to, and tasting objects. A child who is unaware of something in the environment is not likely to learn about it. Sometimes you may need to direct a visually-impaired student's attention to notable aspects of the environment.

Students with visual impairments generally have poorer motor coordination than do other students. Although it is important to give these students opportunities to increase their skill levels, it is important not to set them up for failure. For instance, recess and physical education can be threatening and embarrassing times for visually-impaired students. Discuss with other teachers and coaches possibilities of providing activities to develop motor coordination without putting the students in embarrassing or threatening situations.

Gifted Children

Identification of gifted students for special-education programs usually occurs after students obtain IQ scores above 130. Grades, parent and teacher ratings, and additional test scores may be considered in addition to IQ scores. An IQ test score above 130 is not the sole criterion for assignment to a gifted program. The definition of *giftedness* is quite controversial, and researchers now believe in additional ways of identifying gifted students. Students may demonstrate exceptional performance in one academic area, several academic areas, or in nonacademic areas such as individualized music and art. Are all these classes of exceptional performers "gifted"? Researchers debate whether giftedness should be defined as a single general ability that could be measured with an IQ score, or one or more specific abilities that could be measured with ability-specific assessment instruments. Further, it is not clear if giftedness must be demonstrated specifically on academic tasks (as opposed to music or art). There are also questions about the relationship between giftedness and creativity. Renzulli (1978) defined giftedness as a combination of above average general ability, creativity, and task commitment. Renzulli has also suggested that academic giftedness and "creative-productive" giftedness be distinguished. Today, there are special education programs for the gifted and talented that recognize and accommodate both kinds of gifted students. Current definitions of giftedness are determined by individual school districts. Another current trend is the identification of minority gifted students.

Characteristics and Categories

Typically, gifted children are characterized by above-average intelligence and high levels of performance in academic or special tasks. These students may demonstrate unusual potential in one area while demonstrating average abilities on most tasks. Giftedness is often first demonstrated by unusual alertness and curiosity, advanced development, prolonged attention span, language proficiency, and sometimes advanced reading ability. Generally, gifted children are physically healthy and emotionally stable.

There are two special categories of gifted students: *the underachieving gifted* and *the very highly intelligent* (IQ above 180). Researchers are becoming more concerned with the underachieving gifted student because of the potential that is untapped. However, some researchers contend that underachieving and unmotivated gifted students should not receive special-educational status. Very highly intelligent students tend to have more social and emotional difficulties than do other students. Researchers are endeavoring to understand why these difficulties arise.

Classroom Strategies

There are two traditional approaches to teaching the gifted student: enrichment and acceleration.

Enrichment programs provide greater depth and breadth of content areas than do conventional programs. They may also utilize special curriculum and teaching strategies. Students participating in enrichment programs can be accommodated in the regular classroom by working independently, being clustered (grouped) with other gifted students, and attending special field trips. Students may also attend special classes or special schools on a daily or weekly basis.

Acceleration programs provide the traditional content areas at a faster pace than do conventional programs. There are several acceleration programs: instruction for one content area may be accelerated, an entire year of instruction may be skipped, more than one year of instructional material may be covered in a one-year period, or early entrance to a program (e.g., kindergarten or college) may be granted. Traditionally, there has been concern that skipping grades will be socially difficult for gifted students. Research evidence has not supported this concern. There is also disagreement in the field concerning the placement of gifted students in special classes rather than keeping them in regular classes. Placement in special classes or special schools can provide advanced instruction in particular areas and otherwise benefit the gifted students.

You can provide learning incentives for and prevent boredom in gifted students though supplemental or enriched study programs. You should teach these students to determine how information is derived, not merely present them with facts and figures. Challenge them with "how," "why," and "what if" questions, not rote memorization. Require higher-level learning, which involves analysis, synthesis, and evaluation of information. Provide supplementary reading material to increase the breadth and depth of material you present to the class.

Provide challenge questions that require these students to undertake additional reading or thinking. Get them involved in the design of instruction by asking them what they would like to learn and allowing them to develop their own study plans and to work independently. If you present instruction to a group of gifted students, increase the pace of the presentation to keep the students alert and responsive.

You could arrange with other teachers for gifted students to attend more advanced courses. For example, allow a gifted fourth-grader to attend math class with sixth-graders. Consider assigning special projects that two or more gifted children collaborate on and present to the class. Encourage gifted students to share their special projects and talents with the community through science fairs and other exhibits, letters to newspaper editors, letters to congressional leaders, presentations to parents, and other activities. Also, encourage gifted students to learn about and utilize community resources, such as college libraries, art museums, and industries.

The Education for All Handicapped Children Act

In the 1970s several organizations began publicizing information reporting deficiencies in educational services to the handicapped. The Children's Defense Fund sponsored a project that determined that nearly two million school-age children were not attending school. The National Advisory Committee on the Handicapped estimated that many handicapped students were not receiving special services that were needed. Additionally, the Secretary of Health, Education, and Welfare developed a special project to investigate the effects of labeling special students.

Awareness of these kinds of problems resulted in Congress passing the *Education for All Handicapped Children Act* in November 1975. (This act is Public Law 94-142.) The purpose of the act was to "assure the free, appropriate public education of all handicapped children." The major provisions of this law include the following:

1. An *individualized educational program* (IEP) will be developed for each special-education student. Individualized educational programs describe the current level of achievement, short- and long-term behavioral objectives, criteria used to assess mastery of the

objectives, services that must be provided to the student, and a schedule that specifies when the student will be reevaluated and when the services will be provided. IEPs are developed by a child study team (also called *interdisciplinary assessment team*) that includes the classroom teacher and other professionals, perhaps a special-education teacher, a psychologist, a social worker, a school administrator, and the student's parents or guardians. Other professionals, perhaps physicians, speech pathologists, and occupational therapists, are included on the team when needed. When students are capable, they also help develop the IEP. Together this team assesses the capabilities and needs of the student and develops the IEP. The conference or meeting during which the team discusses the needs or progress of the student or develops the IEP is called a *staffing*.

2. Students will be placed in the *least restrictive environment and mainstreamed* (i.e., placed in classes with nonhandicapped students) whenever possible. The least restrictive environment is typically the regular classroom. As the student is placed away from the regular classroom, the environment is considered more restrictive. For example, special classes are more restrictive than regular classes; special day schools are more restrictive than special classes in a regular school; and special residential schools are more restrictive than day schools. Special institutions and hospitals are considered the most restrictive environments.

When possible, handicapped students are placed in the regular classroom, a practice called *mainstreaming*. When a student is not mainstreamed, the IEP should specify services that will help the student attain skills needed for mainstreaming to a regular class in the future. Mainstreaming special students provides the opportunity for them to interact with nonhandicapped students. This increased exposure to normal behavior and appropriate role models is beneficial to special students. In fact, when teachers implement strategies that accommodate a wide range of student abilities (e.g., individualized instruction), mildly handicapped students attending regular classes can learn better than can handicapped students in special classes (e.g., Calhoun and Elliott, 1977). One problem with mainstreaming is social acceptance of the handicapped students. You can facilitate social acceptance of these students by modeling accepting behavior, openly discussing handicaps, expecting and rewarding cooperative behaviors among students, using role-playing to explore conflicts, pointing out the strengths of the handicapped students, and focusing on the common characteristics and situations the students share.

3. *Legal and civil rights* of students and parents will be protected by due process. This provision ensures confidentiality, allows parents access to school records, and allows an independent evaluation of the student when requested. It also ensures that relevant information will be presented to parents in a way that they will understand. Sometimes this means communicating to the parents in their native language. This provision also specifies that testing procedures will not be culturally biased.

Identification of Exceptional Students

Regular classroom teachers are often the first to suspect that a student needs special education. The teacher then refers the student for testing. Sometimes, especially for physically handicapped and gifted students, parents initiate the referral.

Child Find

Child Find is a recently developed approach that is also used to identify persons from birth to age 21 who might benefit from special education. The approach utilizes telephone interviews, mail questionnaires, news media, posters, and other measures to increase public awareness of various exceptionalities. A phone number and/or address and reporting instructions are provided in the advertisements. The approach also contacts service organizations, public agencies, and day schools asking for names of persons who may need special services. Child Find has helped identify eligible children at an early age.

Early Identification

Identifying persons with possible exceptionalities is obviously a key aspect of effective special education. Currently there is emphasis on early identification and intervention for designing more effective educational programs. Early intervention maximizes the amount of appropriate education. Providing appropriate education as early as infancy and continuing through early childhood is especially important for children with poor muscle tone, speech problems, and cognitive deficits. Early identification also helps education districts with long-term program and services planning.

Assessment of Exceptional Students

Once a person is identified, appropriate screening and assessment are conducted to determine whether he or she qualifies for special services.

Testing

Parental approval must be obtained before tests are administered. Once the referral has been made and parental consent is received, screening test(s) are given to the student. Examples of screening tests are the Minnesota Development Inventory and the Denver Developmental Screening Test. Those instruments are used to determine whether further diagnostic assessment is warranted.   Additionally, parents, teachers, classmates, and the student may be interviewed or asked to complete questionnaires. The interviews and questionnaires are used to validate the need for special education, and better understand the nature of the supposed exceptionality. If results of the screening instruments indicate an exceptionality, additional tests will be used to further determine the severity and nature of the exceptionality. The reason for referral and the expected exceptionality determine which specific tests are administered, but common assessment instruments include the Stanford-Binet Intelligence Scale, the Wechsler Intelligence Scale for Children (WISC), the Wide Range Achievement Test (WRAT), the American Association on Mental Deficiency Adaptive Behavior Scale, the Vineland Social Maturity Scale, the Assessment of Basic Competencies, the Torrance Tests of Creative Thinking, vision and hearing exams, and behavioral checklists. The information obtained from these assessment instruments will be used by the child study team to develop the IEP.

Categorical Labels

Labels are used to classify students and to describe exceptionalities.

Classification can be useful because it aids organization and communication. In special education, however, there are several problems with the existing classification system. In general, most labels do not provide appropriate educational information and, further, they carry negative connotations that affect the well-being of special students.

Disadvantages of Labels. Consider the categorical labels used today, such as "emotionally disturbed," "culturally deprived," and "mentally retarded." These labels are based on psychological, social, legal, or medical assessments. There are three basic disadvantages in the use of these labels.

1. Categorical labels do not help prescribe educational programs. If an emotionally disturbed student were assigned to your classroom for 3 hours each day, for instance, what would your educational objectives and approach be for that student? Obviously, you would need more information, such as the severity of the handicap and the manner with which it interferes with learning.

2. Categorical labels tend to emphasize the negative, or the "problem" with the student. These negative labels can generate self-fulfilling prophecies for students. Students perceive themselves in generalized, negative ways and then act in ways that are consistent with their perception. This particular problem is especially profound because the way students act affects the way they are treated by parents, teachers, and peers. Subsequently, the way students are treated affects the way they behave. The cycle is difficult to break.

3. When people hear a negative label, such as "crippled" or "blind," they generalize that the exceptional person is affected in other ways as well. This might be called a *negative halo effect,* which occurs, for example, when someone speaks loudly to a blind person who has no hearing deficit.

While terms such as learning disability, mental retardation, and emotional disturbance are utilized, the classroom teacher must remain aware of the potential negative consequences of these terms. To reduce the negative impact, use them sparingly. Wherever possible, indicate the specific educational deficit rather than the more general label. For example, instead of referring to Billy's learning disability, indicate that

Billy needs assistance reading large bodies of text because he some-times begins reading from the right side of the page. When other professionals refer to a student's learning disability or mental retarda-tion, ask them to describe the deficit more specifically. Be sure that they refer to the educational implications of the handicapping condition because that is what you are most concerned with. You should draw attention to the positive aspects of a special student's performance. For example, when referring to Billy, point out that his math computation skills are above average for a fourth-grader or that he works well in small groups. Billy needs to hear what he does well, as do his parents and peers.

Alternative classification schemes have been proposed by several special educators and researchers. These alternatives focus on the educational implications of handicapping conditions and avoid general-ized, negative labels. To date, these alternative schemes have not been widely implemented.

Advantages of Labels. There are some advantages to using categorical labels. For example, terms such as mentally retarded and learning disabled indicate that a student needs special-educational programs, and these terms help ensure that a student will qualify for special services. Additionally, the labels can help protect students by accounting for unusual behaviors. For example, a learning-disabled student is frustrated with a reading assignment and becomes fidgety. The teacher investigates to determine whether the inappropriate be-havior is related to difficulty with the reading assignment. By inves-tigating this possible association, the teacher will be able to address the actual source of the problem—the student's inherent learning disability.

Accommodation of Exceptional Students

Special education programs and professional services are available to accommodate exceptional students. Classroom teachers can also do much to enhance the learning potential of these students by following sound teaching principles that work well in the mainstream.

Special Education Programs

There are two main categories of special educational programs:

those in which education is provided outside the regular classroom and those in which services provide assistance to the regular classroom teacher in order to meet the needs of the exceptional student. Most exceptional students are served in regular classrooms in the public schools and do not require placement in special schools. The most appropriate environment is determined by the nature and severity of the exceptionality. The programs are listed from least to most restrictive.

1. The student attends a *regular class* all day. Consultation and support may be provided to the regular teacher. *Consulting teachers* with training in special education may offer suggestions to the classroom teacher. The consultants will probably observe the student and then suggest special materials and teaching strategies for the classroom teacher. The consultant will not work directly with the student.

2. The student participates in a regular class most of the day but attends a special class for about an hour each day and receives instruction from a specially trained professional called an *itinerant teacher* (a teacher who visits a number of schools on a consulting basis). The most typical service provided by itinerant teachers is speech lessons. The classroom teacher is aware of the special training and may be minimally, but not directly involved.

3. The student participates in a regular class for several hours but receives special assistance in a separate classroom called a *resource room* a few minutes or a few hours per day. The student participates with the other students during the regular class but goes to the *resource teacher* for assistance in some subjects. The resource teacher provides services to a small group of students at a time, helping them develop skills and complete work. Typical resource room work consists of math and reading assignments. The regular teacher may give the student(s) assignments to complete in the resource room. Sometimes, a resource teacher will provide services in the regular classroom. Many learning-disabled students receive support services from resource teachers. Communication between the resource teacher and the regular teacher is important. The regular teacher identifies work that needs to be completed and skills that need

to be mastered. The resource teacher helps students develop strategies to deal with their handicaps and learn more efficiently and might suggest instructional techniques to the regular teacher. Resource teachers also trained in counseling and crisis intervention are sometimes called *crisis teachers*. They may be utilized as resource teachers to help students a few hours a day during unusual and difficult situations.

4. The student receives most, if not all, education in a self-contained, special-education classroom from a special-education teacher. Most educable mentally retarded students, many emotionally disturbed students, and some learning-disabled students participate in self-contained classes. Sometimes a student in a self-contained classroom is capable of participating with regular students in music, physical education, or one or two content areas. The teacher may make special arrangements for the student to leave the special class for an hour or so and participate with a regular class. Allowing these students to be mainstreamed on a part-time basis provides a less restrictive environment than the self-contained-only environment.

5. The student receives all education at a *special day school*. When the staffing team determines that a public school cannot accommodate the educational needs or provide for the safety of the student, the student is referred to a special school. The student spends weekdays at the school and spends evenings and weekends with parents or guardians. The day schools are designed specifically to meet the special needs of these students. Some students with visual or auditory handicaps attend special day schools. Many trainably mentally retarded or emotionally disturbed students also attend special day schools.

6. The student receives all education at a *special residential school*. The staffing team (including parents or guardians) may determine that a student is not able to function independently and needs full-time care. Such students reside at the special school. The residential schools are designed specifically to meet educational, medical, and other needs of these students. Students with profound emotional or

mental handicaps attend these schools. Less than 10 percent of all handicapped students are placed in residential programs.

7. The student receives temporary educational services at home (homebound) or in a hospital or other institution. Students recovering from illness may need special services to help them keep up with their work. Teachers will visit the hospital, institution, or the student's home for a few hours each day and provide necessary instruction. This service is generally used on a short-term basis.

Professional Services

In addition to the programs mentioned above, there are several services available to exceptional children and classroom teachers. The professionals who provide these services are interested in the emotional, physical, and educational well-being of the students and can serve as valuable resources for the classroom teacher. These professionals can help you understand the nature, severity, and implications of an exceptionality, work with you to provide appropriate educational materials and presentation of information to students, and offer suggestions to help you manage exceptional students in the classroom.

Psychologists collect and interpret assessment data used to determine whether an exceptionality exists and, if one does exist, to identify its nature and severity. School psychologists administer psychological tests, interview parents, students, and teachers, and sometimes observe students in the classroom. Sometimes, students are referred to psychiatrists, who are trained in both psychology and medicine. Psychiatrists may collect and interpret assessment data and determine whether special medication would help control emotional and/or behavioral problems.

Counselors help gather information about exceptional students from school records, parents, the students themselves, and sometimes other agencies. School counselors also provide educational and vocational counseling for the students.

Social workers collect information from parents and other relevant sources. Social workers learn about the student's home environment, especially aspects that will affect the student's ability to learn and adapt. Social workers coordinate interactions between the staffing team and other agencies, such as day schools and hospitals. They also serve as consultants to parents, teachers, and students.

Physical therapists train students to increase their physical strength, control, and mobility. They may recommend exercises and special adaptive equipment for physically handicapped students. They will help the classroom teacher understand the physical abilities and limitations of handicapped students.

Occupational therapists help prepare students for jobs by teaching students specific skills (e.g., cooking, cleaning, woodworking). Occupational therapists look beyond the academic program to the student's potential role in society and help design educational programs that will allow the student to succeed in the "real world."

Speech pathologists collect speech samples and test students to determine whether communication disorders exists. They train students to communicate, often by teaching them to enunciate and articulate words. Speech pathologists can suggest ways to deal with communication disorders in the regular classroom. They may also suggest that certain communicative behaviors be reinforced in the classroom.

Physicians may provide medication and schedules to be followed during school hours. To ensure appropriateness of the medication and dosage, physicians may request that classroom teachers complete behavioral checklists. Physicians also prescribe and fit prosthetic devices for some students.

School nurses conduct visual and auditory screening exams and collect relevant medical information from parents, physicians, and students. Once a program is designated, the school nurse may be needed to provide medical assistance, such as administering medicine and maintaining prosthetic devices.

Special-education teachers assist in determining appropriate educational goals and placement for students. They can also offer teaching and management strategies. Because of their experience with exceptional students, they are often a good source for support and creative ideas. When a student is assigned to a special-education classroom part-day and a regular classroom part-day, it is important to coordinate curriculum and schedules with the special-education teacher.

Consulting teachers help generate solutions to specific problems. They can suggest alternative teaching strategies, provide special learning activities, list possible reinforcers, and help regular teachers understand the educational deficit.

Parents can also be valuable resources and are an integral part of the education team. Parents can complete behavioral checklists, identify appropriate reinforcers, administer reinforcers, note changes in behaviors at home, and so on. Parental involvement is an important part of special-education programs.

Working with Special Students in the Mainstream

As discussed in the preceding pages, a regular classroom teacher can employ a number of techniques to enhance the learning potential and comfort of special students. The preceding discussion focused on separate teaching strategies and activities for each type of student. A general guide to working with special students incorporates the following principles, which are applicable for most students.

1. Consistently demonstrate a positive attitude and positive expectations.

2. Provide feedback as soon as possible.

3. Implement routine procedures when possible so students learn what to expect and understand responsibilities.

4. Be willing to try alternative approaches.

5. Implement lessons one step at a time (for learning-disabled and mentally retarded students).

6. Use direct, specific instructions (for learning-disabled and mentally retarded students).

7. Provide adequate breaks.

8. Utilize available expertise from other professionals.

9. Facilitate social acceptance in the classroom by modeling accepting behavior, openly discussing handicaps, and rewarding cooperative behaviors among students.

10. Design lessons to meet the educational needs of the students. Do not emphasize categorical labels (e.g., learning-disabled).

Disadvantaged Students

It is difficult to estimate the number of disadvantaged students in the public schools. A very rough estimate is 12,257,000, which is the number of children who were living below the poverty level in 1986. Use this number only as a general indication because poverty, alone, is neither a necessary nor a sufficient condition for classification as disadvantaged.

Characteristics

Outside the school, few disadvantaged students have had experiences that most other students have. This lack of experience affects the student's ability to perform adequately on academic tasks. Disadvantaged students generally are from low-income families, received inadequate prenatal care and inattentive or unresponsive child care, have low career aspirations, and have low levels of motivation and poor self-esteem. For many disadvantaged children, school success is not an important achievement. Teachers need to help these students understand the economic value of education.

Cause of Poor Performance

During the past 25 years, there has been considerable controversy about the causes of poor performance among disadvantaged children. Because many of these students are black and Hispanic, some researchers argued that the performance problems were due to inherent inferiority of these races. Today, however, professional consensus is that performance problems are due largely to environmental deprivation, that is, lack of relevant experiences and appropriate stimulation. Disadvantaged students can be of any race, national origin, or religious belief.

Government-Sponsored Programs

In 1965 Congress passed the Elementary and Secondary Education Act (Public Law 89-10). Title 1 of this act established financial assistance for school districts with a large concentration of low-income students. Federal programs were established to help ensure appropriate education for all students. For example, Head Start was implemented in 1965 as a nationwide educational program for disadvantaged children and also served handicapped children. The purpose of the program was to provide preschool experiences to these children to prepare them for public school. It was designed as a developmental program and was intended to address both medical and educational needs. Longitudinal studies indicate that Head Start helped disadvantaged children achieve in early grades, but the achievement gains were not maintained throughout secondary grades. Home Start was implemented in 1971 as an alternative to Head Start. This was a home-based program that taught parents how to work with young handicapped children.

Classroom Strategies

To accommodate disadvantaged students, teachers should be aware that these students may not have enough relevant experience to understand certain concepts or examples. For example, severely disadvantaged students may have minimal or no sources of entertainment and no learning incentives ouside the school (no television in the home, infrequent or no excursions to shopping malls or museums, no vacations away from home, no discussion of homework, etc.). Try to provide relevant experiences by taking these students on field trips, assigning special projects, showing movies or slides, and having discussions. Extra effort may be needed to motivate these students. Spend time finding out what rewards are particularly reinforcing to them and teach them how to improve their study habits and test performance. Utilize supplemental materials for additional drill and practice. Point out and discuss appropriate role models. If feasible, invite guest speakers who will entertain and stimulate these students.

The most productive teaching techniques for primary disadvantaged children allow the teacher to maintain control over learning activities. However, it is generally not recommended that these students be given a wide choice in learning (Rosenshine, 1976). Have students read texts, complete exercises, and answer specific questions. Provide close supervision during individual seatwork, ample practice, and immediate feedback on all work. Do not have students choose what they want to learn, and do not ask general questions.

Be careful when reviewing test scores. The scores may be influenced by lack of experience and not represent underlying abilities. Also, be careful of labeling these students. Each student has strengths worth finding and developing.

Bilingual Students

Students who do not speak the official or majority language of the country where they are studying may need special instruction to help them become fluent and understand academic tasks. These students need *bilingual education*. Do not confuse the classifications handicapped, disadvantaged, and bilingual. Like the disadvantaged student, the bilingual student is not considered "handicapped." Of course, some bilingual students are also handicapped. Also realize that there are some bilingual students who are also disadvantaged, but not all bilingual students are disadvantaged.

The Bilingual Education Act

The Bilingual Education Act (part of the Elementary and Secondary Education Act) provided federal support for appropriate English education of primary grade students who have difficulty speaking and understanding English. Originally, the intent of the act was to help students move into the regular English curriculum as quickly as possible. In 1974 the act was revised to encourage bilingual programs to help students maintain mastery of their native language as they become more proficient in English. The act was revised again in 1978 to include students who have difficulty reading and writing English and to place more emphasis on becoming competent in English.

Teaching Strategies

There are two approaches to accommodating the educational needs of the bilingual student, the *native-language approach* and the *direct method*. Using the native-language approach, instruction is presented in the native language and the official language (the majority language) is gradually taught. Using the direct method, instruction is presented in the majority language, and the native language is minimized.

The Use of Computers for Exceptional, Disadvantaged, and Bilingual Students

Computers are a valuable resource in the education and development of exceptional, bilingual, and disadvantaged students. They can be used to help students overcome handicaps by enhancing mobility and communication. Computers can be used as instructional aids, tutors, and reinforcers for students, especially learning-disabled and disadvantaged students. There are many classroom management applications as well. For example, computer programs can generate lesson plans, report cards, tests, and IEPs. They can help you locate relevant materials, provide descriptions of those materials, and recommend which materials are appropriate for your students. Computers are also an efficient storage medium for memos, reports, and student profiles. Advances in technology and cost reductions are making microcomputers affordable for most school districts. Additional information on educational applications of computers is provided in Chapter 14.

Public Law 94-142, the Education for All Handicapped Children Act, mandates that all school-age children receive public education in the least restrictive environment. One result of this law is that more exceptional children are mainstreamed into regular classrooms than previously (prior to 1975). These children can benefit from special instructional techniques and modifications to the environment. Students with visual or hearing impairment may require special seating arrangements and special instructional material such as large- print books and specially captioned films. Students with physical disorders may need assistance moving and reaching materials and may require special medical attention at times. Students with emotional and behavior problems can benefit from well-designed behavior management

*practices; these students are quite capable of learning when their
behavior is under control. Mentally retarded and learning disabled
students can benefit from breaking assignments into small parts and
carefully sequencing each part.*

*Gifted children are also classified as exceptional. Providing sup-
plemental exercises and encouraging them to analyze the rationale and
value of lessons can help maintain the interest of these students and
provide them with sufficient challenge to learn and develop in the
regular classroom environment.*

*Disadvantaged and bilingual students also have special needs, not
because of their physical or mental makeup but because of their backgrounds and environments. Extra effort and patience on the part of the
teacher is needed to motivate these students and keep them from
becoming discouraged.*

Recommended Reading

Anderson, W., S. Chitwood, and D. Hayden. (1982). *Negotiating the Special
Education Maze*. Englewood Cliffs, N.J.: Prentice-Hall. (A guide to the special
education process and the development of IEPs; an especially good resource
for parents.)

Ayrault, E. (1977). *Growing up Handicapped: A Guide for Parents and Professionals to Helping the Exceptional Child*. New York: Seabury Press. (An
excellent source for parents and teachers regarding handicapped students; also
provides lists of helpful agencies.)

Axline, V. (1964). *Dibbs, in Search of Self*. Boston: Houghton Mifflin.
(Describes play therapy with an autistic boy.)

Baskin, B., and K. Harris. (1980). *Books for the Gifted Child*. New York:
Bowker. (An annotated reference of books appropriate for gifted children.)

Braithwaite, E. R. (1959). *To Sir with Love*. (Braithwaite describes his experience teaching in a London slum. This story is also available on video
cassette.)

Canfield, J., and H. C. Wells. (1976). *100 Ways to Enhance Self-Concept in the
Classroom*. Englewood Cliffs, N.J.: Prentice-Hall. (An excellent source of
classroom activities.)

Craig, E. (1972). *P.S. You're not listening*. New York: Signet. (Craig describes
her work with five emotionally disturbed children.)

Daniels, S. (1974). *How 2 Gerbils, 20 Goldfish, 200 Games, 2,000 Books and I Taught Them How to Read.* Philadelphia: Westminster Press. (Anecdotes from Daniels's own experience teaching disadvantaged students to read.)

Hayden, T. (1981). *Somebody Else's Kids.* New York: Avon. (Hayden describes her classroom work with emotionally disturbed children.)

Keyes, D. (1966). *Flowers for Algernon.* New York: Bantam Books. (The story of a retarded man who undergoes surgery to raise his IQ.)

Kirk, S. A., and J. J. Gallagher. (1979). *Educating Exceptional Children* (3d Ed.). Boston: Houghton-Mifflin. (A classic text on exceptional children.)

MacCracken, M. (1986). *Turnabout Children.* New York: Signet. (MacCracken recounts her experiences as a learning disabilities consultant.)

McWilliams, Peter A. (1984). *Personal Computers and the Disabled.* New York: Quantum Press. (An excellent source describing computer hardware devices and software available for persons with hearing or speech impairments and learning or physical disabilities.)

Taba, H., and D. Elkins, D. (1966). *Teaching Strategies for the Culturally Disadvantaged.* Chicago: Rand McNally. [A practical book on teaching secondary students (but applicable to all ages) from disadvantaged backgrounds.]

References

Calhoun, G., and R. Elliott. (1977). Self-Concept and Academic Achievement of Educable Retarded and Emotionally Disturbed Children. *Exceptional Children, 44,* 379-380.

Hasazi, S. B., L. R. Gordon, and C. A. Roe. (1985). Factors Associated with the Employment Status of Handicapped Youth Exiting High School from 1979 to 1983. *Exceptional Children, 51,* 455-469.

Renzulli, J. S. (1978). What Makes Giftedness? Reexamining a Definition. *Phi Delta Kappan, 24,* 180-185.

Rosenshine, B. (1976). Classroom Instruction. In N. L. Gage (Ed.), *The Psychology of Teaching Methods.* The 75th Yearbook of the National Society for the Study of Education, Part I. Chicago: University of Chicago Press.

CHAPTER 14

Computers in Education

Computers and their applications in education are discussed in this chapter. In the early 1980s computers were found in approximately 10 percent of the public schools in the United States; in 1987 computers were present in approximately 90 percent of schools. Computers are potentially valuable educational tools. They can be used to tutor, drill, entertain, and challenge students and to manage grade books and lesson plans. Although computers cannot be used for all aspects of teaching and classroom management, e.g., computers cannot perceive students' feelings or potential behavior problems, they can supplement the classroom teacher to some extent.

Brief History of Computers

Early computers were mechanical devices that used relay switches. The Mark I was a prototype developed at Harvard University in 1939.

First-generation computers used vacuum tubes as active elements. Memory devices were mercury delay lines and electrostatic storage tubes. One of the best known of these is the Electronic Numerical Integrator and Calculator (ENIAC) developed at the University of

Pennsylvania in 1947. This computer occupied 1400 square feet of space and cost $500,000.

Second-generation computers used transistors rather than vacuum tubes as active elements. The first major computers in this generation appeared in 1959.

Third-generation computers use integrated-circuit technology, specifically, microchips, or discrete-component technology. *Microchips* are silicon chips manufactured in assorted sizes, some the length of a human thumbnail. Thousands of tiny electronic circuits are implanted on each chip. Two major advantages of microchip technology are reduction in computer size and cost. This generation of computers supports multiprogramming and multiprocessors. These computers are described as using logic technology components. The first computers in this generation appeared in 1964. Some of the better-known computers of this generation are the IBM 360 and 370 and the Univac 1108 and 1110.

Fourth-generation computers are microcomputers, also called personal computers, that fit on top of a desk and typically cost between $500 and $3000. They have appeared on the market since the late 1970s. Some of the most popular personal computers are the IBM PC and PS/2, and the Apple IIe and the Macintosh.

Fifth-generation computers are more "intelligent" than previous computers. They can solve complex problems using some knowledge and reasoning techniques that are similar to human thought processing. This capability to simulate human reasoning (and even learning) is known as *artificial intelligence*. Humans can interact with these computers by using special simple languages.

Computer Terminology

Some basic terms referring to computer structure, function, and operations are explained after a brief discussion of computer literacy.

Computer Literacy

The term computer literacy implies basic knowledge of computers, such as the fundamentals of computer operation and applications. To

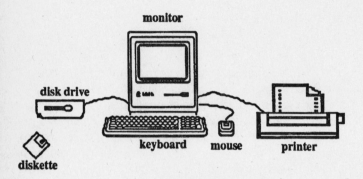

Fig. 14.1 Computer Peripherals

a certain extent computer literacy also implies knowledge of and ability to use computers. Someone who is computer-literate generally knows the relative advantages and disadvantages of using computers for specific applications (e.g., education) and may know how to write computer programs. However, there is some controversy as to whether a person must demonstrate the ability to write programs to be considered computer literate.

Peripherals

Peripherals are equipment used by the computer that are not part of the central processing unit (CPU). Common peripherals are monitors, keyboards, disks, disk drives, printers, modems, and mouse(s).

Monitor–a screen resembling a television set that displays information.

Keyboard–used to input information to the computer; resembles a typewriter.

Disk–a plastic medium used to store computer programs and data.

Disk drive–a device that reads information on disks. Regardless where information is stored on a disk, the disk drive can locate and access that information instantly.

Printer–the device used to print information from the computer in a permanent (i.e., paper) form.

Modem–a device used to transfer data from one computer to another using telephone lines.

Mouse–a pointer device used to locate, select, or transfer information on the computer monitor.

Data

Data is raw information, such as text, numeric values, and special characters, presented to the computer for processing.

Bit (an acronym for *binary digit*)–the basic unit of information content or storage capacity (also known as *memory*) of the computer.

Byte–a group of adjacent bits of fixed number (generally eight in most data processing equipment) that constitute a character, an instruction, or some other logical unit of information, which is usually shorter than a word.

Kilobyte–the most commonly used unit of measure for computer memory, the kilobyte is equal to 1024 bytes (1024 is the round number nearest to 1000 in the binary code); one kilobyte (1K) is the amount of memory needed to store approximately 1000 characters.

Program

A program is a complete set of instructions that tells the computer how to process a given unit of information or perform a specific task. A program is self-contained–that is, it starts at a given point and ends at another given point and contains all the directions necessary to fulfill this purpose–and can run automatically, without direct control or interaction from a human user. System control programs and utility programs perform generalized tasks for the benefit of computer users.

Application

An application is an interactive (i.e., involving two-way communication between the computer and the user) computer program that is run by the user to solve a specific problem or perform a specific function, such as producing bills or spreadsheets (large tabulations of numeric data), printing a report, or entering data into a computer file.

Software

Computer programs and applications are often referred to collectively by the generic term *software*, as distinguished from *hardware*, the physical components or equipment of the computer or data processing system. The term *courseware* is sometimes used to refer to educational software. *Hardcopy* is information printed on paper; *softcopy* is information displayed on a computer monitor.

Terminal

A terminal is a hardware component of the data processing system that enables two-way communication between a human user and a computer. Thus, information is transmitted back and forth between the user and the computer through their interface, the terminal, which is equipped with a monitor and is connected to the computer by either direct attachment or remote control. Some terminals are called "dumb" because they depend on the computer for all control functions and cannot perform or compute independently; other terminals have some computing capacity independent of the computer.

Time-sharing refers to a computing system in which two or more terminals share the resources of one computer. The computer may be located near to (e.g., in the same room) or remote from (e.g., in another room, building, city, state, or country) the terminals and connected to them by means of telephone lines, cables, or electromagnetic waves (microwaves, radio waves, etc.). Time-sharing is usually a business enterprise, where customers pay a usage fee.

Standalone

A standalone is a data processing device capable of operating independently (i.e., outside the control) of a computer. Keypunches and reader-sorters are examples of standalone machines. The term standalone is also used generically to refer to any computer that contains its own CPU, that is, a computer that does not require the use of a modem or another means of accessing another computer. A standalone computer can, however, interface with other computers to form a computer network or to supplement its own computing capacity.

On-Line and Off-Line Equipment

The term *on-line* pertains to equipment (e.g., a terminal) capable of interacting or directly communicating with a computer; thus *on-line information* can be directly accessed by a person using a computer. *Off-line* equipment is not in communication with, or is temporarily disconnected from, a computer. This term should not be confused with *downtime*, which means the amount of time a computer system is down (rendered inoperative, as a result of a malfunction, power failure, etc.), especially during periods when it should be *up*.

Applications in Education

Educational applications of computers are described in the following sections.

Computer-Based Education

Computer-based education (CBE) is an application of computers for educational purposes. As the computer industry expanded from the 1940s through the 1960s, there was an increasing need to quickly train new computer personnel. This need was the major impetus for designing CBE, which has been developing since the 1950s.

A parallel development in the education field was B. F. Skinner's interest in programmed instruction, which is self-paced instruction on a specific topic. This instruction is characterized by subdivision of the material into small units and by provisions for immediate feedback (refer to the section on individualized instruction in Chapter 9). Computers are extremely well suited for presenting this type of instruction.

During the 1960s many corporations and universities developed

CBE applications. However, at that time, computers were so expensive that many schools could not afford them, so many CBE applications were used by large corporations and industries rather than academicians.

The decrease in computer costs over the last 20 years helped bring CBE to the public schools. Some of the early CBE applications were drill and practice exercises. The computer provided questions for the students to answer. The computer was not used to teach new information, only to provide practice.

Today, CBE applications can provide much more than drill and practice. Two major categories of CBE are *computer-based instruction* (CBI) and *computer-managed instruction* (CMI). CBI is the use of computers to tutor students or provide practice exercises and drill. CMI is the use of computers to manage instruction, that is, to plan lessons and manage grade records. Both aspects of CBE can greatly benefit the classroom teacher.

Computer-Based Instruction

Computer-based instruction (CBI) is the direct use of computers to help educate students. Other terms used interchangeably with CBI are *computer-aided instruction* (CAI), *computer-assisted learning* (CAL), and *instructional application of computers* (IAC).

In its most complete implementation, CBI uses the computer as a tutor to present information, then provide practice sessions, then assess the student's understanding of the material, and then provide additional information if it is needed. In theory, this process provides individualized instruction to a student because it assesses the level of understanding and provides more information as needed. Well-written programs can be quite effective at this task. The computer can be used to present nice graphics (illustrations), which appeal to most students. The computer program can be designed to provide frequent reinforcement for persistence at a task and for correct responses. Another advantage is that many children like to sit at a computer to work.

In general, all CBI applications (1) follow a specific, predefined plan; (2) allow students to work at their own pace; and (3) provide frequent feedback at designated locations in the program.

CBI applications developed today take several forms: drill and practice, tutorials, simulations, and games.

Drill and Practice Programs. Drill and practice programs are used to provide practice in areas in which the student has received previous instruction. Typically, the computer presents a problem, the student provides a response, and the computer then informs the student whether the response was correct. These programs are the most common CBE applications. They are similar to flash card and worksheet activities. An example of a drill program is *Mastertype,* produced by Mindscape. *Mastertype* provides typing drills to increase speed and accuracy. This program uses graphics to make the drills more enjoyable and provides a score at the end. Another example of a practice program is *Math Blaster,* produced by Davidson & Associates. *Math Blaster* provides practice sessions in basic math skills: addition, subtraction, multiplication, and division. The program also provides practice in computing fractions, decimals, and percentages. Like *Mastertype, Math Blaster* uses pictures.

Tutorial Programs. Tutorial programs are used to present information, request a response from the student, and provide more information when needed on the basis of a student's response. One major advantage of these tutorial programs is their interactive nature. CBI seems to be effective in helping students learn more quickly and in fostering a positive attitude toward learning (e.g., Kulik and Kulik, 1987).

One of the best known examples of CBI is Programmed Logic for Automatic Teaching Operation (PLATO). PLATO is operated jointly by the University of Illinois at Champaign-Urbana and Control Data Corporation. More than 1000 terminals have access to PLATO, through telephone lines and microwaves. Teachers write lessons using a special language called *Tutor* and store these lessons on the central computer. Other teachers can access the lessons. Students use terminals to view the lessons. Some of the lessons incorporate special graphics and animations. Another popular tutorial is *Typing Tutor IV,* produced by Simon & Schuster Software. *Typing Tutor IV* teaches students to use a keyboard. The program records accuracy, speed, and specific problems. The program then tailors subsequent lessons to develop the student's weaker skills.

Simulation Programs. Simulation programs are used to present information as closely as possible to the way it would appear in real life. For example, flight simulation programs have been developed to help teach prospective pilots to fly. Simulation programs are especially useful when a high skill level is needed and failure at the task has life-threatening implications. Other useful applications are teaching cardiopulmonary resuscitation (CPR) and medical diagnosis of heart disease. These skills are difficult to develop, and there is not much opportunity to practice them in a real-life situation. Additionally, you would not want someone who is first learning CPR to practice on a person who actually needs it. Well-developed simulation programs allow skill level to be brought to a criterion level before practicing in real-life situations. PLATO (mentioned above) has been used to create many simulation programs.

Instructional Games. Instructional games are used to develop problem-solving skills and motivate students to learn. Games can also be used to increase eye-hand coordination. Because these games can be particularly motivating for students, they can be used as rewards for completed homework, good behavior, and other achievements. They can also be used as learning activities in their own right, but it is important to develop specific learning objectives for each program. *Early Games for Young Children,* published by Springboard Software, uses games to teach math and language skills to preschoolers. Several arcade-type games are available. For example, *Mouse Stampede* was published by Mark of the Unicorn to run on the MacIntosh. This is a noninstructional game of cats, rats, cheese, and fast-paced action.

Computer-Managed Instruction

Computer-managed instruction (CMI), a relatively recent development, is the application of computers as classroom management tools. The most popular uses are computerized grade books and testing programs.

Computerized Grade Books and Testing Programs. Computerized grade books are used to add or average student grades, calculate class statistics, and create graphs. Testing programs help by providing possible test items for specific content areas. Teachers can review the items, make changes here and there, and print a test—all in a relatively short period of time. *Elementary Mathematics Classroom Learning*

System, published by Sterling Swift Publishing Company, provides tests and management forms to help teachers keep track of student progress in a math curriculum. *Master Grades: Teacher's Grade-Keeping Utility*, published by Midwest Software, is a grade and attendance management system. This product organizes attendance information, provides three kinds of progress notes for parents, maintains grades, converts scores to grades, and performs several other management tasks. *Lotus 1-2-3*, published by Lotus Development Corporation, is a spreadsheet application that could be used to record and average student grades. *Spreadsheet applications*, as mentioned earlier, are large tabulations of numeric data on which mathematical computations can be performed on rows and columns of numbers. One advantage to using spreadsheet applications rather than calculators is that one can add, change, or delete scores and the results will be recalculated automatically. One does not have to enter all the numbers a second time (or third or fourth, etc.).

Word Processing. One of the most common computer applications is word processing, which is an electronic means of creating and revising text. Information is viewed on the computer monitor. Changes can be made and the information can be formatted with minimal effort (once the program is learned). Also, many word processors include on-line dictionaries that check for correct spelling and identify words that may be spelled incorrectly. Teachers can utilize word processors to maintain lesson plans, memos to parents, permission slips, to-do lists, and a vast number of other tasks. Common word processing programs are: *MacWrite*, published by Apple Computer; *Microsoft Word*, published by Microsoft; and *Writing Assistant*, published by IBM Corporation.

Data Processing. Data processing uses the computer to store, change, and make calculations on sets of information (numbers and text). A *database* is a set of information. A common data processing application in academics is a library database that maintains a catalog of books and periodicals that can be accessed by title, author, and subject. Classroom teachers may have use for a data base of extracurricular or special-interest activities and projects, math problems, test items, or interesting books. *dBASE III* (meaning database 3), published by Ashton-Tate, helps manage large databases. *File*, published by

Microsoft, is a data manager that is especially useful for creating forms and organizing lists (e.g., mailing lists, reference lists, special-interest activities, self-esteem building activities, parents' phone numbers, emergency contacts).

Computer Time as a Reward

As mentioned above, computers seem to appeal intrinsically to many students. Therefore, computer time can be used as an incentive for students to complete other activities. Some schools have programs that create greeting cards and large banners. These programs are quite popular with students. However, one disadvantage of implementing computer time as a reward is the limited availability of the computer.

Educational Software

Today, many educational software packages are available. Some of these products are potentially beneficial to the classroom teacher.

Software Packages

Writing for *Family & Home Office Computing*, Wu (1988) developed a list of the top 10-selling packages. Several of these programs have received awards, and they tend to be highly recommended by educators, parents, and students. The program names, descriptions, and publishers are listed below in alphabetic order. Complete addresses and phone numbers for the publishers are available in the article cited above.

Barron's Computer Study Program for the SAT, published by Barron's Educational Series. Practice questions and drills to prepare students to take the Scholastic Aptitude Test are provided in this package. The package also includes two practice tests.

Early Games for Young Children, published by Springboard Software. Number and letter recognition, matching, counting, addition, subtraction, language skills, and other skills are presented for preschoolers in this package.

Learning DOS, published by Microsoft Corporation. This package provides step-by-step exercises to teach DOS (disk operating system) commands and file manipulation. DOS is an operating system used on many personal computers (PCs).

Mastertype, published by Mindscape. This package provides typing drills designed to increase speed and accuracy.

Math Blaster, published by Davidson & Associates. This package provides practice in basic math skills: addition, subtraction, multiplication, division. It also provides practice in calculating fractions, decimals, and percentages.

The Newsroom, published by Springboard Software. Students develop and print newsletters using this package. Pictures and different type styles can be incorporated in the "paper."

The Print Shop, published by Broderbund. Users create and print banners, stationery, and cards with this package. Pictures and different type styles can be incorporated in the designs.

Reader Rabbit, published by The Learning Company. This package uses a rabbit to introduce over 200 three-letter words, concentrating on visual discrimination and memory skills. It helps young children develop reading skills, vocabulary, and spelling skills.

Typing Tutor IV, published by Simon & Schuster Software. This package teaches students to use a keyboard. The program tailors instruction on the basis of a student's errors.

Where in the World Is Carmen Sandiego? and *Where in the USA is Carmen Sandiego?*, both published by Broderbund. These packages teach students about world and U.S. geography. Students try to find Carmen Sandiego, who is stealing national treasures. Students have to utilize a world almanac and a travel guide to research locations and clues.

Reference Sources for Software Packages

There are many sources available to help you find software packages that teach skills, provide drills, and so on. Provided below are several of those references and a brief description of each.

Software Reviews on File, published by Facts on File, Inc. This document is a collection of previously published software reviews. Reviews of several products are compiled and added to the document on a monthly basis. These software reviews are organized by category. Examples of categories are education, entertainment, and business. For each product, the author, producer, copyright, price, contents, and system requirements are listed.

The Yellow Book: A Parent's Guide to Teacher-Tested Educational Software, published in 1985 by National Education Association Educational Computer Services (NEA Educational Computer Services). NEA Educational Computer Services was formed in 1983 to help students and teachers utilize computer products. Descriptions and reviews of educational software packages are provided in this book. The packages that are mentioned in this book are considered, on the basis of an NEA Educational Computer Services assessment, to be technically reliable, instructionally sound, and easy to use. Packages are organized by preschool, elementary, secondary, postsecondary, and applications software. Special courseware for the learning disabled is also reviewed.

The Software Catalog, published by Elsevier Science Publishing twice a year. This directory includes six editions: *Microcomputers, Minicomputers, Business Software, Science and Engineering, Health Professions*, and *Systems Software*. Microcomputers provides descriptions of approximately 25,000 microcomputer programs. Programs are listed within subject categories. Educational software is one subject category. Examples of categories within the educational subject are Addition/Subtraction, Aptitude Testing/Counseling, Cognitive Development, French, Math, Special Education, Speed Reading, and Computer Literacy. The programs are cross-referenced by company, computer system, operating system, language, microprocessor, application, and keyword. A toll-free phone number is provided for help with questions about software and price information. This publication is a comprehensive source. It lists and describes virtually all available software products. However, the products are not reviewed; therefore, the quality of products is unknown.

Psychware Sourcebook (Krug, 1987). This book is a reference guide to computer-based products for psychological and educational assessment.

Answers Online: Your Guide to Informational Data Bases (Newlin, 1985). Many online databases are described, including a Yellow Pages for the United States, encyclopedias, mail services, and journal abstracts. Additionally, the author describes the process of gathering information that is stored on other computers (going online). She identifies the types of hardware and software needed; types of database; and how to access, search, and evaluate these.

The Free Software Catalog and Directory, published by Crown Publishers (Froehlich, 1984). This book lists over 5,000 software programs that run under the CP/M (Control Program for Microcomputers). All programs listed in this book are in public domain. Public domain means the software can be used and distributed without payment to the owner.

The Book of Macintosh Software, published by Arrays (McCrosky et al., 1985). This book lists, reviews, and "grades" software products that run on a Macintosh. For exclusive Macintosh users, it is a more efficient source than the other publications.

In addition to these books, there are numerous periodicals that provide useful information, including software reviews such as *Family & Home Office Computing, Electronic Learning, Electronic Education, BYTE, MacWorld,* and *PC Magazine*. These magazines are available in school libraries, public libraries, and some supermarkets.

Software packages are investments. Among the thousands (over 10,000) of available packages, many are of poor quality. Several sources on purchasing software for personal or school use are available. Consulting the sources listed below and reading professional software reviews (from the sources listed above) can increase one's likelihood of making profitable investments.

How to Buy Software (Glossbrenner, 1984). This book was designed to present all the information needed to make good purchasing decisions. The author discusses where and how to purchase educational software or obtain free software, and discusses important concepts and terminology.

Educational Microcomputing Annual: Volume 1, 1985, published by Oryx (Tashner, 1985). This book is an easy-to-follow presentation of microcomputers in education, including uses, trends, software selection, a glossary, relevant journals, and societies.

Use of Computers in Schools Today

The implementation of computers in public schools is in its infancy. Today, there are more computers in secondary schools than in elementary schools. In secondary schools, computers are used primarily for learning about computers and learning to program in BASIC (beginner's all-purpose symbolic instruction code) language. In elementary schools, computers are used primarily to learn and practice arithmetic and English skills.

Effectiveness in the Classroom

Students seem to achieve roughly the same amount when computers or teachers present information. However, students seem to learn somewhat more quickly, have a more positive attitude toward learning, help each other more, and be less dependent on the teacher when they work with computers. Although these preliminary results are encouraging, it will be many years before comprehensive evaluations of computer effectiveness will be complete and reliable.

Helping Handicapped Students

The potential utility of computers for helping handicapped students is just beginning to be realized. Computers can be used to help speech-impaired students "speak." The student types a word or presses a symbol, and the computer generates speechlike sound. Computers can also be used to recognize speech for hearing-impaired students. A computer is programmed to recognize voice input (voice recognition) and then print the words on paper to enable the student to read what the computer heard. There are a few problems with voice recognition technologies used today. Affordable computers can interpret a limited vocabulary, and even within the limited vocabulary, the computer does not recognize words with 100 percent accuracy. Computers are also being used to help physically handicapped students gain more control over their environment. Students can give instruction to a computer by blowing air through a tube, sucking air from the tube, moving a lever that is held in the mouth, and in other ingenious ways. Computers help physically handicapped students turn pages in a book, complete homework exercises, turn on lights in a room, operate automobiles, turn on a television, and many other daily activities.

Current Problems with Computer Use

There are several problems with the use of computers in educational settings today. For example, the number of computers is insufficient to provide easy access for students. There are serious limitations on funding for computer-related purchases. When schools obtain funding for computers, administrators often purchase computers without a well-developed plan. Most educational software packages are of poor quality. In general, there is not enough computer and educational expertise to utilize fully the capabilities of computers. Appropriate computer literacy training and introduction to available software is not provided for teachers. Therefore, teachers may not know any more about the computers than the students.

Teacher Training for Computer Use

To help teachers learn how computers can be used in classrooms, well-designed teacher training needs to be developed and implemented. Training should include computer literacy, potential uses of computers in the classroom, what software is available, how to use that software, how to teach students about computers, and so on. Computers should be integrated in both classroom management and curriculum. Administrators should stay abreast of technological advances and current research on computer implementation. Administrators should work closely with computer specialists to plan the use of computers in schools. Administrators should identify potential uses in each school and work with computer specialists to determine how those needs can be met (i.e., what hardware is needed, what software is appropriate, what software is of high quality, what peripherals are worth spending money on, which students will use the computers). Administrators, teachers, and computer specialists should work closely together to determine objectives for computer use. Long-term plans for fund raising and computer acquisitions should be developed. Communication is vitally important. Teachers and computer specialists should develop special means of informing each other about computer-related purchases, ideas, successes, and problems. Similarly, parents should be included in decisions and kept informed. Parents, especially those with experience or special interest in computers, should be asked to help evaluate software, plan purchases, and educate teachers.

Expectations for Educational Use of Computers

Computers are here to stay. Schools that do not have computers now will purchase them. Schools that have one or two will probably purchase more. Hardware will become more affordable. Personal computer systems will continue to offer increased amounts of computing power for the buck.

Advanced Technology

Additional technology will mean more exciting presentations in the next 5 years. For example, CD-ROM (compact disk-read-only memory), videocassette recorders, and computers will be used together to integrate video images, high-quality audio signals, and computer graphics. Therefore, tutorial programs can be created to contain much more information, real-life pictures and sounds, and greater ability to individualize instruction. Information that could not be communicated by means of earlier technologies will be incorporated in newer software packages and implemented using computers, video players, and compact disks. For example, software programs that demonstrate scientific experiments, cooking, and automobile repairs will be developed. This technology also offers potential for increased interaction between the student and the computer. Students will be able to get more detailed information about concepts and terms they do not understand. They will be able to watch moving pictures (the video technology) on the computer monitor. For example, a program on automobile repairs will have moving video images of a mechanic actually fixing an automobile. The student will be able to see and hear what the mechanic does. The student will be able to control the rate of the presentation, skip parts, back up, and control other maneuvers. More information will be available so the presentation can be tailored to the individual's learning style and skill level.

Increased Usefulness for Handicapped Students

Computers and related products will become increasingly important tools in the education of handicapped students. Robotics applications will be developed to aid students with physical handicaps. Computerized speech and voice recognition technology will continue to improve and become more available for vision- and speech-impaired students. Advances in telecommunications will allow special students at home to communicate easily with classroom peers and an instructor during actual classes.

Improved Computer Programs

Higher-quality software programs will be developed. More teachers will write software and work with software developers to create specialized educational applications. Textbook publishers will offer computer programs to supplement student reading material. They may also provide sample tests on-line. More teachers will learn to use authoring languages, which allow teachers to create their own computerized drill and instruction. Computer education in the schools will continue to grow. In addition to learning BASIC, Pascal, and LOGO, students will learn artificial intelligence languages such as PROLOG and LISP.

More Individualized Instruction

Applications utilizing artificial intelligence will be developed to tailor tutorials to individual students, thereby providing more useful instruction than that available through current programs. These programs will be able to identify patterns of errors and strengths and adapt instruction to correct the errors and reinforce strengths.

Development of Computer Neworks

Computer networks will be created within and between schools. Within a given classroom, teachers will be able to monitor student work on computer screens and students will be able to view the teacher's computer screen. Between classes and schools, networking will allow more students to access special information and software. By connecting two or more computers together, students and teachers will be able to exchange data and share peripherals, such as special printers. Increases in telecommunications technology will also provide more information online. Encyclopedias, special books, and other databases will be available to students through modem connections.

Training in Computer Use

Graduate programs will require education and psychology students to demonstrate computer literacy. Undergraduate teacher education courses will be developed to familiarize teachers with available software products. The involvement of industry in academics will continue. Major corporations will continue to offer educational discounts, donate equipment, and conduct cooperative research programs.

Program Evaluation

Program evaluation of the effectiveness of computers will help educators understand where computers can offer the greatest benefit in classroom instruction. These studies will help identify components of effective computer education and areas that need further investigation. As the novelty begins to wear off, we will have a more accurate assessment of the utility of computers in the schools.

Demand for Educational Specialists

With the increase in computer technology and the subsequent increase in CBE applications, the demand will increase for specialists who can develop effective CBE applications. Persons trained in educational psychology have a great deal to contribute to this work.

Today computers can be found in almost all public schools in the United States. Computer-based education (CBE) is the application of computers to help educate students. CBE has been demonstrated to be an effective instructional media. Computer-based instruction (CBI) utilizes computers to tutor students, provides drill and practice, simulates complex tasks, and entertains students. Computer-managed instruction (CMI) utilizes computers to help maintain grade books and create tests. There are many potential benefits to using computers in the classroom. Computers can be used to help handicapped students complete tasks that most people take for granted, such as hearing and speaking, turning equipment on and off, and turning pages in a book. Computers can be used to provide special practice and attention to students when the teacher is not available. Learning about computers, specifically how to use them in the classroom, which software is useful, and similar information, can seem overwhelming. Teachers should utilize any available resources, such as libraries, computer retail stores, continuing-education courses, advice of experts in the computer industry, and assistance from other teachers, to tackle this task.

Recommended Reading

Alessi, S. M., and S. R. Trollip. (1985). *Computer-Based Instruction: Methods and Development*. Englewood Cliffs, N.J.: Prentice-Hall. (A history of computer-based instruction and a summary of the current state.)

Bork, A. (1983). *Personal Computers for Education*. New York: Harper & Row. (A short, easy-to-read introduction to computer- based education.)

Glossbrenner, A. (1984). *How to Buy Software*. New York: St. Martin's. (Book designed to present all information needed to make good purchasing decisions; discusses where to buy software, how to get free software, how to buy educational software, and important concepts and terminology.)

Kulik, J. A., and C. C. Kulik. (1987). Review of Recent Research Literature on

Computer-Based Instruction. *Contemporary Educational Psychology, 12*, 222-230. (Review article summarizing research on the effectiveness of computer-based education in elementary schools, high schools, and colleges.)

McWilliams, Peter A. (1984). *Personal Computers and the Disabled.* New York: Quantum Press. (An excellent source describing computer hardware devices and software available for persons with hearing or speech impairments, and learning or physical disabilities.)

Papert, S. (1980). *Mindstorms: Children, Computers, and Powerful Ideas.* New York: Basic Books. (A description of LOGO—how it was created and how it works.)

Surviving the High-Tech Hype (September 1983). *Principle,* pp. 4-5. (Presents a brief, humorous history of computers and two views by educators.)

Tashner, F. H. (Ed.). (1985). *Educational Microcomputing Annual: Volume 1, 1985.* Phoenix, Ariz.: Oryx. (Easy-to-follow source describing microcomputers in education, including uses, trends, software selection, a glossary, and list of relevant journals and societies; book consists mostly of reprinted articles from educational magazines.)

Thornburg, D. D. (July 1984). Technostress, *Compute!,* pp. 96-99. (An argument against the view that computers create social and psychological distress; suggests that computers are being used as "scapegoats.")

Walker, D. F., and R. D. Hess. (1984). *Instructional Software: Principles and Perspectives for Design and Use.* Belmont, Calif.: Wadsworth. (Provides criteria for evaluating computer hardware and software.)

References

Froehlich, R. A. (1984). *The Free Software Catalog and Directory.* New York: Crown.

Glossbrenner, A. (1984). *How to Buy Software.* New York: St. Martin's.

Kulik, J. A., and C. C. Kulik. (1987). Review of Recent Research Literature on Computer-Based Instruction. *Contemporary Educational Psychology, 12*, 222-230.

Krug, S. (Ed.). (1987). *Psychware Sourcebook,* (2d ed.). Champaign, Ill.: MeriTech.

McCrosky, M., M. Mellin, and R. Ritz. (Eds.). (1985). *The Book of Macintosh Software.* Van Nuys, Calif.: Arrays.

Newlin, B. (1985). *Answers Online: Your Guide to Informational Data Bases.* Berkeley, Calif.: Osborne McGraw-Hill.

The Software Catalog (1987). New York: Elsevier.

Software Reviews on File. New York: Facts on File.

Tashner, F. H. (Ed.). (1985). *Educational Microcomputing Annual: Volume 1, 1985.* Phoenix, Ariz.: Oryx.

The Yellow Book: A Parent's Guide to Teacher-Tested Educational Software. (1985). New York: National Education Association Educational Computer Services.

Wu, L. (1988). Top Ten Educational Programs: Software that Families Like Yours Are Buying. *Family & Home Office Computing, 6,* 24-26.

CHAPTER 15

Designing Instruction for Specific Subject Areas

Skills that are important for reading, writing, and mathematics are discussed in this chapter. Contemporary educational psychologists strive to provide specific recommendations to improve teaching in specific subject areas. To develop these recommendations, researchers attempt to determine which subskills are needed and what problems students encountered in mastering those skills. Two ways of investigating problem areas are observing differences in performance between high and low performers and completing detailed error analyses.

Subject area research is certainly more comprehensive and complex than the material presented in this chapter. The objective here is to provide an introduction to this aspect of educational psychology.

Reading

Reading is obtaining meaning from printed text, an important skill for students. Once students learn to read, they apply this ability to study academic subject areas, as well as to learn about current and extracurricular events. Psychologists have studied the reading process in detail. Many of their research findings can be applied to the teaching of reading skills.

Reading Readiness

A child must develop several skills before acquiring a functional ability to read. Collectively, these skills are called reading readiness.

Prereading Activities

Some researchers (e.g., Spache, 1981) consider general factors like vision and hearing acuity and age to be important for reading readiness. These researchers advocate programs that help develop physical, visual, and auditory skills. Examples of activities included in these programs are jumping rope, gymnastics, art, story-telling, and musical games. Other researchers (e.g., Venezky, 1980) consider specific prereading skills to be important for reading readiness. Venezky, for example, advocates programs that increase students' awareness of the order of letters (e.g., nap versus pan), the orientation of letters (e.g., d versus b), and the details of individual words (e.g., kit versus kite). Venezky also recommends phonetics-oriented programs to help students learn to match and blend sounds.

The Age Factor

There has been some controversy among researchers regarding the age factor in reading readiness. Morphett and Washburne (1931) noticed that most students made satisfactory reading progress at the mental age of 6½ years. They thus suggested that reading instruction begin at that age, and many specialists still believe that is appropriate. However, methodological problems in the Morphett-Washburne study limit the applicability of their findings. Some contemporary researchers (e.g., Hodges & Rudorf, 1984) have demonstrated benefits of reading instruction before age 6, and a number of children do develop the ability to read before that age. Although research in this area continues, the "right" time to learn to read probably varies among individuals.

Classroom Applications

Teachers should help young children develop a positive, receptive attitude toward reading and help them master reading readiness skills. The following steps are suggested for enhancing reading readiness.

1. *Help children develop a positive attitude toward reading.* Model and reinforce good reading habits. Encourage parents to model good reading habits. Discuss with children topics or events that you learned about from books, emphasizing, if possible, that you acquired information from *books* and not other sources. Read to them and encourage parents, siblings, and friends to read to them also. Reading stories and other material to children at bedtime can help them relax and prepare to sleep. Some public libraries provide reading services for young children during which a librarian or volunteer reads a story to a group of children at the library. However, do not pressure or try to force children to read as this could damp their enjoyment of reading.

2. *Help children develop or utilize physical, visual, and auditory skills.* For instance, encourage them to draw, clap, sing, work with clay or string beads, and differentiate between similar objects, sounds, and so on. Suggest that parents engage their children in these activities as much as possible at home and elsewhere outside the school.

3. *Have young students screened for vision and hearing disorders.* Early identification of any existing or potential problems in these areas of perception is important. Any perceptual problems can cause unnecessary frustration and interfere with development of reading skills.

4. *Help children learn to pay attention.* Children who cannot sit still or focus on one topic or object for a reasonable amount of time (say, a few minutes) generally will have difficulties learning to read. Children should be able to concentrate on reading skills without being distracted by extraneous impulses or stimuli when they begin reading.

Decoding

Once students can pay attention to printed information, can discriminate between letters, and generally have mastered other reading readiness skills, they are ready to decipher whole words and sentences. Reading can be divided into several subtasks. The two primary components are decoding and comprehension. *Decoding* involves translation of printed symbols into sounds that represent meaningful information. One looks at a word, pronounces it, and searches long-term memory for the meaning of the word.

Phonics versus Whole-Word Approach

Phonics Approach. One of the most common ways to teach decoding is the phonics approach, in which students are taught letter-sound relationships. You may remember "this is an 'a' and sounds like a, a, a, apple" and "ch, ch, chair." These familiar phrases exemplify attempts to teach common sounds and the letters that are used to represent them. One problem with using this approach to teach the English language is that certain letters have multiple or hidden sounds. For example, an "a" may have a long vowel sound as in "gate" or a short, flat vowel sound as in "hat" and the "k" in "know" or "knee" is not heard in speech. Readers must learn rules that specify when a given letter or letter combination produces a particular sound. Learning these rules can be difficult, but additional problems can develop when clearcut rules do not exist. To eliminate this ambiguity, the Initial Teaching Alphabet (also known by its acronym, ITA) was developed with 44 characters, each character producing a single related sound. Although this system was designed to eliminate ambiguity, it potentially introduces new problems for students who must subsequently transfer their decoding skills to the English language. Moreover, it is sometimes difficult to find materials published in the Initial Teaching Alphabet; although this system includes 44 characters, the number of unique sounds taught in different programs varies.

Whole-Word Approach. In contrast to the phonics approach is the whole-word approach in which children learn to recognize words on the basis of their appearance. Children initially learn a sight-word vocabulary which includes simple, common words such as "ball" and "hat" and they subsequently add words. One way to add words to a sight vocabulary is to teach children to recognize word families such as "hat, cat, pat, mat, chat."

Eclectic Approach. The relative merits of the phonics approach versus the whole-word approach have been a great source of controversy for teaching reading (Chall, 1967). This controversy is reflected in historical trends shifting between the two approaches. The phonics method, using *The New England Primer*, was taught in the 1700s. Children were first taught the alphabet, then letter combinations, then words, and then sentences. The whole-word approach, using the *McGuffey Readers*, was popular in the mid-1800s. Children were taught new words by seeing them in written form, hearing them spoken, learning to spell them, and seeing pictures related to those words. Similar to contemporary basal readers (graded series of books and activities), there were different *McGuffey Readers* for children of different ages and ability levels. In the 1880s there was a resurgence of the phonics approach. In the early 1900s there was renewed interest in the whole-word approach and in silent (nonverbal) reading. Today, most basal readers utilize an eclectic approach, which includes both phonics and whole-word instruction.

Language-Experience Approach

Another way of beginning reading instruction is the language-experience approach. As a child tells a story, the classroom teacher records it on paper. Children may be asked to "read" the story or copy it on paper. Some teachers record the story verbatim. The language-experience approach helps children understand the relationship between oral and written language and is especially useful for children who do not speak standard English. Additionally, this approach helps children learn to recognize words.

Matching and Recoding

Irrespective of the method of beginning reading instruction, it is important for students to develop decoding skills. There are several examples of recent research that further investigates the decoding process. Ehri (1982) suggests that there are actually two decoding processes: matching and recoding.

Matching occurs when a printed word is part of one's sight vocabulary. In this case, a person tries to match the pattern of the written word with the representation of the word in long-term memory.

Recoding occurs when a person must decode an unfamiliar word by sounding it out (reciting it orally). Researchers have demonstrated that skilled readers can match and recode words more quickly than less skilled readers (e.g., Ehri and Wilce, 1983; Frederiksen, 1981).

The implications of this research are the need to provide practice time for less skilled readers so that the decoding process can become automated. There also seems to be a relationship between decoding speed and comprehension. Perfetti and Hogoboam (1975) found that students who scored low on an standardized reading comprehension test take about 1 second longer than do other students to decode unfamiliar and nonsense words. A plausible explanation is that the more time students have to spend decoding words, the less time they have to comprehend the meaning of the information.

The Word Superiority Effect

An interesting, and related, psychological phenomenon is the word-superiority effect. People can read letters in words faster than letters alone or letters in nonsense words (nonwords) (e.g., Reicher, 1969). This effect has been used as support for the whole-word approach (e.g., Singer, 1981). However, current theorists (e.g., Johnston, 1981) maintain that the word is still analyzed in parts and thus do not justify support for the whole-word approach. One implication of this finding is that you can use familiar words to provide letter clues when students have difficulty decoding new words.

Decoding Strategies

Understanding how skilled, adult readers decode words can provide clues for teaching decoding strategies to new readers. Baron (1977) asked adults to read aloud pronounceable nonsense words and then explain how they decided how to pronounce each word. Baron identified three decoding strategies: similarity, analogy, and corresponding. The *similarity strategy* was used to make a nonsense word sound like a real word (e.g., "blud" = blood). The *analogy strategy* was used to make a nonsense word partially rhyme with a real word (e.g., "rotion" = rhymes with motion). The *corresponding strategy* was used to sound out words, similar to a phonics approach. This strategy was used most often. This finding lends support to the importance of effective phonics instruction. Baron's research suggests that students be encouraged to apply alternative decoding strategies as needed.

Suggestions to Facilitate Decoding

The following suggestions may be used by the teacher to help children learn to decode words.

1. *Do not correct every minor mistake.* Reinforce effort and pay attention to the correct words. Try to correct minor errors in a casual, unintentional manner, rather than drawing attention to each little mistake.

2. *Encourage students to make educated guesses based on story context, pictures, and common sense.* The important goal of reading is to understand the printed word, not pronounce every word correctly (although that would be desirable).

3. *Allow students to reread familiar material.* This experience can build self-confidence. Once students understand the gist of the material, they can concentrate on unfamiliar words. Additionally, repeated exposure to words seems to facilitate decoding skills (e.g., Samuels, 1979).

4. *Devote time to reading and promote positive attitudes.* To develop proficiency in reading with the ability to automatically decode many words, students need time to practice. Computer programs can be used to tutor students and provide practice exercises (Frederickson et al., 1983).

5. *Teach students to employ alternative decoding strategies.* For example, a student may be able to figure out an unfamiliar word by determining if it is similar to known words.

Comprehension

In addition to decoding words, reading requires pulling words together to understand the intended meaning of the complete message.

The second major component in reading is comprehension (also called *literal comprehension*), which means understanding a printed message. Literal comprehension requires an understanding of the words in a passage.

Comprehension Research

One important research issue is how educators can help readers efficiently access word meanings (called *lexical access*). *Inferential comprehension* requires integrating, summarizing, and assimilating the printed words to infer meaning.

Bartlett (1932) investigated how people learn and remember meaningful prose. Bartlett discovered that people do not always remember things precisely but do try to derive sense or meaning from things they remember. More specifically, he found that people

1. Remember the gist of a story, not the details.

2. Remember a few particularly interesting details, and sometimes emphasize those details.

3. Modify or alter a story to make it more compact and consistent with expectations.

Bartlett's work helps us think of comprehension as an active and constructive process. This work demonstrated that existing knowledge plays a role in comprehension of new material. Bartlett used the idea of schema, a general-knowledge structure used to select and organize information, to indicate that existing knowledge is important for comprehension and memory.

Components of Comprehension

The comprehension process can be divided into a number of components. Rosenshine (1980) reviewed basal readers to identify the following eight components: locating details, recognizing the main idea, recognizing the sequence of events, drawing conclusions, recognizing cause-and-effect relationships, understanding words in context, making interpretations, and making inferences.

Classroom Applications

To demonstrate literal comprehension, students are typically asked to recall information from a story. Memory, therefore, plays a part in comprehension. A well-demonstrated finding in psychological studies is that memory is influenced by prior knowledge. Even the title of a story can influence what information will be remembered about the passage. The important point is that reading skill alone does not account for comprehension. One implication is that reading material should be consistent with the experience and interests of the students.

Another applicable finding in memory research is that readers are more likely to remember the most crucial or pertinent information. Brown and Smiley (1977) demonstrated that third-, fourth-, and fifth-graders are unable to recognize the important ideas in a story but that seventh-graders and college students can. Taylor (1980) further determined that skilled sixth-grade readers recalled 75 percent more main idea information (as opposed to subordinate information) than did less skilled sixth-grade readers. The implications of this research are the need to train young students and less skilled readers to find the main ideas and supporting details. Taylor and Beach (1984) developed a successful training program. They taught seventh-graders to develop an outline of social studies material, identifying the thesis, main ideas, and supporting details. Students who received training recalled more information about the social studies material than did students who did not receive training. Similar to the word-superiority effect mentioned above, researchers have demonstrated a context effect: words in a meaningful sentence are recognized more quickly and accurately than other words (e.g., Tulving & Gold, 1963). Furthermore, Frederiksen (1981) demonstrated that skilled readers take better advantage of context cues than do less skilled readers. Researchers believe that using context cues to determine word meaning is more automatic for good readers. In other words, less skilled (or younger) readers spend more time trying to understand the meaning of words than other readers. Therefore, they have less time to concentrate on the gist of the material.

Less skilled readers seem to be less proficient at integrating information than skilled readers. For example, Perfetti and Roth (1981) noticed that less skilled readers did not utilize information from one sentence to fill in information missing in a subsequent sentence. Less skilled readers also have more difficulty with pronoun references (e.g., Frederiksen, 1981). Early researchers attributed the integration problems to a working memory deficit that would be difficult to overcome. Contemporary researchers attribute the integration problems to inadequate training and practice. Educators can help students automate the integration process.

Skilled readers are also more adept at monitoring their comprehension; that is, they are more likely to notice when information does not make sense or is erroneous. They will review the text to validate the information. This relative difference between readers can be studied and applied to develop methods of training less skilled readers to monitor their comprehension more effectively.

Suggestions to Facilitate Comprehension

The following suggestions can be used by the teacher to facilitate literal and inferential comprehension.

1. *Use advance organizers, questions, and discussion.* Each of these tools can help increase comprehension.

2. *When you expect students to learn specific information, provide objectives.*

3. *Provide practice and feedback.*

4. *Encourage students to highlight information, take notes, and develop summaries.*

5. *Teach students to choose an appropriate reading rate.* A slow, careful rate is needed for learning subject areas. A normal rate is appropriate for learning the main plot and extracting details. A faster rate is appropriate for reviewing familiar material. A *skimming* (i.e., scanning) rate can be used to overview material and get the general gist.

6. *Ensure that students have appropriate prior knowledge.* One suggestion is to coordinate material between subject areas. For example, after a social studies unit on American Indians, use reading passages about American Indians during reading units. Alternatively, provide class discussions, films, or demonstrations to provide prior knowledge.

7. *Give older students practice finding inconsistent information in reading passages.*

Eye Movements

Contrary to what might seem logical, one's eyes do not move smoothly and slowly as one reads. Instead, the eyes fixate (focus) at a particular point for about 200 milliseconds and then jump to another point. People tend to fixate longer on unfamiliar words and the end of sentences. A fixation span typically includes 3 to 10 letters. These rapid eye movements are called *saccades*. During saccades, no information is gained. Eye-movement research provides interesting clues about the reading process. Skilled readers will experience fewer eye fixations than less skilled readers on equivalent material. As students develop reading skill, they tend to have shorter fixations and fewer regressions (looking back at previous material). For related information see Carpenter and Just (1981).

Writing

Writing, like reading, is typically a meaningful activity. The purpose of writing is to communicate and thus to influence one's audience. To influence an audience, the writer must have good command of the topic and understand who the audience will be. The writer should determine what education, background, goals, and perspectives the audience has. The writer will need to communicate adequate knowledge of the material. Without establishing credibility, it is difficult, if not impossible, to influence an audience. The writer must also develop a well-written (i.e., grammatically correct) document. If a paper or presentation is poorly written, the audience may notice the poor quality more than the intended message.

Cognitive Processes in Writing

John Hayes and Linda Flower (1980) developed a model of the cognitive processes in writing that includes three major tasks: planning, translating, and reviewing. This model emphasizes the interactive nature of each process. Even during the review process, one refers back to goals established during the planning process.

Planning

In the planning process, writers set goals, generate information, and organize material. The goals that are set depend on the particular writing assignment and the relevant information in long-term memory. Other planning activities include obtaining the needed information and organizing the material. Most skilled writers consider the primary goal of writing to be the communication of meaningful information and identify the purpose of the assignment before writing. Less skilled writers are more likely to have a goal of avoiding errors and tend to "dump" information from memory onto paper. They also tend to be more concerned with superficial appearance than communication.

Translating

A second process in this model is translating thoughts into sentences. Often the writer will develop a phrase or sentence, return to the planning task, then translate another phrase or sentence, return to the planning task, and so on.

Nystrand (1982) identified five factors important for translation; these factors potentially affect communication between writer and reader.

1. *Graphic factors* that affect legibility, including penmanship, spacing, and spelling.

2. *Syntactic factors,* including grammar and punctuation.

3. *Semantic factors,* including the writer's assumptions, if any, regarding the reader's prior knowledge and expectations.

4. *Textual factors* that affect the cohesiveness of the writing.

5. *Contextual factors* that affect the style of the writing; an example would be sarcasm.

From an educational perspective, it is important to know how much and when teachers should concentrate on these factors. There is evidence (e.g., Glynn et al., 1982) that students should concentrate on content, not mechanics, during the first draft. Because text can be revised and reformatted quickly and easily with word processors, this is an appropriate approach. Many people find it tempting to correct every typographical error, and fuss with formatting as they write. A more efficient approach (which results in higher-quality writing) is to first write the main ideas and as many details and transitions as possible. Teachers working with young children should emphasize planning and organization rather than the mechanics of writing. Forcing students to concentrate on developing polished sentences during initial writing exercises limits their ability to plan, retrieve, and organize information.

Reviewing

The final process is reviewing what has been written by reading and editing. During reading, one looks for missing and extra information. During editing, one rewrites, rearranges, and rewords to clarify the message.

Researchers have learned several things about this aspect of the writing process. Many students who lack specific training do not review their papers. When they do review, they fail to detect a number of problems. Bartlett (1982) found that young children, especially, have difficulty identifying and correcting referent errors (misuse of pronouns). People in general seem to have more trouble finding errors in their own writing than errors in others' writing. When students revise their papers, they tend to notice mechanical rather than organizational errors. Nold (1981) identified several types of revision: cosmetic, mechanical, grammatical, continuational, informational, stylistic, transitional, and organizational. Nold determined that 13-year-olds made more revisions than do 9-year olds in each category. Of particular interest was that 9-year-olds made very few transitional and organizational changes. Skilled writers make meaningful revisions, while less skilled writers make superficial changes. This research indicates the need to teach revision strategies. If teachers don't offer feedback and guidance, they should not hand a paper back and expect the quality of a student's writing to improve suddenly and dramatically.

Guidelines for Teaching Writing

The following suggestions are offered as steps or objectives in teaching writing:

1. *Teach students to set goals.* To ensure that students set goals, have them write down the meaning or ideas that they want to convey. When the assignment is complete, have children compare the goal statement to the finished product.

2. *Teach students to develop outlines.* After students identify a goal, ask them to develop outlines. Review their outlines (especially the first few times) and offer feedback.

3. *Provide practice time.* To become skilled writers, students must practice and receive feedback. Like reading, writing should be required in several classes, not only in English class. Writing is a difficult skill, however, and learning new content can be difficult. Students generally write best about things they know or have studied in depth.

4. *Have students revise their essays and papers.* Request that students incorporate your feedback in a revision. Consider grading the revised paper rather than the initial paper (or both). The revision process can be facilitated by putting the paper aside for a day or two before editing, and by reading the paper aloud to another person. Teach students to look for the following common problems:

   a. Information that is not presented clearly

   b. Necessary information (e.g., to support argument) that is missing

   c. An "Introduction" that does not introduce the topic

   d. A "Conclusion" that does not pull information together or is not supported

   e. Appropriate transition that is not provided

   f. Style or content that is inappropriate for the audience

   g. Any goal that is not met

5. *In general, provide direct instruction on the writing process*

(establishing goals, developing outlines, translating information, and revising text). Writing is a complex task, and students need instruction on these individual processes. Instruction should also be provided on grammar and simple rules of good writing, but additional and specific emphasis must be placed on the writing process.

6. *Encourage students to write for a specific audience.*

7. *Emphasize planning and organization during the first draft.* Encourage students to work on mechanical details and polish the work on a subsequent draft.

8. *Prompt (directly encourage) young students to provide more information.* Sometimes young students have more to say than they write. Review the work and ask students to explain more where needed.

9. *Teach students to provide support for their arguments.* Young writers are likely to make their position clear without presenting arguments. Stress the importance of substantiating positions with evidence. Providing evidence helps influence the audience.

Training Programs for Teaching Writing

Although the research on writing is in the early stages, several educators have implemented successful training programs for improving writing performance.

Hillocks' Cooperation Program

Hillocks (1984) reviewed available studies on writing and provided recommendations for the instructional method and content of writing programs. He found that cooperation between student and teacher during the writing process was the instructional method producing the most improvement. Alternative methods required students to work independently or a teacher to present a lecture. Teachers should provide specific assignments and work with small groups to help students develop support for their ideas.

Hillocks determined that the content most likely to help students improve is to teach them to (1) build complex sentences from simple ones, (2) apply checklists or other procedures for reviewing work, and (3) discuss how they write and to work on specific problem areas. Focusing on grammar, providing models of good writing, and allowing students to write about anything they choose did not turn out to be effective ways to improve writing skill.

De Beaugrande's Writing Training Program

De Beaugrande (1982) has developed a writing training program. Students write essays and revise ones written by other students. Students are requested to detect and correct errors and discuss the revisions with the teacher. De Beaugrande uses separate sessions to focus on different revision techniques, such as removing "fillers" (irrelevant or superfluous information that increases the length of the paper without adding substance), reordering information, adding information, and providing details.

Computer Programs

Computer programs are becoming sufficiently sophisticated to analyze style and find inappropriate sentences. One example is *Writer's Workbench*, which was developed and used at Bell Laboratories (Macdonald et al., 1982). In addition to these more complicated tasks, many computer programs are available that check for spelling, punctuation, double words, and other grammatical errors. The utility of these programs for teaching writing skills is not clear at this time. However, they can be used to allow students to focus on developing content and organization rather than concentrating on the mechanics of writing.

Mathematics

Mathematics is a subject area that generates anxiety for many students. Nevertheless, expertise in mathematics is important in adulthood, and educators should help students acquire the needed skills. To solve math problems, students must be able to understand a problem, determine which computations are appropriate, perform accurate calculations, and verify the derived solution.

Types of Math Errors

Typical stumbling blocks in math include borrowing, carrying, adding fractions, solving for the unknown, and setting up word problems. Students sometimes make errors because they either do not know how to proceed in solving a problem, apply incorrect rules, lack the prerequisite skills, or are careless or work too quickly. An important aspect of effective mathematics instruction is the ability to determine specifically the nature of a student's difficulty, that is, the reason for the error. Error analysis is a useful tool for teachers to pinpoint a given student's deficiencies.

Representational problems are particularly difficult for students. Representational problems contain statements that express a quantitative relationship between variables. Consider the following example: the apple costs twice as much as the plum cost last year. The apple costs 0.80. How much did the plum cost? The source of the problem seems to be the relative ability to translate the statement into an equation. One implication is the need to provide specific drill and assistance in translating problems into equations.

Expert versus Novice Problem Solvers

Researchers have identified differences between expert and novice (nonexpert) math problem solvers. These differences provide important pedagogical information. For instance, speed and accuracy are important in many problem-solving situations; experts (e.g., professional mathematicians) solve problems more quickly than do students. Lewis (1981) gave experts and novices linear equations to solve and determined that expert mathematicians used fewer steps to solve the problems than did the novices; thus experts probably use slightly different problem-solving procedures than do novices.

Expert problem solvers also seem to have mathematics information organized better than do nonexperts. For example, Silver (1981) determined that expert problem solvers could sort (organize) word problems according to how the problems would be solved whereas poor problem solvers did not do this. The expert problem solvers seemed to be able to read word problems and understand them well enough to determine how they should be solved.

Guidelines for Teaching Mathematics

The following suggestions are offered as steps or objectives in teaching mathematics.

1. *Teach students to estimate solutions.* Students should estimate solutions and verify the derived solution against the estimate. This procedure may help students detect careless errors.

2. *Determine where in the problem-solving process errors occur.* Ascertain whether a student has the prerequisite knowledge, makes careless errors, does not know how to represent the problem, or does not know how to proceed to solve the problem.

3. *Conduct error analyses to determine exactly what procedural or computational problem a student has.* Review a student's work on paper or have a student talk aloud while working through a problem. Students frequently make similar errors consistently rather than random errors. You can discover the pattern and develop a specific strategy to remedy that problem. For example, once you notice that a student performs poorly on borrowing problems, review that student's work to determine what kinds of errors are being made. Common errors include: borrowing from a zero without reducing the number in the next column, subtracting the smaller number from the larger number even when the smaller number is on top, and skipping columns rather than borrowing from zeros. When you determine which error is made, provide specific remedial instruction.

4. *Help students recognize different problem types.* Mayer (1981) reviewed algebra textbooks and identified types of word problems, such as amount-per-time, cost-per-unit, portion of total, amount-per-amount, number stories, and geometry. Recognizing that a problem belongs to a particular family of problems can a help student solve the problem (assuming that the student knows how to solve that type of problem). However, a student who incorrectly identifies the problem family will probably apply an inappropriate procedure. Instruct students to read through a problem completely before assuming that it belongs to a particular family. After initial instruction, do

not group similar problems together all the time. Give students practice figuring out what kind of problem they have to solve.

5. *Teach students to identify and use only relevant information and to draw pictures.* Sometimes students do not correctly solve word problems because they utilize irrelevant information. Give students practice sorting relevant from irrelevant information. Then, for example, teach them to draw a picture to represent the problem.

6. *Ensure that students are skilled in basic addition and multiplication facts (at the appropriate level).* When the basic facts are not automatic, the student must spend time and effort working through them, rather than determining how to represent or solve a more complicated problem.

A Mathematics Training Program

Madeline Hunter (1982) developed the Hunter Mastery Teaching Program, which provides ideas to help prepare students for learning and suggestions to help teachers present material effectively. Another system was created by Tom Good and Doug Grouws (1979) after many years of studying the methods and results used and obtained by effective math teachers. Their system, the Missouri Mathematics Program, emphasizes that students should understand the material, not merely be able to use formulas correctly. Clear presentations using demonstrations, concrete examples, models, and other techniques are also important to this system.

The Missouri Mathematics Program can be divided into five components:

1. *Opening*—Review, collect homework, and assign mental exercises.

2. *Development*—Focus on meaning and understanding.

3. *Seatwork*—Ensure uninterrupted work, get everyone involved, and check the work.

4. *Homework*—Assign every day except Friday; include review.

5. *Special reviews*—Provide one per week or month.

Educational psychologists have conducted many studies to determine the cognitive processes and skills needed in content areas such as reading, writing, and mathematics. Researchers investigate differences between skilled and less skilled performers and carefully analyze errors. Reading seems to involve a decoding process during which words and word meanings are determined. Teachers should be tolerant of minor mistakes and offer ample opportunity for practice. Reading also involves comprehension, during which the reader endeavors to understand the intended meaning of the passage. People tend to remember the gist of a passage rather than the specific details. Teachers should give students specific objectives for reading assignments and ensure that students have the prerequisite information. Writing is intended to communicate. A cognitive model of writing includes three processes: planning, translating, and reviewing. Teachers must work with students on the writing process, not simply mechanics. Problem solving in mathematics involves understanding the problem, determining which computations are appropriate, performing accurate calculations, and verifying the derived solution. Teachers can conduct error analyses to determine what kind of remedial work is needed.

Successful training programs based on cognitive principles have been implemented in public schools. This area of educational psychology will continue to grow over the next few years, and educational psychologists will strive to offer specific recommendations for more successful teaching.

Recommended Reading

Carpenter, T. P., J. M. Moser, and T. A. Romberg. (Eds.). (1982). *Addition and Subtraction: A Cognitive Perspective.* Hillsdale, N.J.: Lawrence Erlbaum. (A collection of papers by mathematics education researchers.)

Crowder, R. G. (1982). *The Psychology of Reading: An Introduction.* New York: Oxford University Press. (A textbook summarizing relevant psychological research.)

Gagné, E. D. (1985). *The Cognitive Psychology of School Learning.* Boston: Little, Brown. (Contains several chapters presenting current research on teaching reading, writing, mathematics, and science.)

Gregg, L. W., and E. R. Steinberg. (1980). *Cognitive Processes in Writing.*

Hillsdale, N.J.: Lawrence Erlbaum. (An excellent, readable introduction to the psychology of writing.)

Meyer, R. E. (1987). *Educational Psychology: A Cognitive Approach.* Boston: Little, Brown. (Contains several chapters presenting current research on teaching reading, writing, mathematics, and science.)

Nystrand, M. (Ed.). (1982). *What Writers Know: The Language, Process, and Structure of Written Discourse.* New York: Academic Press. (A collection of papers written by psychologists and linguists.)

Pearson, P. D. (Ed.). (1984). *Handbook of Research on Reading.* New York: Longman. (Collection of papers with contributions from leading researchers on reading.)

Resnick, L. B., and W. Ford. (1981). *The Psychology of Mathematics for Instruction.* Hillsdale, N.J.: Lawrence Erlbaum. (An introduction to mathematical problem solving research.)

References

Baron, J. (1977). What We Might Know about Orthographic Rules, In S. Dornic (Ed.). *Attention and Performance VI.* Hillsdale, N.J.: Lawrence Erlbaum.

Bartlett, F. C. (1932). *Remembering: A Study in Experimental and Social Psychology.* Cambridge, U.K.: Cambridge University Press.

Bartlett, E. J. (1982). Learning to Revise: Some Component Processes, In M. Nystrand (Ed.). *What Writers Know.* New York: Academic Press.

Brown, A. L., and S. S. Smiley. (1977). Rating the Importance of Structural Units of Prose Passages: A Problem of Metacognitive Development *Child Development, 48,* 1-8.

Carpenter, P. A., and M. A. Just. (1981). Cognitive Processes in Reading: Models Based on Readers' Eye Fixations. In A. M. Lesgold and C. A. Perfetti (Eds.). *Interactive Processes in Reading.* Hillsdale, N.J.: Lawrence Erlbaum.

Chall, J. S. (1967). *Learning to Read: The Great Debate.* New York: McGraw-Hill.

de Beaugrande, R. (1982). Psychology and Composition: Past, Present, and Future In M. Nystrand (Ed.). *What Writers Know.* New York: Academic Press.

Ehri, L. C. (September 1982). Learning to Read and Spell, paper presented at the American Psychological Association annual meeting, Washington, D.C.

Ehri, L. C., and L. C. Wilce. (1983). Development of Word Identification Speed in Skilled and Less Skilled Beginning Readers *Journal of Educational Psychology, 75,* 3-18.

Frederiksen, J. R. (1981). Sources of Process Interactions in Reading, in A. M. Lesgold and C. A. Perfetti, (Eds.). *Interactive Processes in Reading*. Hillsdale, N.J.: Lawrence Erlbaum.

Frederiksen, J. R., P. A. Weaver, B. M. Warren, J. H. P. Gillotte, A. S. Rosebery, B. Freeman, and L. Goodman. (1983). *A Componential Approach to Training Reading Skills*. Cambridge, Mass.: Bolt Beranek and Newman. Report No. 5295.

Glynn, S. M., B. K. Britton, D. Muth, and N. Dogan. (1982). Writing and Revising Persuasive Documents: Cognitive Demands *Journal of Educational Psychology*, *74*, 557-567.

Good, T., and D. A. Grouws. (1979). The Missouri Mathematics Effectiveness Project: An Experimental Study in Fourth Grade Classrooms *Journal of Educational Psychology*, *71*, 355-362.

Hayes, J. R. , and L. S. Flower. (1980). Identifying the Organization of Writing Processes. In L. W. Gregg and E. R. Steinberg, (Eds.). *Cognitive Processes in Writing*. Hillsdale, N.J.: Lawrence Erlbaum.

Hillocks, G. (1984). What Works in Teaching Composition: A Meta-Analysis of Experimental Treatment Studies. *American Journal of Education*, 93, 133-170.

Hodges, R. E., and E. H. Rudorf. (1984). *Language and Learning to Read: What Teachers Should Know about Language*. Langham, Md.: University Press of America.

Hunter, M. (1982). *Mastery Teaching*. El Segundo, Calif.: TIP Publications.

Johnston, J. C. (1981). Understanding Word Perception: Clues from Studying the Word-Superiority Effect. In O. J. L. Tzeng and H. Singer, (Eds.). *Perception of Print*. Hillsdale, N.J.: Lawrence Erlbaum.

Lewis, C. (1981). Skill in Algebra. In J. R. Anderson (Ed.). *Cognitive Skills and Their Acquisition*. Hillsdale, N.J.: Lawrence Erlbaum.

Macdonald, N. H., L. T. Frase, P. S. Gingrich, and S. A. Keenan. (1982). The Writer's Workbench: Computer Aids for Text Analysis *Educational Psychologist*, *17*, 172-179.

Mayer, R. E. (1981). Frequency Norms and Structural Analysis of Algebra Story Problems into Families, Categories, and Templates *Instructional Science*, *10*, 135-175.

Morphett, M., and C. Washburne. (1931). When Should Children Begin to Read? *Elementary School Journal*, *31*, 496-503.

Nold, E. W. (1981). Revising. In C. H. Frederiksen and J. F. Dominic, (Eds.. *Writing:* Volume 2. Hillsdale, N.J.: Lawrence Erlbaum.

Nystrand, M. (1982). An Analysis of Errors in Written Communication. In M. Nystrand (Ed.). *What Writers Know.* New York: Academic Press.

Perfetti, C. A., and T. Hogoboam. (1975). The Relationship between Single Word Decoding and Reading Comprehension Skill *Journal of Educational Psychology, 67,* 461- 469.

Perfetti, C. A., and S. F. Roth. (1981). Some of the Interactive Processes in Reading and their Role in Reading Skill, In A. M. Lesgold and C. A. Perfetti (Eds.). *Interactive Processes in Reading.* Hillsdale, N.J.: Lawrence Erlbaum.

Reicher, G. M. (1969). Perceptual Recognition as a Function of the Meaning-fulness of Stimulus Material *Journal of Experimental Psychology, 81,* 275-280.

Rosenshine, B. V. (1980). Skill Hierarchies in Reading Comprehension. In R. J. Shapiro, B. C. Bruce, and W. F. Brewer (Eds.). *Theoretical Issues in Reading Comprehension.* Hillsdale, N.J.: Lawrence Erlbaum.

Samuels, S. J. (1979). The Method of Repeated Readings, *The Reading Teacher, 32,* 403-408.

Silver, E. A. (1981). Recall of Mathematical Problem Information: Solving Related Problems, *Journal for Research in Mathematics Education 12,* 54-64.

Singer, H. (1981). Teaching the Acquisition Phase of Reading Development: An Historical Perspective. In O. J. L. Tzeng and H. Singer (Eds.). *Perception of Print.* Hillsdale, N.J.: Lawrence Erlbaum.

Spache, G. B. (1981). *Diagnosing and Correcting Reading Disabilities.* Boston: Allyn & Bacon.

Taylor, B. (1980). Children's Memory for Expository Text after Reading, *Reading Research Quarterly, 15,* 399-411.

Taylor, B. M., and R. W. Beach. (1984). The Effects of Text Structure Instruction on Middle-Grade Students' Comprehension and Production of Expository Text *Reading Research Quarterly, 19,* 134-146.

Tulving, E., and C. Gold. (1963). Stimulus Information and Contextual Information as Determinants of Tachistoscopic Recognition of Words. *Journal of Experimental Psychology, 66,* 319-327.

Venezky, R. L. (1980). *Orthography, Reading, and Dyslexia.* Baltimore: University Park Press.

Glossary

Abstraction A method used to solve complex problems whereby the original complex problem is reduced to a simpler case, the simpler case is solved, and then an analogy is made to the original complex problem to facilitate solving it.

Acceleration A program designed for gifted students allowing or encouraging them to progress through regular course material in less time than is typically allocated.

Accommodation According to Piaget, altering the existing schema to handle (accommodate) a new experience; also refers to the ability of the lens of the eye to change shape for focusing on objects, an ability that young children often lack.

Achievement Motivation An attitude or action related to the need for achievement, that is, the need to perform successfully.

Achievement Tests Tests designed to measure how much students have learned (knowledge or skills) in a particular subject area.

Acronym A word formed from the first letters of other words.

Acrostic A sentence created such that the first letter of each word in the sentence represents a word that is to be remembered.

Advance Organizers Statements presented at the beginning of a new section of material; used to introduce the material and provide a bridge between what the student already knows and what is to be learned.

Algorithms Rules guaranteed to result in the correct solution of a problem.

Analogies Comparisons that can be used to guide the solution of novel problems when similar problems have already been solved.

Anticipatory Set A receptive attitude toward learning; may be established by presenting interesting and pertinent topics or points.

Approximations Small incremental steps designed to lead a person gradually into a specific new situation.

Aptitude Tests Standardized tests designed to measure abilities that have been acquired over a long period of time and to indicate how well a student is expected to perform in a particular area (cognitive or psychomotor).

Aptitude-Treatment Interaction A relationship between a given student's ability and a particular teaching method (the treatment); indicates which teaching methods are more effective for certain students.

Artificial Intelligence The capability of a computer to simulate human reasoning and thought processes.

Assimilation According to Piaget, the process of adapting new information or a new experience so that it will fit in with (be assimilated into) the existing schema.

Associative Play Children's play with each other in an unorganized manner.

Attending Receiving a stimulus, focusing on it, and interpreting it mentally.

Attribution Theory Explanation of behavior or performance on the basis of how people perceive their success and failure; that is, attribute it to factors such as ability, effort, luck, and task difficulty; has implications for motivation to succeed.

Auditory Impairments Hearing disabilities that are classified as either hard of hearing or deaf.

Autonomy Ability to function and perform some activities independently.

Babbling Producing sounds without specific meaning.

Behavior Content Matrix A planning tool used to pair instructional objectives with course content; a systematic strategy for covering each level of learning in an educational taxonomy.

Behavior Modification An approach to changing behavior that advocates rewarding appropriate behavior and withholding reinforcement for or punishing inappropriate behavior; focuses on observable behaviors rather than mental events.

Behavioral and (or) Emotional Disorders Conditions or attitudes inducing behaviors that may be aggressive, impulsive, disruptive, withdrawn, isolated, extremely fearful, or self-mutilating to the extent that they interfere with learning.

Behavioral Theories Theories that emphasize how persons and objects in the environment influence a person's behavior; focus on observable behavior rather than internal, mental events.

Bell-Shaped Curve A theoretical statistical curve, also known as the *normal distribution curve,* which represents the frequency with which a variable occurs; most of the scores are clustered near the mean, scores are distributed symmetrically about the mean, and the mean, median, and mode are the same number.

Bias Occurs if persons from an identified population are more likely to perform better (or worse) than those from other populations.

Bilingual Education Instruction offered in a second language (e.g., Spanish) to accommodate students not proficient in English.

Bottom-Up Reasoning See Inductive Reasoning.

Centration Rigidity of thought caused by focusing on only one aspect of a topic.

Chain Method Method that uses visual links created between the items in a list to aid recall of those items.

Chunking A memory strategy that involves grouping several individual pieces of information into a single piece.

Class Inclusion Suggests reasoning of the following nature is possible: If three boys and two girls are in the family, there are more family members than either boys or girls alone.

Classical Conditioning A technique introduced by Ivan Pavlov in which an unconditioned (response-producing) stimulus is paired with a conditioned (previously neutral) stimulus until the response is produced from the conditioned stimulus alone.

Client-Centered Therapy An approach to psychotherapy developed by Carl Rogers in which the therapist provides unconditional positive regard, congruence, and empathy allowing the client to grow in mental health.

Cognition The act or process of knowing.

Cognitive Behaviorism The study of how covert (concealed) behavior affects observable behavior; utilizes behavioral methods of analysis.

Cognitive Consistency Theories Theories that describe the motivation to maintain a balance between how one acts and what one believes. See also Cognitive Dissonance.

Cognitive Development The growth and development of the abilities to think, learn, remember, perceive, and solve problems.

Cognitive Dissonance An uncomfortable psychological state resulting from conflict; according to Leon Festinger, people will try to reduce dissonance by changing attitudes or behavior.

Cognitive Models Models that explain how people learn, retain, and retrieve information.

Cognitive Psychology The study of cognitive processes such as thinking, learning, remembering, and problem solving.

Competency Tests Usually criterion-referenced tests used to determine whether the students have mastered a designated set of basic skills.

Comprehension A stage in reading during which one gains understanding of the information.

Computer-Based Education (CBE) The application of computers for educational purposes.

Computer-Based Instruction (CBI) The use of computers to tutor students or provide practice exercises and drill.

Computer Literacy Having basic knowledge of how a computer operates and what some computer applications are.

Concrete Operational Stage The third stage (at approximately 6 to 12 years of age) designated by Piaget and characterized by reversibility of thought and an understanding of conservation.

Conditioned Response (CR) An unconditioned response such as salivation that has been paired with a conditioned stimulus such as a bell so many times that now only the bell is necessary to elicit the response.

Conditioned Stimulus (CS) A novel event that does not already elicit the desired response.

Conservation The ability to realize that certain properties of an object (e.g., quantity or amount) remain the same even though the appearance of the object has changed. (Inability to conserve is characteristic of the preoperational stage.)

Construct Validity The extent to which a test measures a hypothetical construct, or quality, such as creativity.

Constructive Memories Memories that are recalled the same way they were interpreted when the event occurred.

Content Validity The extent to which a test covers the material representatively.

Context-Dependent Retrieval The finding that people remember best when they learn and recall while located in the same environment.

Continuous Reinforcement A reinforcement schedule requiring that the reinforcer be presented every time the behavior occurs.

Convergent Thinking The direction of the thinking process toward one solution.

Cooperative Play Children's play in an organized fashion, each taking a certain role.

Correlational Data Data that are related but have not been manipulated experimentally.

Courseware Educational computer programs or software.

Criterion-Referenced Tests Tests designed to provide a means of comparing each person's level of performance against specific criteria.

Criterion-Related Validity The extent to which test scores can be used to predict performance in specific situations.

Crystallized General Intelligence Abilities such as reading, writing, and balancing a checkbook that require the application of prior knowledge, are highly useful, and are influenced by cultural values.

Cueing Signaling or gesturing that provides a stimulus designed to elicit the appropriate behavior.

Culture-Fair or Culture-Free Tests Tests that are designed to be free from bias.

Data Processing Use of the computer to store, change, and make calculations with large amounts of data (information).

Decay Term used to describe forgetting due to a fading memory trace.

Declarative Knowledge Knowledge that includes facts and beliefs.

Decoding Translation of printed symbols into sounds that represent meaningful information.

Deductive Reasoning Manipulating general information to deduce specific information.

Deficiency Needs Conditions or items necessary to health such as food and water, safety, love and belonging, and self-esteem; according to Abraham Maslow people are motivated to satisfy these needs.

Depth of Processing The finding that the more information is analyzed and associated with other information, the more likely it will be remembered.

Descriptive Statistics Statistics used to summarize and organize data.

Developmental Psychology The study of human growth along several dimensions, such as cognitive, emotional, and physical.

Deviation IQ A converted score on an intelligence test derived from the percentage of individuals in each age group who obtain a given score.

Diagnostic Evaluation Evaluation during instruction used to determine the strengths and weaknesses of a student's performance.

Diagnostic Tests Tests designed to measure particular strengths and weaknesses in a student's learning process.

Difference Reduction A problem-solving method in which a person tries to reduce the difference between the problem state and the goal state.

Direct Instruction A teacher-centered, structured approach by which the students are made aware of the goals, instruction is comprehensive, performance is monitored, and feedback is given.

Direct Method A method of teaching bilingual students during which the majority language (e.g., English in the United States) is used during instruction; the educational goal is for the students to become proficient in that language.

Discovery Learning An approach to learning developed by Jerome Bruner in which students learn by doing and discover general principles from specific examples and details.

Distribution of Practice The distribution of information over time to help people remember.

Divergent Thinking Thinking that is not directly focused and that produces several approaches to a problem.

Echoic Memory A brief sensory storage of incoming auditory information.

Echolalia Repetition of what is heard.

Echolalic Babbling A child's attempts to imitate sounds others make.

Educational Goals Statements that describe in general terms the information to be taught.

Educational Psychology A branch of psychology concerned with human learning and development in educational settings. It is a scientific study of techniques that can be used to affect learning. Studies in this field center on the teaching process, the learner and learning process, and the environment.

EG-Rule Method A teaching method that facilitates students' inductive reasoning skills by beginning with specific examples and moving toward general information.

Egocentrism A characteristic of Piaget's preoperational stage; a child's view is based only on that child's own perception.

Encoding Taking in information and representing it as thoughts or memories.

Enrichment A program designed for gifted students providing greater depth and breadth of content areas than in conventional programs.

Epigenetic Principle The development in the fetus of bodily organs over time.

Episodic Memory Long-term memories of specific events.

Equilibration The process of restoring balance between what was expected and what was actually experienced.

Evaluation A quantitative or qualitative appraisal of performance that includes value judgments.

Exceptional Children Either handicapped or gifted students.

Expository Organizers Strategies or measures that do not activate old information but provide new information that will be needed to understand the lesson.

Expository Teaching A method of learning developed by David Ausubel involving deductive reasoning and receptive learning (as opposed to discovery learning).

Extinction The decrease and eventual disappearance of a learned behavior due to the absence of reinforcement.

Extrinsic Motivation Motivation that is not directly related to the behavior.

Eye Fixations The brief periods during reading when the eyes remain on the printed material.

Face Validity The extent to which a test appears to measure what it is intended to measure.

Field Theory A theory describing the importance of understanding behavior from the viewpoint of the learner because at any given time the learner is attracted to some objects and repelled by others.

Figure-Ground Principle The finding that as one looks at or hears complex stimuli, one will focus on a basic figure and let the rest of the stimuli remain less distinct.

Fine Motor Activities Activities that require manual dexterity and, to a certain extent, precision.

Fixed Interval Schedule A reinforcement schedule requiring that the reinforcer be presented after the first occurrence of a behavior when a specified amount of time has elapsed.

Fixed Ratio Schedule A reinforcement schedule requiring that the reinforcer be presented after the desired behavior occurs a specified number of times.

Fluid General Intelligence Abilities such as reasoning, dealing with abstractions, and problem solving that require the ability to adapt to new situations and are not dependent on formal or specific education.

Formal Operational Stage The fourth stage of cognitive development (usually between age 12 and adulthood) designated by Piaget and characterized by hypothetical or abstract thinking.

Formative Evaluation Analysis or assessment during instruction that is intended primarily to help teachers modify their instruction to help students meet instructional objectives.

Frequency Distribution A representation that indicates the number of people obtaining particular scores.

Functional Fixedness A barrier to problem solving that occurs when someone is intent on taking a particular perspective on a problem and cannot (or will not) view it differently.

g Factor A term used by Charles Spearman that stands for general ability, an inherited aspect of intelligence.

General Transfer The application of information learned in one situation to new problems or novel situations.

Gestalt German word for pattern, form, or configuration.

Gestalt Psychology A system of psychology based on the notion that the whole is more than the sum of the parts; explains how people recognize information even when it is distorted and how they perceive patterns; forerunner of cognitive psychology.

Goal State The outcome that is desired.

Good Behavior Game A game that requires students to form teams and compete to demonstrate good behavior.

Grade-Equivalent Scores Scores expressed in terms of grade levels.

Gross Motor Activities Activities involving major muscle groups.

Group Tests Tests administered to several students at the same time.

Growth Needs Needs in Abraham Maslow's hierarchy such as knowing and understanding, aesthetic, and self-actualization that can be met only after the deficiency needs have been met.

Guided Discovery The teaching method whereby teachers provide some guidance (e.g., asking leading questions and giving feedback) in the process of discovery learning.

Hardware The physical component(s) of a computer or data processing system.

Heuristics Rules of thumb that may lead to the correct solution of a problem.

Higher-Order Questions Questions that require hypothetical or abstract thinking.

Histogram A bar graph showing the number of times each score was obtained.

Holophrase A single word used to express an idea.

Humanistic Theories Theories that emphsize the effect of emotional and interpersonal behavior on learning.

Hyperactivity A behavior disorder characterized by excessive activity, impulsiveness, or inattentiveness.

I messages Statements a teacher makes regarding feelings or thoughts that result from student behaviors.

Iconic Memory A brief sensory storage of incoming visual information.

Imagery A representation in the mind of an event or object.

Incubation Effects A process that occurs when someone has worked unsuccessfully on a problem for a long time, puts it aside for a few hours, days, or weeks, and on returning to the problem, finds that the solution is almost immediately apparent.

Individualized Educational Programs (IEP) Programs describing behavioral objectives or criteria used to assess mastery of the objectives and services that must be provided to handicapped students.

Individual Tests Tests administered to one student at a time and designed to discover very specific information regarding a student.

Individualized Instruction Instruction or classwork based on a student's specific needs and abilities.

Inductive Reasoning (also known as *bottom-up processing*) Reasoning that starts with specific details and moves toward more general principles.

Information Processing Model A model that facilitates understanding of how people store and retrieve information; based on how computers process information.

Initial State The state in which a problem is recognized.

Insight A sudden ability to perceive new relationships and find a solution to a problem.

Instructional Games Programs used to develop problem-solving skills and motivate learning.

Instructional Objective A statement that identifies the information, skill, or attitude to be learned; the manner in which the information will be presented; and sometimes the means of measuring whether the information is learned.

Instrumental Conditioning See Operant Conditioning.

Intelligence The ability to reason and adapt to one's environment; the ability to comprehend, assimilate, and retain information.

Intelligence Quotient (IQ) A relative quantitative value calculated by dividing mental age by chronological age.

Intentionality A child's attempt to make certain events occur over and over again.

Intermediate State A state that occurs when the person begins to solve the problem.

Intermittent Reinforcement A reinforcement schedule requiring that the reinforcer be presented frequently but not after every occurrence of the desired behavior; very effective for maintaining a given behavior.

Interrater Reliability The consistency of results when two scorers grade the same test independently.

Intrinsic Motivation An attitude or action that leads someone to behave in a certain manner because of the inherent value of doing so.

Irreversibility A term Piaget used to describe an inability to back up or perform a mental operation in reverse; characteristic of children in the preoperational stage of cognitive development.

Itinerate Teacher A visiting teacher called in for consultation or to observe specific students in a classroom environment.

Keyword Method A memory aid technique that utilizes associations between new words and known words that sound similar.

Language Experience Approach A teaching method used to help students understand the relationship between oral and written language; especially useful for children who do not speak standard English.

Lateral Transfer The application of previously learned skills in new contexts.

Law of Closure The tendency to perceive figures as if they were complete even though they are not complete (i.e., they contain gaps).

Law of Contiguity The tendency to perceive unconnected points as if they were connected provided that they would create a straight or smooth line when connected.

Law of Effect The finding that actions which produce satisfying states will be repeated in similar situations.

Law of Good Figure The finding that patterns are seen in the simplest way possible; also referred to as the law of *Prägnaz*.

Law of Proximity The tendency to perceive things that are physically close together as units.

Law of Similarity The tendency to organize together things that appear similar.

Learned Helplessness The feeling or belief (based on past experience) that one will not be successful or cannot be independent.

Learner-Centered Approach An approach to learning presented by Carl Rogers in which a learner is allowed more control in the educational process.

Learning Centers Areas around the classroom that are used for special projects and activities.

Learning Disability A common description for students with near average to above-average intelligence who have difficulty in certain academic tasks such as reading, language skills, and math.

Learning Probe A brief check on how much students have learned.

Lecture Format The oral presentation of instructional material.

Lesson Plan An organized description of the content of a lesson, the method of delivery, the evaluation strategy, and the amount and nature of practice exercises.

Life Space Everything in one's environment that contributes to one's behavior.

Loci Method A memory aid that utilizes associations between to-be-remembered items and familiar places.

Locus of Control Location or place where responsibility for an outcome is attributed.

Long Term Memory (LTM) The permanent storehouse of information in the brain.

Mainstreaming Placing handicapped persons into a regular public school in an attempt to give them a better opportunity to develop.

Massed Practice The attempt to store large quantities of information in a short period of time (cramming).

Mastery Criteria Standards that define acceptable levels of performance.

Mastery Learning An instructional approach to learning requiring an established level of performance on a given skill before a student can progress to a subsequent skill.

Mean The arithmetical average of a set of scores.

Mean Length of Utterance (MLU) The average number of words or morphemes in an utterance; calculated by dividing the total number of words or morphemes in a speech sample by the total number of utterances in the sample.

Meaningful Verbal Learning A teaching approach advocated by D. Ausubel by which information and relationships among ideas are presented together in a meaningful manner.

Means-Ends Analysis A problem-solving method in which the goal state is broken into several problems and any method may then be used to solve each of the problems.

Measurement The quantitative (numeric) assessment of performance.

Measures of Central Tendency Measures indicating the typical score for the group of people who took the test; include the mean, median, and mode.

Median The middle score in a given distribution.

Mental Age A person's intellectual age calculated by comparing that person's performance on a test with the performance of others of different ages and then ranking that person in terms of the chronological age level on which that person performed.

Mental Retardation Below-average intellectual functioning (usually an IQ below 70) and social skills.

Metacognition Thinking about thinking; an awareness of the mental processes that take place and (or) developing strategies to change them.

Mnemonics Strategies used to help people remember new words or a list of several words.

Mode The score that occurs most frequently in a given distribution.

Model A proposed concept of the relation between variables and (or) a graphic representation of the way something works.

Modeling Learning by observation; behavior is acquired or increased after an observer sees another person demonstrating the behavior.

Morphemes The smallest meaningful units of speech.

Motivation The influence of factors or conditions such as needs and preferences on the initiation and continuation of behavior.

Native Language Approach A method of teaching bilingual students during which the student's native language (e.g., Spanish) is used for instruction and students gradually learn the majority language (e.g., English in the United States).

Natural Observation A research method in which researchers observe and record behavioral changes without interfering.

Nature/Nurture Issue Controversy regarding the degree to which genetics and environment influence traits and development.

Negative Reinforcement The removal of an aversive or unpleasant stimulus that increases the strength or likelihood that a specific behavior will be repeated.

Negative Transfer A process that occurs when information learned in one situation interferes with learning new information.

Network Model A model that attempts to mimic human memory through associative networks.

Nondirective Therapy See Client-Centered Therapy.

Norm-Referenced Tests Tests designed to provide a way to compare each person's level of performance with that of others who have taken the same test.

Normal Distribution Curve (also called *normal curve* and *bell-shaped curve*) A theoretical bell-shaped distribution of scores that represents the frequency with which a variable occurs; most of the scores are clustered near the mean, scores are distributed symmetrically about the mean, and the mean, median, and mode are the same number.

Norming Sample A large group of people, similar to the students who will take a given test, who serve as a comparison group when tests are scored.

Object Permanence Piaget's term for the realization that an object actually exists even though it is hidden; most often occurs during sensorimotor stage of cognitive development.

Onlooker Behavior Behavior involving observation of a group rather than participation with the group.

Operant Conditioning (also called *instrumental conditioning*) An explanation of how people learn voluntary responses; involves strengthening or weakening behavior in response to consequences (reinforcers) of the behavior.

Operation A word used to describe a mental process that is reversible.

Operators The courses of action a person can take to achieve a given goal state.

Overlearning Practicing a skill or working with information beyond the point of mastery.

Overregularization The application of rules where they do not apply.

Parallel Play Play in which a child plays beside another child but does not interact with the other child.

Pattern Matching A problem-solving method in which one attempts to match a pattern in memory with the current problem.

Peer Tutoring Instruction by a peer (a classmate or another person of approximately the same age as the student).

Pegword Method A memory aid that uses modified images of to-be-remembered items associated with known words to facilitate recall.

Percentile Rank A ranking that indicates the percentage of students who scored at or below a given student's score.

Peripherals Hardware equipment used by the computer but not part of the central processing unit.

Phonics Approach A common method of teaching beginning reading in which students are taught letter-sound relationships.

Physical Handicaps Orthopedic and health-related disabilities warranting special equipment or assistance to enable students to communicate or function in normal physical activity; examples of such handicaps are missing or malformed arms or legs, epilepsy, cerebral palsy, asthma, and heart problems.

Placement Evaluation Evaluation that occurs prior to instruction; used to match students with programs appropriate to their interests and abilities.

Positive Reinforcement The presentation of a given stimulus after a behavior occurs that results in strengthening the behavior.

Positive Transfer A process that occurs when information learned in one situation aids in learning (or applying) new information.

Prägnaz See Law of Good Figure.

Premack Principle The principle of requiring work first, then providing a reward the student chooses.

Preoperational Stage The second stage (at approximately 2 to 6 years of age) designated by Piaget and signified by symbolic thinking, increased vocabulary and language skills, and a vivid imagination.

Presentation Punishment The presentation of an aversive stimulus (e.g., spanking) after the appearance of an undesirable behavior that causes a decrease in the behavior.

Primacy Effect The finding that memory for information that is presented at the beginning of a list will be superior to memory for information presented in the middle of the list. See also Serial Position Effect.

Proactive Interference Term describing what occurs when old information makes it difficult to remember new information.

Problem Representation The manner in which a person mentally represents (understands) a problem.

Problem-Solving The application of knowledge or skills to achieve a specific goal.

Problem Space All possible solution paths that a person considers.

Procedural Knowledge Memories of processes (things one knows how to do).

Proximity A term used to describe the spatial relationship between two people or objects.

Proximity Searches A method of problem solving in which a person will continue to narrow the possibilities until a solution is reached.

Public Law 94-142 The Education for All Handicapped Children Act, passed in November 1975 to ensure public education for all handicapped children.

Punishment Any stimulus that occurs after a given behavior and decreases the strength of that behavior.

Random Search The search for a solution at random; generally the least efficient means of problem solving because only chance determines the occurrence of the solution.

Range Extent or gamut of a set of numeric values; interval from the lowest to the highest score.

Raw Score Term referring to the number of correct answers on a test.

Reading Readiness Skills and general abilities (such as awareness of order and orientation of letters and visual acuity, respectively) that are needed before one will be able to read.

Recall The process of remembering information that has been learned.

Recency Effect The finding that memory for information that was presented at the end of a list will be superior to memory for information presented in the middle of the list. See also Serial Position Effect.

Recoding Decoding an unfamiliar word by sounding it out.

Reconstructive Memories Memories based on inferences made at the time of recall together with some of the original information.

Reflex Behaviors Reactions that do not have to be learned.

Rehearsing Repeating something in one's mind over and over for the purpose of retaining it in memory.

Reinforcement Any event of consequence of a behavior that increases the frequency or intensity of that behavior.

Reinforcement Schedules Schedules that determine the timing of the presentation of the reinforcers.

Reliability A measure of the consistency of scores when the same person takes the same test on different occasions or an equivalent form of the test under different conditions.

Removal Punishment The removal of a desired stimulus after a behavior that causes a decrease in the behavior (e.g., a fine).

Repression Unintentional forgetting of information as a result of unpleasant experiences.

Response Set Effect The tendency to respond in a certain way (become biased or rigid) even though the response does not solve the current problem.

Retrieval The recall or recognition of information stored in memory.

Retroactive Interference Term describing what occurs when new information makes it difficult to remember old information.

Ripple Effect A term coined by Kounin to describe a situation where a teacher reprimands one student and the rest of the class feels the effect and responds to it.

Schema An organized pattern of thoughts or behaviors that is developed as a result of interacting with objects or people in the environment.

Self-Actualization Attaining one's ultimate goal in life or realizing one's potential.

Self-Fulfilling Prophecy Tendency for someone who expects something to happen to act in a way that would make the event happen.

Semantic Memory Memory of information regarding facts, concepts, and principles.

Sensorimotor Stage The first stage of development (approximately birth to 2 years of age) described by Piaget during which exploration occurs through the motor skills.

Sensory Receptors Those organs of the body that receive input or stimuli from the environment.

Sensory Register Holding system for visual or auditory memory.

Serial Position Effect The finding that people are more likely to remember the first and last bits in a set of information than the parts in between.

Set Effect See Response Set Effect.

Shaping Gradual modification of behavior by reinforcing approximations of the desired behavior until the desired behavior is achieved.

Simulation Programs Computer programs used to present information as closely as possible to the way it would appear in real life.

Skinner Box A small cage with a built-in lever or bar and a tray; used in operant conditioning studies.

Small-Group Format Instruction or educational projects designed for a group of students who may be assigned to work together on the basis of a common characteristic or need.

Social Learning Theory A behavioral theory which maintains that behavioral changes (i.e., learning) occur as a result of observation and imitation.

Software A program written to run on a computer.

Solution Paths Routes or strategies connecting the initial problem state with the goal state.

Specific Transfer Term that describes what occurs when information learned in one situation is applied in a similar situation.

Split-Half Reliability A measure of reliability in which items from one test are divided in two groups and a correlation is generated between performance on items in both groups.

Stages In developmental psychology, a concept which suggests that growth of mind and body occurs sequentially.

Standard Deviation An measure of dispersion, that is, how spread out from the mean a set of scores are; calculated as the square root of the variance.

Standardized Tests Carefully (usually professionally) developed tests administered under predefined conditions and scored according to predefined specifications.

Stanine Score Representation of a raw score on a standardized 9-point scale.

State-Dependent Retrieval The finding that people remember best when they learn and recall while under the same conditions (states) such as sobriety or intoxication.

Stimulus Discrimination A learned response made to one stimulus is not made when similar stimuli are presented.

Stimulus Generalization A learned response to one stimulus also occurs when a similar stimulus is presented.

Student-Centered Approaches Teaching methods designed to interact with a student.

Summative Evaluation Evaluation after instruction that is used to determine how well learning objectives were met.

T Score A standardized score with a mean of 50 and a standard deviation of 10 that indicates the extent of deviation from the mean of the distribution.

Table of Specifications A table that relates instructional objectives to test items; useful for test construction.

Tabula Rasa John Locke's term for the notion that a child is born with the mind as a blank tablet or slate.

Task Analysis The process of analyzing large or complex tasks and breaking them down into fundamental simpler components, called subtasks.

Taxonomy of Educational Objective Devised by Benjamin Bloom, a classification scheme involving knowledge, comprehension, application, analysis, synthesis, and evaluation.

Team Teaching A teaching method involving two or more teachers who share in or contribute to the teaching process.

Telegraphic Speech A stage of language development during which an idea or thought is communicated using only key words (e.g., "Mommy, down") and is usually understood by another person even though it is not presented in correct grammar.

Test An instrument used to measure performance of an individual or group.

Test-Retest Reliability The consistency of results when identical tests are given to the same student on two separate occasions.

Theory A set of related statements that explain a given phenomenon, synthesize existing data concerning that phenomenon, and allow one to predict performance in situations where data have not been collected.

Third Force Psychology Humanism; the proposal of Abraham Maslow that education should incorporate awareness of emotions and feelings.

Tip-of-the-Tongue Phenomenon The feeling of knowing something without being able to retrieve it from memory.

Token Economy A classroom scenario in which students are reinforced for certain behaviors with a token that they can trade for some reward, such as free time.

Top-Down Processing See Deductive Reasoning.

Transfer of Learning The application of information learned in one context to solve a problem in another context.

Trial-and-Error Learning Problem-solving behavior where a student makes mistakes and learns from them.

Tutorial Programs Teaching methods and computer programs that present information, request a response from the student, and provide more information when needed.

Unconditioned Responses (UCR) The reflex actions that occur naturally and do not have to be learned.

Unconditioned Stimuli (UCS) Events that elicit involuntary, reflex actions, such as fear and salivation.

Valences Positive and negative forces that affect human behavior.

Validity The extent to which a test measures what it purports to measure.

Variable Interval Schedule A reinforcement schedule requiring presentation of reinforcement (after the first occurrence of the behavior) at predefined time periods that vary in length for the duration of the schedule.

Variable Ratio Schedule A reinforcement schedule requiring presentation of reinforcement after the behavior occurs a predefined number of times (which varies for the duration of the schedule).

Variance A measure of deviation (variability) from the mean.

Vector A symbol of motivation, the direction of a valence.

Verbal Reports Orally presented descriptions of one's thought processes.

Vertical Transfer A term that describes what occurs when information learned in one situation facilitates learning of more complex information.

Vicarious Conditioning Learning in which behavior increases or decreases in relation to the rewards or punishment that someone else received for similar behavior.

Visual Impairments Opthalmologic problems that cannot be adequately corrected by glasses or contact lenses and cause a student to need special materials to be able to perform academically. "Partially impaired" and "blind" are the two categories of visual impairment.

Vocational Interests Tests Tests designed to measure career areas that students might be interested in.

Whole-Word Approach A method of teaching beginning reading in which students learn to recognize words on the basis of their appearance.

Word Processing An electronic means of creating and revising text.

Working Backward A popular method of problem solving in which a person starts with the desired answer and gradually works backward.

Working Memory That part of the memory used for thinking or reasoning.

Z Score A standardized score with a mean of 0 and a standard deviation of 1 that indicates the extent of deviation from the mean of the distribution.

Zero Transfer Occurs when information learned in one situation has no effect on acquisition of subsequent information.

INDEX